ONE WEEK
LOAN

- 4 FEB 1997   2 4 OCT 1997   2 4 APR 1998

1 1 DEC 1997

3 0 APR 1997   - 8 MAY 1998

1 7 DEC 1997

1 0 NOV 1998

1 4 MAY 1997

10 MAR 1999

-9 JAN 1998

2 8 MAY 1997   1 6 FEB 1998   1 7 MAY 1999

- 4 MAR 1998   1 JAN 2001

26 SEP 1997   3 0 MAY 2002

2 3 FEB 1999

1 2 FEB 2004

Housing and social change in Europe and the USA

There is a growing structural crisis in the provision of housing in advanced capitalist countries, and the steady improvement in housing conditions since 1945 is unlikely to continue. The dilemmas facing housing policy-makers can no longer be seen just as distributional questions, but as problems generated by the restructuring of key elements of housing provision, including private housing finance and the housebuilding industry.

This book looks at housing markets, housing policies and specific institutions connected with housing provision in many advanced capitalist countries, including Britain, the USA, France, West Germany, the Netherlands and Denmark. It considers the different sectors and the changes taking place within them, using case study material where appropriate to support its varied and convincing arguments. Its conclusions will interest all students of social policy and of housing.

The Editors
Michael Ball is Lecturer in Economics at the Department of Economics, Birkbeck College, University of London; Michael Harloe is Reader in Sociology at the University of Essex: and Maartje Martens is a researcher for the Research Institute for Housing at the Technical University of Delft in the Netherlands.

Housing and social change in Europe and the USA

Michael Ball, Michael Harloe and
Maartje Martens

London and New York

First published 1988
by Routledge
11 New Fetter Lane, London EC4P 4EE
New in paperback 1990

Simultaneously published in the USA and Canada
by Routledge
a division of Routledge, Chapman and Hall, Inc.
29 West 35th Street, New York, NY 10001

Printed and bound in Great Britain by
Billings and Sons Limited, Worcester

British Library Cataloguing in Publication Data

Ball, Michael, 1948–
   Housing and social change in Europe
   and the USA.
   1. Housing policy—Europe 2. Housing
   policy—United States
   I. Title II. Harloe, Michael
   III. Martens, M.
   363.5'56'094   HD7332.A3
   ISBN 0-415-00510-8
       0-415-04994-6 (pbk)

Library of Congress Cataloging-in-Publication Data

Ball, Michael.
     Housing and social change in Europe and the USA / Michael Ball.
Michael Harloe, and Maartje Martens.
       p. cm.
     Bibliography: p.
     Includes index.
     ISBN 0-415-00510-8
     ISBN 0-415-04994-6 (pbk)
     1. Housing policy — Europe. 2. Housing subsidies — Europe.
3. Housing policy — United States. 4. Housing subsidies — United
States. I. Harloe, Michael. II. Martens, Maartje; 1953–
III. Title.
HD7332.A3B35   1988
363.5'8 — dc 19   88-4403

Contents

Tables and Figures

Acknowledgements

This work draws on the results of a series of research projects carried out since the late 1970s by the three authors jointly and severally: on house building, social rented and owner-occupied housing, mortgage finance and innovations in housing policies and markets. Much of this work has focused on developments in six countries: Britain, West Germany, Denmark, the Netherlands, France and the United States (although some has only been concerned with a narrower range of countries and some has ranged more widely). The work involved the extensive collection of published data and other documentary sources as well as many interviews (the number running into well over three figures) with those involved in housing provision in these countries.

It is impossible to thank and acknowledge, either here or in the rest of this book, all those who have co-operated in this research over the years. But the following have been centrally involved, either as consultants or in other ways: Andrew Cullen, Peter Marcuse, Chester Hartman, Christian Topalov, Ruth Becker, Klaus Novy, Hedvig Vestergaard, Jan van der Schaar, Jos Smeets, Helga Fassbinder and Eberhard Muhlich. In addition we thank officials of the Danish Ministry of Housing for special help with Danish housing data and Knud-Eric Skouby for similar help regarding Danish house building. They are, of course, not responsible for the uses to which we have put the data and information which they have supplied. In addition, we are very grateful to Nigel Foster of the Department of Economics, Birkbeck College who produced the computer-generated figures for us, at short notice and under great pressure of time.

Finally, we wish to thank and acknowledge those who have funded our research: the Economic and Social Research Council, formerly the Social Science Research Council (housing construction and mortgage finance), the Leverhulme Trust (social rented housing and owner occupation), the Anglo-German Foundation for the Study of Industrial Society (mortgage finance) and the Joseph Rowntree Memorial Trust (housing innovations). Again, they are of course not responsible for the analysis and conclusions contained in this book.

Introduction

Over the past five years a considerable number of books about housing have been published. While some of them have been textbooks surveying the existing literature, a number have increased our understanding of the ways in which housing provision operates. Renewed interest in housing research has come at a time when housing policy in many advanced capitalist countries overwhelmingly favours owner occupation above other tenure forms. Attempts are still being made to encourage the new building of rental housing for those that cannot afford home-ownership, but in ways which are as private market orientated as possible. Governments ideologically wedded to the benefits of market relations have spearheaded these shifts in housing policy, but in most countries all the major political parties accept the broad approach to housing provision, even if they utilise different rhetorics in their policy statements.

Much of the renewed interest in housing research can, therefore, be put down to concern at the narrowness and folly of some of the contemporary policy experiments. A major theme of the new housing literature has been investigations of the extent of subsidy and state intervention into the so-called private market. The results of even casual inspection of governments' roles in those markets belie views that the state is actually withdrawing from intervention in housing provision. There have been shifts in the forms of state intervention rather than wholesale withdrawal. Another area of interest has been focused around a variety of attempts to devise new forms of state intervention into rental housing, particularly through a rejigging of housing subsidies, rent structures and new forms of finance.

1

Such trends are common to most countries. Debates relating to the changes have been taking place in European countries and in the USA. The content of the discussions, of course, varies, reflecting the differing frameworks of housing provision, political debate in each country and certain structurally unique policies (such as the selling off of council housing by the Thatcher government in Britain). But it would be fair to say that the whole role of the state in the housing sphere, as formulated in the years after 1945, has been questioned from virtually every conceivable political perspective in most advanced capitalist countries. Usually the debates take place in splendid isolation from each other, rather than drawing on the experience of other countries. Even so, there is a remarkable consistency in the themes raised.

Most explanations of the reasons for the consistency of trends in housing policy debates place overwhelming emphasis on political ideologies in the face of a changing world economy. Economic crises since the early 1970s have had a disastrous effect on social democratic style consensus politics and have encouraged a flowering of market liberalism as the dominant political ideology. In practice, governments have continued to intervene in economic and social affairs as much as they did in the past. Their intervention now, however, is overlaid with that market-based ideology and an acute awareness of the need to offer economic plums to prospective voters. Changes in housing policy consequently can be said to be a clear example of the shifts in political terrain. Housing policy, in such explanations, can be analysed from entirely within the terrain of politics. Governments changed and so did their policies, with good or bad consequences for the rest of social and economic life.

Our reason for writing this book is to challenge this excessively political explanation of the changes in housing policy. While the new political terrains have to be a major part of any analysis, in isolation they ignore the substantial transformation of the whole nature of housing provision that has occurred because of developments in the institutions associated with them and problems arising in the detailed workings of housing and construction markets. In particular, some erroneous assumptions underlie such explanations of why housing policy has changed. There are three basic assumptions in most housing research which, we feel, severely limit its usefulness.

1. Housing tenures encapsulate uniform ways of providing housing. One implication of this assumption is that any major change in a tenure can come about only through altering the level and form of state subsidies or controls. The assumption can be shown to be false through international comparison. There is a diversity of housing provision in nominally similar tenures between countries. Not surprisingly, as a result, the development of tenure forms and their social roles has varied considerably between countries. Tenure by itself, therefore, does not delimit a way of providing housing, nor the economic and social consequences of providing housing in that way.

2. Changes in housing provision arise from politically induced responses by the state to general social and economic problems. While we would not deny the importance of the state in influencing the nature of housing provision, we would suggest that major influences are ignored in this assumption. In particular, we would like to suggest that the principal non-governmental agencies involved in particular forms of providing housing and the ways they interreact have a considerable effect on what housing is provided, to whom, at what cost and with what level of state subsidy.

3. State subsidies go to consumers, therefore the question of housing subsidies is primarily a distributional one. In contrast to this assumption we would suggest that, frequently, consumption subsidies do not solely benefit their immediate recipients, housing consumers, but private agencies within particular forms of provision. Those private agencies could be landlords, landowners, builders, financiers and exchange professionals. The distributional question, in other words, has to encompass a wider set of social agents than simply consumers with different income levels and social characteristics. The issue is more than a distributional one as the existence of subsidies can affect the behaviour of housing agencies and so the nature of housing problems. House price rises, for instance, are not solely caused by patterns of demand, while subsidy levels are *dependent* on the costs of providing housing rather than determined through the whim of government.

When stated, these points undoubtedly seem obvious and

trivial and do not in themselves provide an explanation of why or how housing provision is changing. But failure to break out of such restricting assumptions, we feel, has been a major inhibitor in housing debates.

We further question generally held views about *the objective of housing policy*. A major presumption that runs through housing debates is that consumers with housing difficulties should be helped by the state, but in ways that have the minimum possible impact on pre-existing forms of provision and the agencies associated with them. We would argue instead that intervention will only be successful if it confronts and questions the operation of those institutions.

THE ROLE OF COMPARATIVE RESEARCH

Comparative research offers a way of demonstrating how the assumptions underlying much housing policy debate do not correspond to the actual nature of housing provision. It is easy to provide counter-examples from other countries to the entrenched beliefs of housing commentators in a particular country. But comparative research also has a positive role. Lessons can be learnt from the experience in other countries, and from policy innovations and suggestions being made there. It is possible to see the pressures that develop on particular tenures and structures of housing provision (where similar ones exist) as internationally they are placed in different social and economic contexts, and they may have distinct rules of operation. In addition, international trends in the activities of particular agencies involved in housing provision can be investigated, particularly with respect to finance and house building where international competitive pressures are likely to be greatest.

Comparative work, like any other form of housing research, needs a method by which to proceed. Much housing research, we feel, has neglected questions of method to its detriment, relying instead on implicit assumptions like those criticised above and a naive hope that empirical investigation can avoid all the disputes surrounding social theories. Comparative work brings out starkly the inadequacy of an empiricist's seat-of-the-pants, data-grubbing, tape-recording approach to empirical work. Given the overwhelming mass of information and

4

potential interpretations of it, comparative research needs a method by which to proceed. A theoretical perspective must inform the questions asked, their frame of reference and the means by which pieces of information are juxtaposed and analysed.

STRUCTURE AND SCOPE OF THE BOOK

The issues raised above have strongly influenced the framework of this book. The question of comparative method is tackled in the first chapter with a survey of earlier work, and a presentation of our own approach. The method of housing analysis we suggest is based on the concept of structures of housing provision. A structure of housing provision encompasses the interrelations between all the agencies involved in the production, exchange, finance and consumption of housing in a particular way. Generally, they are related to particular tenures, although tenures can be associated with more than one structure of provision. Each housing tenure in a country has a structure of provision (or more than one) which differs from that in other countries, to a greater or lesser extent. International variations in forms of housing provision help to explain the different experiences of housing tenures and why they have developed in separate ways.

Chapters 2 and 3 take up the theme of differences in the nature of housing provision and the varied experiences and fortunes of housing tenures between countries by looking at trends in social housing and owner occupation respectively. Chapters 4 and 5 then illustrate the substantial changes that have taken place in mortgage finance and house building over the past 20 years. Here general international trends can be discerned, but it is also clear that they do not lead to the same consequences in each country. The reasons for the differences are not accidental and their causes are explored. The final chapter, in the light of the previous ones, examines cross-national developments in housing policies.

What is being attempted in this book is a questioning of traditional approaches to housing issues through the framework of a comparative investigation, and an analysis of some of the main developments in housing provision in advanced capitalist countries. No attempt is made to explain all the major developments that have occurred, partly because that is not the book's object, and partly because such an exercise would anyway be beyond the scope of just one book. It is highly unlikely that such a definitive history could ever be provided, requiring as it does an exhaustive social and economic history of many countries stretching over two centuries. The purpose of such an endeavour is also questionable. We would argue that the object of research is to provide explanatory frameworks to enable processes of change to be understood and affected. Key elements require isolation through theoretical abstraction and empirical investigation. The holy grail of a definitive history of housing provision could easily turn out to be a battered colander of over-ambitious relativism, where everything depends on everything else whilst consideration of the motors of change drains away.

The three authors have been working together on housing issues for many years and have jointly been involved in a number of comparative projects. The chapters of this book represent some of the results of that co-operative work. Each chapter, however, has been the responsibility of one author, although we have jointly discussed the contents of each chapter. To avoid any confusion, as the nuances of individual contributions are bound to vary, we decided to name the authors of each chapter.

1

Housing Provision and Comparative Housing Research

Michael Ball

INTRODUCTION

Analysis of different countries' housing problems and governments' responses to them is a field of enquiry that is as old as housing research itself. Seeing how they do it 'over there', plus strong doses of national pride and rivalry, have always led politicians and researchers to venture to other lands or to read potted summaries of different housing systems.

In the post-Second World War era, with much greater state intervention into the housing sphere and the formalisation and dramatic expansion of applied social science, comparative housing research has reached new heights. Within that growth, fashion and funding have led to research cycles. A vast outpouring of data, official reports and academic studies can be seen during the long boom of housing research in the 1950s and 1960s, followed by a downswing, then a partial revival in the 1980s. It is now possible to scan through the library of many an academic institution and in the course of a few days get a rough idea of housing differences and similarities across countries. The Third World invariably and unreasonably gets lumped together with a strong emphasis in the literature on squatting and self-building. But for individual advanced capitalist countries reasonable pictures are available, either as individual studies or as comparisons between countries. And it is comparative housing analysis in the advanced capitalist world that is of concern here.

What concerns us, and it is the theme that will run throughout the book, is what is achieved by making comparisons? General trends may be discerned but what do they mean? Is generalisation in fact the central concern, or are differences in housing provision more interesting? What, in fact, do we want to find out by undertaking comparative work? We will argue that the objectives of comparative research and the methods by which it is approached strongly influence the information gathered and the answers reached. The implications of adopting specific methodologies can be seen in comparative housing research. Most of it is narrowly concerned with housing policy and tenure and consequently blinkered in its conclusions. The problem arises because the role of the state in determining patterns of housing provision is exaggerated.

Questions of method in housing research are rarely discussed. Pragmatism generally rules, and it has been particularly evident in comparative work. But beneath the veneer of pragmatism, particular theoretical perspectives and political concerns have determined the nature of research and frequently limited its usefulness. Pragmatism has not been adopted on the grounds of being the best and simplest practical methodology, instead it is the product of particular conceptions about the role of housing research. More detailed examination of the issue will follow later, but our objections can initially be summarised. We believe that a *liberal-interventionist* problematic has determined the focus of research and led to uncritical acceptance of the narrow lines of a policy debate, formulated as conventional wisdom by housing reformers, politicians and state functionaries.

With respect to the international scene, politicians and policy-makers frequently hope to find in comparative analysis easy solutions to political dilemmas. 'In country X they have such-and-such schemes, if we had them here perhaps things would be better, and people would stop complaining' is an accurate parody of a recurrent political view of comparative research. Sometimes, complacency is offered as a justification for inaction. The British population, for instance, is forever being told that it is better housed on average than people in other West European countries, which must sound very hollow to the millions living in poor and costly accommodation. 'Better housed' is, of course, fundamentally unquantifiable — but never mind, national pride and never-had-it-so-good take precedence over statistical reality.

The problem with such perspectives is not just their cynical use of the results of social research when they prove politically expedient. Like much of the research itself, there is also an implicit assumption that aspects of housing provision can be treated in isolation, rather than a recognition of their inter- connectedness and mutual determination. Between countries, there are contrasting general economic, social and political contexts, and differences specific to housing provision itself — such as in sources of finance, tenures, subsidy systems, housing production, consumption, location and design. The impact of one part becomes misunderstood when it is isolated from the whole. A policy, for instance, that 'works' in one country might have radically different effects in the social context of another.

In addition, within such discourses the description of housing provision is seen as unproblematic, provided that the informa- tion is available. If it is there, the data is generally accepted at face value. But information has to be selected and interpreted, and the theoretical framework from within which those tasks are undertaken influences the conclusions reached. Believers in the efficiency of markets and the effectiveness of their allocative and distributional roles, for example, would classify as a subsidy any form of intervention into the market which reduces price below its supposed free market value (see Odling-Smee, 1975 and Aaron, 1972). Such definitions lead to the calculation of vastly different 'subsidies' from those appearing in official government statistics, which are themselves subject to varia- tions in accounting conventions between countries.

Because method and explanation are interlinked, our analysis of international trends in housing provision starts with an essay on theory and research methods.[1] To many, this might seem tedious and unnecessarily academic. In contrast, we feel that avoidance of the issue has limited the usefulness of much comparative work, contained the area of political debate over housing issues, fuelled the frustration many feel over the failures of state intervention to live up to the ideals once claimed for it and contributed to the sense of hopelessness shared by many over a seeming inability to create socially worthwhile change.

The rest of the chapter will be divided into four main sections. The first will examine the general thrust of housing research, in particular its overwhelming concern with consump- tion processes and patterns. In much of the literature it seems that state housing policy only affects consumers, as winners or losers. Other agencies in the process of provision usually are part of a shadowy 'institutional context'. The focus on consumption has led to distorted interpretations of particular forms of housing provision. The next section maps out the evolution of the liberal-interventionist perspective in housing research, after which there is a survey of trends in comparative work. The subsequent section outlines an approach, based on the concept of structures of housing provision, which offers some ways out of the dilemmas of earlier research perspectives. The final section suggests ways in which such an approach can be used in comparative research, and indicates the ways in which we have used it in our analysis in this book.

THE LIBERAL-INTERVENTIONIST TRADITION
IN HOUSING RESEARCH

There have been substantial changes in housing provision over the last 50 years, and considerable theoretical shifts and debates within housing research. Within those developments, a number of common trends can be identified. The most significant was the acceptance in most advanced capitalist countries by the 1940s of the need for substantial state intervention into housing provision. Intellectual justification for such action was usually based on recognition of the problems associated with private housing. In 'industrial' societies, unfettered markets could not create sufficient adequate working-class housing. The problem was seen as one of a high cost of even minimally acceptable housing in relation to working-class incomes. Capitalism and market mechanisms were regarded as the best general forms of economic organisation, but situations arose where the state had to intervene to relieve the burdens experienced by those who bore the costs of market failure. With regard to housing, the issue was not simply a matter of individual welfare. A poorly housed workforce could also have adverse consequences for general economic development. The philosophy underlying this prescription for state intervention can be described as *liberal-interventionist*.[2]

The actual history of the development of state intervention into housing provision and the forms it has taken has varied widely between countries (see Harloe, 1985; Merrett, 1979; Duncan et al., 1985; Burnett, 1978; Sutcliffe, 1981; and Bullock and Read, 1985). To understand the reasons for that intervention, its timing and the forms it took requires detailed investigation beyond the scope of this chapter. But the political processes leading to state intervention were generally couched in terms of a common ideological framework: the nature of the housing problem as perceived by liberal-interventionists. That framework has influenced both the forms of state intervention and successive investigations of its success or failure. This does not mean that all who espoused the cause of the need for state action over housing were liberals, many in fact were not. Social democracy has been the dominant ideology of housing interventionists in Europe. Such supporters of state intervention, however, accepted the general terms of the contemporary housing debate, and that was laid down by liberal-interventionists. Liberals in Britain were particularly influential at the time because, despite relatively high working-class standards of living prior to .1914, housing was notoriously bad and a major political issue. It is the terms of the debate that are of interest here, because most housing research has followed its ideological lines.

The liberal-interventionist perspective has a long tradition stretching back into the nineteenth century. Housing and planning reformers, like Seebohm Rowntree and Ebenezer Howard in Britain, posed the housing problem in this way and argued for interventionist solutions in the years prior to 1914. Such antecedents were to set the ideological framework of the debate well into the 1950s. Seebohm Rowntree expressed the perceived problem and potential solutions to it particularly succinctly (Swenarton, 1981).[3] Working-class incomes were too low in relation to the market price of housing, which itself was determined by the profits of its providers, landlords, and the high cost of new house building. So, the state had to intervene in one form or another to right the inequality. But it should do so in ways which minimised interference with previously existing agents involved in housing provision and the rights of private property.

Either side of the wage/housing cost inequality in theory could be tampered with, but in practice only one option was open: housing costs had to be reduced. If wages were low, in theory they could be raised but that was practically impossible because it meant intervening in the labour market and raising wages substantially, threatening company profitability and undermining the very basis of capitalist society. Modern neo-classical economists are more sanguine about the robustness of the capitalist system and argue for the converse strategy. They suggest that raising the incomes of the poor is the only efficient (i.e. non-market distorting) way of improving bad housing conditions (Robinson, 1979 and Muth, 1969). The arguments of such economists, however, have been put forward in a context where social security systems are widespread and the taxation of incomes substantial and all pervasive. (Income redistribution is, in fact, often couched by neo-classical economists in terms of a negative income tax). In Rowntree's time, working-class incomes were hardly affected by such state redistributive mechanisms, so the wages paid by employers would have had to be forced up, or tax burdens on capital and the middle class raised substantially: neither option was a viable proposition for the liberal-interventionist. Even though housing costs had to be reduced through state intervention, Rowntree's subsidy expedients were only to be temporary, lasting until such time as working-class incomes rose to levels where they could purchase or rent housing on the open market. For Rowntree, the market only failed because of the contemporary existence of widespread poverty.[4]

What was to be done on the housing supply side? As noted above, whatever was done had to result in the minimum of intervention into pre-existing market processes commensurate with improving working-class housing conditions and limited additional state expenditure. Subsidies and regulatory controls were the best means of achieving those goals. As a corollary, to ensure the efficient use of subsidies and regulation, the state might also have to encourage a reordering of the contemporary institutional framework of housing provision.

Rent control, as opposed to either an unregulated market or a state take-over of rental housing, fits perfectly within the liberal-interventionist formula (though it was not proposed by Rowntree himself). Rent control, apart from some minor administrative and policing expenses, cost the state nothing. It benefitted housing consumers at the expense of one relatively small group in society, landlords. Later commentators were to highlight important feedback effects ignored by rent controllers. One particularly adverse effect of rent control was said to be the impact on new supply and maintenance levels, caused by the reduced profitability of landlordism: although the empirical importance of such supply factors in the face of competing modern forms of housing provision is the subject of much dispute (Robinson, 1979).

Early liberal-interventionists were aware of one of the problems of subsidies. If they were given to private agencies, a significant part of the subsidy would end up enhancing their profits, so that the final outcome of subsidies in terms of the quantity and cost of housing would be uncertain. Agencies had to be found which avoided the problem. The obvious candidates were the state or non-profit housing associations. In West European countries with strong traditions of social democracy blame was, in fact, often placed on one of the agencies within the process of working-class housing provision. The agency in question could be the private landlord, financiers or landowners (see Bullock and Read, 1985) but invariably one of the main means of tackling the problem was to take rental housing out of the private market in the form of social housing while leaving other aspects of provision, like the actual building of the housing, to market forces (although such private agencies' actions were frequently regulated).

It is possible to speak overall of two forms of liberal-interventionism. There is the *strong* form, where the state overrides the interests of specific private agents by imposing strict controls, such as rent controls, or takes one aspect of provision out of the market altogether, as with social housing. A *weak* form avoids confronting the private agencies of provision, relying instead on regulatory controls (minimum standards, etc.), state support agencies (like the FHA and VA housing programmes in the USA), and direct and indirect housing subsidies.

In terms of actual developments in housing provision, the years of strong and weak interventionism varied between countries and in the institutional structures adopted. An example of a strong form of intervention is the development of state landlordism in Britain (with local authorities as the providers of housing) and to an extent in the USA (particularly during the New Deal era and its aftermath). In other European countries, greater emphasis was put on non- or low-profit housing associations, whose growth was strongly encouraged by the state. Although such institutional structures reduced the threat of subsidies being dissipated in private landlord's profits, the narrow focus of the liberal-interventionist strategy on the direct point of consumption meant that other private agencies, especially financiers, builders and landowners, still operated within the framework of the new landlordism and could derive extra revenues from subsidies. The fundamental reason for the consumption focus, as was noted earlier, was to avoid threatening previously existing property relations.

In some countries, because of associated political developments (often temporary), constraints were put on other private agencies, apart from landlords. In Germany, for instance, municipal acquisition of suburban land was instigated from the turn of the century; while in Britain at times there has been low-interest funding of local authority capital works and a limited creation of local authority building departments. But, in general, such innovations were piecemeal and small scale, and not systematically introduced through recognition of the interlinked nature of housing provision. In addition, despite the arguments about the efficiency of social housing as the vehicle for improving working-class housing conditions, political consensus could rarely be achieved simply by subsidising rental housing. Governments, particularly those on the Right, have often over the past 50 years wanted to encourage home-ownership, so subsidies have been given, either as tax reliefs or as production subsidies. New private rental housing was also sometimes subsidised in attempts to revive flagging markets.

Although there have been shifts in political emphasis in every country during and since the inter-war years, the principles of subsidy and state regulation have generally survived intact. Considerable changes, however, have occurred in both the patterns of subsidy between tenures and the instruments used to put them into operation; some of these later chapters will consider.

Subsidy and tenure have been the main instruments in the liberal-interventionists' armoury of housing policy tools. But a variety of other schemes has been used, schemes which, interestingly, do take account of specific agencies involved in the process of housing provision.

Land-use planning has been another form of intervention. Early proponents of land-use planning primarily couched their arguments in terms of the beneficial effects of planning on housing provision (Sutcliffe, 1981 and Bullock and Read, 1985). Planning would reduce land and infrastructure costs and produce better estate layouts and urban spatial structures, it was claimed. Again, for its principal theorists, the prime role of planning has been seen as directing the market rather than going against it; an approach which contains fundamental logical contradictions (Ball, 1983). The high cost of land has also been tackled in some countries at various points in time through taxation schemes, the cheap purchase of land for privileged uses, or through the large-scale acquisition of land, the latter often being associated with the development of new towns and suburbs.

Design has been another area of active interest, particularly from the nineteenth century until the early 1970s. Initially, interest was strongly associated with projects like the Garden City movement, while later projects were linked to Modern Movement attempts to rationalise dwelling design and the construction process and to the development of industrialised building systems. Breakthroughs in house-building technology for many years held great fascination for liberal-interventionists, until crisis hit so many countries' building industries in the 1970s.

In the sphere of housing finance, regulatory rules and other devices, such as preferential interest rates and borrowing conditions, have been extensively used to encourage specialist housing finance institutions to channel funds into housing. Frequently, they have been associated with the encouragement of specific housing tenures, as is the case with the Building Society Movement in Britain and the Savings and Loans Associations in the USA (see Chapter 4).

Each intervention into the institutional structure of housing provision had a clear purpose. The reforms were undertaken to improve the consumption possibilities of households, either in general or for particular targeted social groups. Institutional reform was consequently based on an instrumentalist methodology in which institutions are treated in isolation and regarded as having particular functions with respect to the delivery of housing as a consumption good. Constraints faced by those institutions could be removed through partial reform or selective encouragement. The basis for institutional reform, in other words, fell firmly within the liberal-interventionist world view: markets should be constrained or restructured but never fundamentally questioned. Again, there was little understanding or exploration of agencies as operating within complex and interlinked economic and social environments. Institutions were not seen as having interests which could distort or negate the wishes of the policy-maker. The possibility of reverberations

15

of partial reforms on other agencies within a structure of housing provision was also ignored. Perennial complaints about the impact of planning and zoning constraints on house building is a good example of the neglect of interlinkages. Builders quite simply do not operate as policy-makers might wish them to; either the mode of operation of building enterprises has to be changed or the policy modified.

To jump ahead in history for a moment, it is interesting to note that many earlier fashions about state intervention into the institutional structure of housing provision had lost credibility by the late 1970s/early 1980s. Although a general rightwards drift in the political spectrum could account for some of the retreat of governments away from intervention, the failures of earlier experiments have played a strong part. Few now believe, for example, that the state can induce radically new forms of building technology. The state still plays a key role in many West European countries by funding research and development in construction, but now the aim is a more gradual, piecemeal transformation of the house-building process. The retreat, however, is not only a political and ideological one. It is also a severe defeat for the strong 'statist' version of the liberal-interventionist philosophy. Yet, in general, the failure of state intervention is not seen as the bankruptcy of one form of intervention but as denying the feasibility of any major initiative. Ideologically speaking, there is generally a simple binary scale with state intervention and market forces as opposite and unchanging poles. Such ideologies allow no intellectual space for more complex analyses of the nature of housing provison and how it is being, and can be, transformed.

NEW RHETORICS AND OLD STRUCTURES OF PROVISION IN THE POST-WAR ERA

After the Second World War, in virtually all capitalist countries, governments embarked on large-scale housing drives. The instruments used for the expansion of housing consumption were usually the institutional structures that had emerged in housing provision over the previous 50 years or even earlier in the case of private rental provision.

In the USA, a little public housing and, overwhelmingly, owner occupation expanded on the lines of the mass consumption forms emerging out of the 1930s' New Deal restructuring. In Britain, council housing was concentrated upon first, but with no fundamental alteration to the model of provision assembled under the aegis of local authorities prior to the First World War. Later, owner occupation was to be the prime vehicle for mass housing; the only substantial change to its pre-war structure of provision being the introduction of effective suburban land-use controls. In other European countries, pre-war forms of housing provision re-emerged, often with a greater emphasis on rental housing than in Britain and the USA. To a great extent the ideologies associated with European social democracy encouraged the use of non-profit social housing institutions, even if the governments in charge of the housing drives themselves were not social democrat, as in West Germany in the 1950s and 1960s and in France during the 1960s. Social housing was to be the mass housing form for urban dwellers, and often did not cater for the poorest social groups. The aim instead was to overcome the limitations of private landlordism.

Major changes did occur in the post-war decades in the percentages of new housing provided through different structures of housing provision. A drift towards home-ownership can be seen in many countries from the mid-1970s onwards. Despite a number of innovations in institutional forms and subsidies, however, the framework of housing provision as perceived and developed by earlier liberal-interventionist strategies remained fundamentally the same.

It is wrong to see the enormous post-1945 expansions of housing output solely as a consequence of conscious government housing policies. Numerous governments were obviously prepared to appropriate any successes in housing provision as being consequences of their own actions, while opponents placed blame for failures squarely on the party in power. Governments apart, large-scale expansions in housing output owed much to general social, economic and demographic trends and to pent-up housing demand. War-ravaged Europe inevitably experienced high demand for new housing even during the reconstruction years of low income growth. But everywhere rising real incomes during the long boom led to buoyant demand, which subsidies added to rather than created.

Rising effective demand had many important consequences for the nature of housing provision. Rents for new social housing for many years could, if governments wished to minimise subsidies, be raised at least as fast as the increasing cost of providing this housing. In a number of West European countries, however, rents were kept low as part of anti-inflation strategies. High demand for rental housing in the prevailing political contexts meant that existing structures of social housing provision were reinforced. Change was associated primarily with varying levels of subsidy, new formulae for deficit financing and a frequent association of social housing with experiments in urban renewal (particularly in Britain) and house-building techniques. The take-off of mass home-ownership, particularly in the USA and Britain, owed much to improving living standards. Overall, with substantial and generalised economic growth, housing provision could draw in successively larger amounts of national resources without posing either a major threat to capital accumulation or to the liberal-interventionist world view. Not surprisingly, the focus of liberal-interventionist strategies moved away from concern with the housing conditions of the working class. For many years, the extent of the housing shortage in Europe led to social housing being provided for a wide spectrum of the population, particularly in Scandinavia, West Germany and the Netherlands. Middle-class households also benefitted from the growth of social housing in such countries. This was not the case in Britain, where slum clearance was seen as a key aim. In Britain and elsewhere, attention was increasingly given to specific groups classified as being in need (e.g. large as well as single-parent families and the elderly). Implicit within the redefinition of need, away from class to household types, were highly contentious views of desirable household structures and heavy doses of social engineering and control.

The years following the collapse of the long boom in the early 1970s were to see a gradual breakdown of the liberal-interventionist consensus in its explicitly statist form. Incomes no longer automatically rose, state budgets were under pressure and inflation wrought havoc with historic cost-based housing finance systems. Inflation and recurrent speculative booms also put key housing institutions in some countries under threat. The crisis of the Thrifts in the USA was one of the most publicised cases (see Chapter 4).

By the late-1970s, it was apparent that the models of housing provision idealised during the earlier concensus faced significant problems. Those problems were often incorrectly seen as simply failures of state intervention. Models derived from idealised views of market process gained greater sway; although, as was argued earlier, market-based forms were always central to liberal-interventionist views of housing provision. A shift towards greater reliance on the market ensued in most countries. Rarely did this lead to a withdrawal of the state from housing provision. Instead, there was a shift of tenure emphasis in policy, particularly away from subsidised rental housing towards subsidised owner occupation. In addition, some restructuring of major institutions was encouraged by governments, particularly in the fields of housing credit and social housing, as later chapters will show.

Widening disparities in income distribution arose with the collapse of the long boom. The increasing number of unemployed felt the impact of growing inequality most strongly, while the new urban professionals were to be one of its main beneficiaries. Shifts in state intervention in housing provision exacerbated the trend in inequality. State housing intervention now blatantly favoured higher-income groups. Burgeoning middle-class housing demand led to a substantial spatial restructuring of housing provision in processes often dubbed as gentrification. Lower-income households not surprisingly faced increased 'housing affordability' problems (to use the US phrase). Such wholesale shifts of patterns of housing demand coincided with, and contributed to, a redrawing of the institutions of housing provision. Indeed, after the early 1980s' slump, many capitalist institutions became aware of the profitable opportunities arising from involvement in owner-occupied housing provision, at least if it could be done in low-risk forms (as mortgage credit seemed to be).

POST-WAR HOUSING RESEARCH

Housing researchers in the 1950s and 1960s lost much of their advocacy role with regard to the structural reform of housing provision. Research still focused on government housing policy by producing assessments of the successes and failures of policy in terms of the quantity and cost of housing and its distributional implications. Some research did advocate shifts of emphasis, the private rental sector in particular came in for much criticism but, unlike previous periods, there was little advocacy of new models of provision.

Liberal-interventionism had achieved its main goals of institutional and subsidy reforms, so monitoring, piecemeal change and keeping up the pressure on governments were now seen as the main issues. Governments, consumers and tenure were virtually the only aspects of housing provision considered in research. Explanations for state actions were couched almost entirely in terms of the power of pluralist-style pressure groups, with home-owners leading the pack. Other agents in the process of provision were virtually ignored; whereas in fact many of them were determining the costs, quality and availability which so concerned governments and researchers.

During the 1960s, growing disquiet developed about the role of the state in housing. Things were not working quite as well as hoped for. Pockets of extreme housing disadvantage were still around, and increasingly publicised. A growing number of studies in the 1960s and 1970s showed that subsidies were often wasteful and regressive and the forms taken by state intervention were highlighted as being unnecessarily bureaucratic, poorly targeted and remote from the users whose lives they were supposed to improve. These criticisms were particularly pertinent with respect to social rented housing.

Survey, analysis and policy commentary were the bread and butter of housing research. Quite what form intervention should take was strongly influenced by intellectual and political fashion. There have been two prime strands of policy advocacy in post-war housing research. One calls for substantial and strong state intervention — through subsidies, rent controls and social housing provision. The other argues for weaker forms of intervention — with the state regulating the various markets associated with housing provision, adopting redistributive policies where necessary and dealing with any perceived market failure. In the main, the stronger form of state intervention has been associated with writers from the disciplines of sociology and politics, and the weaker variant with neo-classical economists. Although there have been fierce disputes, virtually all antagonists in policy debates have seen the state as the great housing orchestrator. State policy towards tenures was the central question.

A tradition of Marxist-inspired research grew up in the 1970s, but again much of that, particularly in the earlier years, simply altered the role of the state, rather than the parameters of research. The state was no longer benevolent, as liberals and social democrats believed it to be, but in the control of capital or the site of a very unequal class struggle. Demands were made for much greater state expenditure on housing and more control over housing resources by their working-class users. In general, little criticism was made of the ways in which housing was provided. Instead, emphasis was put on the unreasonable and consumption-distorting profits made by private agencies in housing provision, and on housing as a key item in the distributional struggle over collective consumption. In many respects, such analyses could be regarded as radical variants of traditional liberal-interventionist themes, as they tended only to question the functions of state involvement in housing rather than criticising the means through which it was undertaken.

COMPARATIVE RESEARCH

Comparative research, not surprisingly, has followed the same intellectual lines as housing research in general.[5] Much work has been undertaken of a general descriptive nature outlining basic housing market structures, policies or specific innovations. Often, comparative studies take the form of quick, consultancy-style overviews. They contain implicit theoretical perspectives that are rarely specified, and provide potted, descriptive snapshots of what are regarded as the major relevant issues. Though often useful, to an outsider such studies can give a highly distorted impression of the overall nature of housing provision in the country in question and little understanding of how the various elements of housing provision interact there. Invariably, strong emphasis is given to housing policies with little explanation of why such policies emerged and their current impact. The survey of foreign housing finance policies in the 1977 *British Housing Policy Review* (DOE 1977) is a good example of the approach. While useful information was provided, the review suffered from the lack of a common, coherent theoretical structure; its individual parts reflected the interests and concerns of the expert authors drawn together and the policy issues discussed were influenced by current political debates in the country in question, which may not have much long-term relevance to understanding how housing systems function.

21

Comparative analysis, however, has not just been limited to superficial descriptive work. There have been a number of academic studies dealing with aspects of housing provision in depth and attempting to explain the broader political and economic context in which housing policies arise. It is important to note at the outset that virtually all academic comparative work has focused almost exclusively on housing policy and has neglected analysis of systems of provision themselves.

Most of the comparative literature argues from a presupposition of the need for substantial state intervention. Politically much of it has been associated with the liberal wing of the Democratic Party in the USA and social democracy in Europe. Theoretically, most has fallen, explicitly or implicitly, within the traditions of structural-functionalist sociology and adopted a pluralist view of politics (see Abrams, 1965; Donnison, 1967; Mandelker, 1973; Fuerst, 1974; · Headey, 1978; Duclaud-Williams, 1978; and Donnison and Ungerson, 1982). Those sociological and political theories have been subject to extensive criticism (see Lukes, 1974; and Westergaard and Resler 1975). Specific assumptions underlie their use in comparative housing research, as Harloe and Martens (1984) argue:

1. Industrialisation is the motor of social change, creating complex social structures which are subject to periodic 'restructurings', especially during periods of crisis.

2. Industrial societies, no matter what were their initial social structures, converge towards similar forms of 'mixed economy' with substantial state intervention. In industrial society, social and economic problems are essentially technical matters.

3. Social interests are represented by pressure groups and political parties, with the state as neutral arbiter. The basic value system for arbitration is, or should be, equality or equality of opportunity

4. Applied social science is a key policy tool, as it helps to provide unbiased, factual analysis of the issues at hand.

The dynamic of capitalist societies and the class structures associated with them are ignored within this approach. Despite the concern with inequality, no systematic theory of its existence is provided. So the list of assumptions on which comparative work is based is in reality a series of wishes from within the liberal-interventionist perspective about how societies should operate and change. Given these absences and aspirations, the explanatory power of such comparative work is limited.

Neo-classical economists favour widespread state intervention less as they believe in the general efficiency of markets.[6] The state can still play a key role in housing provision, however, by ensuring the efficient running of markets, resolving distributional questions and solving externality problems. Some texts accept that the state can also intervene because housing is a merit good, although this argument went out of fashion with the increasing free-market orientation of mainstream economics after the mid-1970s. But even free marketeers accept some role for the state in creating the conditions under which markets can operate efficiently. Most economists working in the housing sphere are prepared to tolerate substantially more state intervention than that, so most work by economists falls within the liberal-interventionist tradition, albeit of a weak state interventionist type.

Like sociologists, neo-classical economists in studies have relied on a variety of idealised assumptions about the workings of capitalist societies.

1. An ideal-market model is used, explicitly or implicitly, as a device through which to evaluate housing policies and occasionally the role of specific institutions. That ideal model is the standard one of perfect competition, with its claimed distributive and allocative efficiency with respect to the criterion of Pareto optimality. Real world markets, and perhaps especially housing markets, do not conform to the assumptions of perfect competition. Even so, statements about the general efficiency of markets are based on its ideal constructs.

2. Consumers and producers within housing markets have standard behavioural responses and parameters, which hold across different countries and points in time, although the constraints on them vary between countries. Burns and Grebler (1977), for instance, feel able on the basis of assumed similar consumer behaviour to calculate a world consumption function for housing.

3. Countries' housing policies and institutional structures within this framework are treated as part of the empirical specificity overlying the universality of market mechanisms. A corollary of this approach is that simple parables from neo-classical theory are often unquestioningly applied in comparative analysis. Specific housing subsidies, for instance, are often said to bias the interaction of demand and supply (see Hallett, 1977). That statement itself is frequently treated as sufficient

policy commentary, although in fact it is a truism of neo-classical theory and so hardly warrants the claim of being an analysis of the actual impact of subsidies. A similar use of the results of abstract models without questioning their applicability to specific countries' institutional contexts can be seen in the role given to competition. It is always good for you, and never seems to involve agencies with unequal power. Such uncritical generalisation can be seen in statements like ones that suggest that institutional structures, like protected circuits of mortgage finance, weaken the coercive effects of competition, leading to inefficiency (see Roistacher, 1986). Protected financial circuits may lead to such results, but it is an empirical question rather than a theoretical deduction. As an empirical question, it surely is necessary to consider the degree of competition or other efficiency incentives within the protected circuit, the existence of other compensating benefits and the consequences of alternative market structures — all of which could discredit the 'more competition is good for you' parable.

4. Economists' comparative analysis, because of its reliance on the ideal constructs of neo-classical theory, rarely explores the detailed operation of forms of housing provision. Textbook-style stable demand and supply curves are the heuristic tools of analysis with no evaluation of their applicability to the specific context. Similarly, the operation of agencies may be sketched but their interaction is not evaluated. Classic instances are statements about the impact of housing subsidies. Often they are seen as only influencing the behaviour of households, not that of other agencies in the market process, even though considerable amounts of any consumption subsidy, as early liberal-interventionists were aware, leak into the revenues of non-consumers in structures of provision.[7]

5. Like other housing analysts, economists concentrate on housing policy and its effects on consumers. Sometimes producers are considered, but the models used are static and consider only limited aspects of housing markets, such as land supply or the impact of consumption subsidies on effective demand. Housing provision is rarely examined as a dynamic process of interaction between markets and the agencies operating in those markets.

6. The theory of the state used to evaluate housing policies is generally crudely instrumentalist. The state has, or should have, objectives and a range of instruments through which to

achieve those objectives. On occasions, strong pressure groups might stand in the way of achieving particular aims. The purpose of applied economic analysis is to reveal the effects of using certain instruments in relation to the objectives set, and to consider the distortions caused by their ineffective use or non-use. Viewed from the instrumentalist perspective, government policies invariably exhibit a lack of clarity, reveal conflicts between objectives and show the use of inappropriate instruments to achieve specified goals. Not surprisingly, therefore, neo-classical economists tend to be highly critical of government policies, particularly on the grounds that governments fail to let markets 'work', either because of excessive interference with market processes (in social housing, for example, and through excessive controls on the private rental sector and the release of developmental land) or through failing to have tenure-neutral subsidy and taxation systems.

Like sociologists and political scientists, neo-classical economists provide only limited comparative analysis and explanations of differences in housing provision between countries. Their perspective leads them to look almost entirely at a misspecified housing policy/housing consumption interface and their use of ideal market constructs results in analysis generally being limited to comparisons of parts of structures of housing provision with the ideal. By using such idealised structures, neo-classical economists reproduce in a different form a cross-country convergence theory of systems of housing provision, as 'real' structures of housing provision should be altered as closely as possible to conform to the ideal model.

McGuire (1981) in his review of many countries' housing policies illustrates the use of idealised systems particularly clearly. At the conclusion of his chapter on housing finance, he describes the perfect system of housing finance as follows:

After reviewing the major housing-finance systems of the world, one might at this point attempt to describe the perfect system. First of all, such a system would have assets and liabilities that were evenly matched in terms of maturity. There would be neither premature redemption of bonds on the liabilities side, nor of mortgages on the assets side. Balances on deposit in savings accounts would not be withdrawn. There would be variable interest rates that would tend to match cash flows of both assets and liabilities. There would be stable operating expenses. There would be a secure regulatory environment that would positively encourage both savings and mortgage lending. This is the perfect system, but of course it does not exist (McGuire (1981), pp. 49–50).

Whatever the merits of McGuire's view of perfection, such ideal constructs are of little help in understanding the evolution, operation and problems of actual financial systems.

MARXIST COMPARATIVE RESEARCH

There has been little comparative housing work in the Marxist tradition, but what exists suffers from a number of the pitfalls described above. Politically, there is a tendency, similar to that of the liberal-interventionists, to idealise consumption forms which the state should help to create. The two works to be surveyed here, those by Kemeny (1981) on home-ownership, and by Dickens et al. (1985) on housing provision in Britain and Sweden, both have only limited specification of the nature of housing provision in the countries they consider, using ideal constructs instead, and try to formulate universally applicable hypotheses about aspects of housing provision which are empirically tenuous.

Kemeny (1981) tries to demonstrate that owner occupation is not the ideal mass tenure it is portrayed as being in many countries. He argues instead for greater availability of non-profit rental housing. Comparison is made between Australia, Britain and Sweden, and the benefits of non-profit renting are argued for primarily by reference to Sweden. Initially, Kemeny criticises traditional sociological housing studies for being narrowly empiricist and for failing to relate housing to the wider social structure. Yet, in a number of respects, he does not break out of the theoretical strait-jackets he initially criticises. Tenures are seen as universally the same and unchanging. They are ideal-types, which can be compared on the basis of highly controversial calculations of their financial effects and the extent to which they achieve what he sees as socially desirable goals; a methodology reminiscent of the sociological studies surveyed earlier. The nature of the way in which houses are actually provided is hardly considered, nor, despite his earlier strictures, is housing policy placed in the context of the social and economic history of the country in question. General statements, such as countries having 'privatism' or 'collectivism' established in their social structures, are used as explanations of differences in tenure distributions between countries. Yet, such descriptive categorisations explain little, nor help to show how his preferred tenure-balance system could be achieved.

Duncan et al. (1985) build on work within the political economy of housing tradition. Much of the 'success' of housing provision in Sweden as compared to Britain is explained, it is suggested, by the greater productivity of the Swedish building industry. Intervention by the state into key aspects of housing production is said to be a prime cause of the higher productivity. The authors are also keen to emphasise the importance of housing policy variations at the sub-national level, which they explain primarily in terms of local political differences in Britain; the only one of the two counties where 'locality' is considered.

An initial chapter on methodology outlines Duncan et al.'s approach to comparative research. The explanation at times is unclear, but the general approach suggested seems to be sum-marised by the following statement. It is said that 'comparative analysis can achieve some control over real world variability and so contribute in establishing the process links between structural mechanisms and historical events' (Duncan et al., 1985, p. 30). Such a statement would find considerable support amongst logical positivists and econometricians in its attempt to discover regularities beneath the variability of actual financial events. Where Duncan et al. differ from such epistemologies is that the underlying regularities they search for are structural dynamics which they claim exist under capitalism. Actual variation — 'how the structural becomes the particular' as they put it (ibid., p. 10) — is then explained by historical accident, the political process and particular agencies' responses to the constraints imposed on them by the state.

In housing provision, Duncan et al. claim that the important underlying structural dynamic, which they have managed to isolate through a comparative analysis of Britain and Sweden, is the level of productivity in the building industry. 'In Sweden, the building industry is much more productive and more closely follows the normal model of capitalist rationality' (ibid., p. 3). The reason suggested is that land speculation holds back house-building productivity in Britain, whereas in Sweden the state has intervened to remove that impediment. Theoretically, their notion of a 'structural dynamic' seems a device for elevating one aspect of housing provision, production, to an unwarranted primacy. Causality itself is then reduced to one, highly questionable, hypothesis — rational capitalist development in housing production can be held back by land speculation. Within their mono-causal explanation, moreover, is an implicit, universally applicable, model of a capitalist industry; for without it no claim could be made about the retardation of development in the British construction industry. Yet it is unreasonable to suggest that all capitalist industries follow the same pattern of development; a point which holds as much for construction industries as any others (Ball, 1988). Not surprisingly, the main policy suggestion emanating from Duncan et al.'s book is the need for effective land development taxation. This might seem ultra-radical in the 1980s, but previously it had been a major plank of liberal-interventionists' housing strategies for decades; a fact which ironically helps to account for the land policies adopted in Sweden itself.

The reason for these criticisms of Kemeny and Duncan et al. is to highlight the difficulty of breaking out of the framework of comparative housing research as set up within the liberal-interventionist framework. Confronting the tradition on its own terms by questioning contemporary political ideologies associated with the politics of tenure, as Kemeny does, is useful but leads only to the championing of other tenure forms within essentially the same theoretical and policy-orientated framework. To isolate housing production and bestow on it some universal norm, which then gets distorted by the murky world of land speculation, as Duncan et al. do, again fails to break out of the theoretical framework. Strictures about the evils of land speculation on the cost of housing provision seem to take us closer to the worlds of Henry George, Ebenezer Howard and the early town-planning movement than towards an analysis of social relations in housing provision deriving from the Marxist tradition.

SOCIAL RELATIONS AND COMPARATIVE HOUSING RESEARCH

So far this chapter has given a negative view of comparative research. The point of doing so is to highlight the overwhelming influence of the theoretical and political presuppositions of liberal-interventionism. Housing research and comparative work within it has a history and one of the objects of earlier sections was to show the continuing influence of this perspective throughout years of substantial social and economic change, wide-ranging theoretical dispute, and a much-changed housing scene and political environment within which it works.

This does not mean that all the conclusions of comparative work are of little use. Instead, it is the absences in the liberal-interventionist framework which are most worrying. Its focus on the housing policy/housing consumption interface was suggested above to be a major theoretical weakness (albeit one which favours the political presuppositions of many who adopt the approach). This is not to say that either state policy or consumers are the wrong things to look at. Quite the contrary, for any progressive change in housing provision to occur, it is precisely to those areas that attention must be addressed. The point is that liberal-interventionism misspecifies the connection between the state and housing consumer, and in doing so fails to propound the policies required for change towards the housing goals they espouse. Other theories, such as Marxism, applied by analysts with different political perspectives face similar difficulties if they remain within the remit of housing research as laid down by liberal-interventionism. Elsewhere, I have termed housing research which focuses solely on the housing policy/consumption interface as the consumption-orientated approach to housing research (Ball, 1986a).

What should replace the narrow and misleading frame of reference for comparative research dictated by liberal-interventionism? The major absence in this perspective is a lack of analysis of structures of housing provision, and it is utilisation of this concept which offers ways out of the impasse.

A structure of housing provision specifies the nature of the social agents involved in the provision of a particular form of housing and their interlinkages. Producers, consumers and financiers in different guises all have their place within structures of provision. Actual structures of housing provision, however, are empirical constructs and cannot be theoretically deduced, although obviously theory has to be applied in their analysis.

From within this perspective, it can be seen that there are not universal forms of provision whose efficacy can be analysed through international comparison of their operation. Cross-country comparisons of tenure, one of the bread-and-butter subjects of comparative research, must be aware that distinct structures of provision are being examined even though they exist within apparently common tenure forms. In other words, it is not just variations in wider social and political processes which explain differences in tenure patterns between countries and consumers' experiences of living in them. In addition, there are important variations in the internal processes of provision. Owner occupation, for instance, involves a wide variety of structures of provision between countries and sometimes within a country, as Chapter 3 will show.

What is clear from the development of housing provision over the past 50 years is that structures of housing provision have been changing substantially. Often, the changes are not consequences of government policy but of shifts in the nature or roles of agencies within a process of provision and the subsequent reaction of others to those changes. Such dynamic interaction is continually occurring, so structures of provision never stay constant. They cannot, in other words, simply be described and used as the backdrop against which the real discussion of housing policy and consumption can be undertaken. The evolution of housing policy and consumption are occurring in a continually changing environment.

The example of some developments in home-ownership in Britain and the USA can be used to illustrate the point. From the early 1970s onwards in both countries existing home-owners became increasingly important as purchasers and sellers in the housing market. To an extent, the relative shift away from first-time buyers was an inevitable consequence of the earlier growth of home-ownership. Another contributing factor was periodic affordability problems for potential new entrants. The changing composition of both purchasers and sellers has had substantial implications for the development of the home-ownership market in both countries. House-builders, for instance, now have to compete with existing home-owners as well as renovators of stock transferred from other tenures. In addition, the housing market has become more volatile and sensitive to changes in macro-economic circumstances, such as interest rates and rates of change in disposable incomes. Market volatility, however, has had distinct consequences in the two countries because of variations in the nature of home-ownership provision.

In the USA, increasing market volatility was one of the contributory factors causing the crisis of the Thrifts in the early 1980s, whereas British building societies reacted differently (see Chapter 4). Another contrast would seem to be the fragmentation of the US home-ownership market and the increasing differentiation of housing consumers. There are distinct regional markets and sectoral markets. Custom building, retirement homes and mobile homes, for instance, all contribute to the complex pattern of home-ownership in the USA. This helps to explain the wide variety of types of housebuilder and their small size relative to the overall scale of the US housing market (see Chapter 5).

In Britain, historically the housing market has been very unified, principally because of the widespread existence of trading-up by home-owners to better accommodation. Extensive trading-up itself reflects the poor quality accommodation offered to most British first-time buyers. In mid-1980s Britain, considerable regional variations in the rate of house price increase are occurring for the first time in many years reflecting the unevenness of the revival of the British economy, but it is difficult to predict whether this will lead to strong segmentation of the British housing market or whether it simply reflects contemporary local variations in the balance of supply and demand. What is clear is the different response of producers in Britain to the changed housing market compared with their US counterparts. For instance, there has been a major process of centralisation of production under the control of a handful of producers, as Chapter 5 shows.

An outcome of the distinct patterns of change in US and British home-ownership provision, not surprisingly, are separate patterns of price and output change. In both countries, moreover, all the major policy initiatives with respect to home-ownership have to a great extent been forced on governments because of the developments in its structure of provision — be they mortgage reform, the consequences of burgeoning subsidies and tax reliefs, or growing pressures to subsidise or support low-income owners because of the rising costs of home-ownership. This type of explanation of housing policy change, of course, contrasts substantially with the liberal-interventionist one which, as was argued earlier, sees policy changes as more or less rational responses to problems of consumption inequality in an essentially static institutional framework. For it, the possibility that changes in agencies in the market actually create the problems that need resolving is ruled out prior to analysis.

USING STRUCTURES OF HOUSING PROVISION
IN COMPARATIVE ANALYSIS

Detailed exposition of the notion of structures of housing provision has been presented elsewhere and will not be repeated here (Ball, 1986a and 1986b). But three comments are worthwhile to highlight what is being suggested as an approach to comparative housing research.

The first concerns the determinants of change. The approach could be misinterpreted as suggesting that one or more of the agencies associated with housing provision are the 'real' determinants of change, everything else being mere epiphenomena or expressions of that underlying relation. Building production, for instance, could be assigned that role, as Duncan et al. (1985) did. It should be emphasised that no such essentialism is being suggested. The determination of changes in housing provision is a complex historical process whose explanation can only be investigated through detailed empirical analysis. Changes in structures of housing provision may at times have little or no effect on the empirical issues being investigated (though such an event can perhaps be assumed to be relatively rare). What is being suggested is not a conclusion to research but a method through which it can be conducted; one which more accurately maps real processes in housing provision than do the methods implicit within much housing research, including comparative work.

There is particularly a need to downgrade the autonomy and power of the state, which is assumed to exist in the housing sphere. It may be true that the state as the repository of legitimate violence in capitalist societies does have ultimate power if the forces controlling the state choose to use it. But in the housing sphere, despite large-scale state intervention, it is perhaps remarkable how little the state has interfered with the evolution of structures of provision in ways which contradict the aims of the major private agencies involved, despite frequent major political pressure to do something about housing provision. In most countries, only the private landlord has significantly lost out from state intervention, and even then the pattern has been highly varied.

The second point concerns the scope of research. It could be retorted that use of the concept of structures of provision seems either to mean that everything has to be known about housing provision in the countries in question before research can start, or alternatively that all research must endeavour to map out detailed structures of provision and their dynamics in order to consider any more specific topic. As both approaches to research are obvious non-starters, the method is doomed as unworkable and idealistic. The point of the approach in fact is not to suggest that housing research should have such an impossibly enormous scope. Instead, it suggests that when looking at an aspect of housing provision it should be put in the context of how provision actually works rather than of some idealised construct of how it is believed to work. The subsequent chapters on mortgage finance and house-building, for instance, explain some of the differences between countries' institutional structures in these spheres, suggesting that they arise from the distinct types of structure of provision in which the institutions operate. It does not require total or even detailed knowledge of those countries' structures of provision in order to be able to make such points.

It should also be remembered that every statement about housing provision explicitly or implicitly includes some view about the processes involved in it. As was pointed out, for example, strong state liberal-interventionists assume that the agencies providing housing are very pliant to the wishes of the state and do not change in ways that affect the topic of concern. Such views implicitly are assumptions about structures of housing provision, ones which empirically seem unrealistic.

The third and final point concerns the purpose of the research. Housing research frequently seems to conflate the issues of research with approaches to research. Analysis of structures of provision, for instance, could be said to neglect the importance of the family or give unwarranted privilege to the power of institutions over that of people. In part, the conflation arises because of the enormous variety of feasible topics within the housing sphere. But it also arises from a failure to specify adequately the object of research and the methods by which it is to be approached. Again, all that is being suggested is that any issue has to be put in context if unwarranted generalisations or over-inflated causal linkages are to be avoided. Structures of provision are simply a theoretical device for putting things in context, not a substitute for adequate empirical analysis.

CONCLUSION

Comparative housing research is an important means of understanding the nature of housing provision in capitalist societies. It focuses attention on the economic, social and political pressures creating change in people's housing circumstances. It can help to highlight the fundamental mechanisms of housing provision and bring into focus the complex pressures on any government's strategies in the housing sphere. Comparative work is useful in enabling a broader range of circumstances to be considered than is possible within one country. Policy ideas may be gleaned from such cross-country perspectives, but as important is the greater ability to distinguish between broad patterns of social change, government policy and institutional restructuring through the juxtaposing of developments in countries with similar forms of economic organisation and dominant political ideologies but different types of housing provision. The object of such research should not be solely to draw out the common elements and trends, and use those generalisations as some 'higher-level' explanation. General trends may have some bearing on housing developments in a particular country, but conflicts and struggles between social agencies outside and within the sphere of housing provision actually determine the content of housing change there. General trends might help elucidate the context in which those conflicts are played out, but they are not a substitute for investigation of them.

In conclusion, it is perhaps worthwhile illustrating the difference between a liberal-interventionist perspective on current trends in housing policies and the type of conclusion which comes out of the analysis presented in later chapters of this book. One of the major general trends in housing policies, especially in Western Europe, is often said to be a movement away from subsidising the housing of lower-income households towards the subsidy of higher-income groups (see Chapter 2). Such trends fly in the face of all that liberal-interventionists see as being the rational role of governments in industrial societies.

There are two standard 'liberal-interventionist' responses to the perceived shift. One is essentially a moral critique, sometimes dressed up in 'efficiency' clothes. It is said to be wrong that governments subsidise higher-income groups at the expense of lower-income ones (and that subsidies are wasteful and distorting anyway). It is difficult to disagree with the moral statement, but it faces two problems.

The first problem concerns the practical feasibility of creating greater equality of income (or consumption possibilities) by subsidising consumption goods. Redistribution has been attempted in many countries through policies associated with the welfare state in the post-war years, and housing has been seen by many as a key means to achieve such an aim. It has unfortunately proved impossible to achieve much redistribution without tackling severe inequalities in wealth and income at the same time. In practice, what has happened in a number of countries, such as Britain (Le Grand, 1982), is that consumption subsidies have benefitted the better off more than the poor. The reasons seem obvious once stated (see Le Grand, ibid.). Richer people often benefit more from the welfare state because they consume more, are more able to take advantage of tax reliefs, health programmes and educational facilities, and have greater success at dealing with bureaucracies and political processes.

Housing is a clear example of the regressiveness of subsidies. Owner-occupiers and the middle-income groups who enjoyed the benefits of social housing programmes in a number of West European countries have been the main recipients of subsidies (though much of the subsidy is subsequently channelled through the associated structure of provision to other social agents). The changing patterns of subsidies in the 1980s could consequently be argued to be reflecting shifts in the patterns of housing consumption by such middle-income households (towards home-ownership) and the generally higher cost of housing rather than a deliberate increase in the regressiveness of housing subsidies. Of course, this explanation does not make the effects of subsidies any the less regressive and reprehensible. One consequence is that liberal-interventionists have increasingly veered back towards market solutions on the grounds of the supposed superior efficiency of market over bureaucratic allocative mechanisms. Such a shift does not represent a break with earlier trends, if anything it represents a reinforcement of the views of early proponents like Rowntree, who argued that income redistribution was the best way of improving working-class consumption opportunities. Non-market mechanisms should only be used when there was no other means available. The growing emphasis on market mechanisms in capitalist societies, therefore, should not be seen simply as a political and ideological drift to the Right, but as a logical consequence of the very ideology that spearheaded the earlier moves away from the market. The argument that real standards of living for most people are much higher than they were in earlier decades, so more people are able to use the market to get adequate levels of consumption of 'welfare' goods is a perfectly consistent liberal-interventionist position. Housing subsidies in this framework have become an anachronism. A similar argument is usually made against subsidising public transport on the grounds that higher-income households travel more and therefore benefit from subsidised public transport more than the poor (see Le Grand, 1982).[8]

The second liberal-interventionist explanation of the subsidy shift eschews the high ground of morality for the cynicism of the political arena when arguing about the causes of the subsidy change. Housing subsidies, it is often claimed, are no longer really about housing provision but about right-wing parties reasserting market-orientated ideologies and building up client groups of voters. Again, it is difficult to dispute the cynicism of most political parties, nor the growing strength of views about the power of the market. Problems still arise, however. Explanation of housing policy change cannot simply be found in the political itself. Conditions must have arisen to enable such cynical manipulations of voting intentions to come to the fore, if voters are in fact so gullible (and it is doubtful whether they actually are (see Ball, 1985)).

Most forms of housing provision prevalent in advanced capitalist countries have changed in significant ways over the past 40 years, as later chapters will argue. Changes in the nature of housing provision, therefore, must be part of the explanation of shifts in housing policies and subsidies. Understanding the causes, for instance, of cutbacks in new social house building or in the tenure as a whole cannot avoid recognition of the failings of the structures of provision associated with it. The problems, in other words, of the liberal-interventionists' models of non-profit rental housing provision have to be confronted in any explanation, rather than ignored as a pure political ideology as client-voter explanations tend to do.

We would argue that the most important difficulty with the distributional, client-voter type of explanation is the lack of understanding implicit within it of the enormous changes that have gone on within housing markets and the institutions operating within them over the past decade. Major developments, such as new forms of housing finance and new types of house-builder, favour a fragmentation of housing provision. Rightwards shifts in housing policy, in other words, have flowed along with developments amongst the major housing-related institutions in a mutually supporting way. Within the much vaunted shift of subsidies towards higher-income households, moreover, new mechanisms for channelling state funds towards the activities of these institutions have been found. The restructuring of housing provision in advanced capitalist countries, however, has not been a simple or even clear process, and it has been highly variable between countries, as the following chapters will show.

A corollary of the conclusion about the interwoven nature of contemporary changes in housing policies and structures of housing provision is that in many respects piecemeal reform of housing provision is becoming increasingly more difficult. Any significant change, such as a more equitable subsidy policy, is likely to have enormous repercussions on the new institutional structures of housing provision. There is no need to believe in a conspiracy theory of the state to expect that such entrenched interests will resist change which threatens them. Liberal-interventionists have always felt that major social reform could be achieved without jeopardising major private interests. Time, it would seem, is proving them wrong.

NOTES

1. The arguments contained in this chapter have been strongly influenced by the earlier comments in Ball (1983 and 1986a and 1986b), Harloe and Martens (1983) and Ball, Martens and Harloe (1986). Detailed referencing will not be made of them in this chapter.

2. In an interesting recent book on the failure of Keynesian and Beveridgite economic and welfare policies in post-war Britain, Cutler, Smith and Williams (1986) call a similar type of political philosophy, liberal-collectivist. However, in the field of housing provision justi-

fication for state intervention is so dressed up in the framework of market failure, and never entirely supercedes market relations and forms of calculation, that the term liberal-interventionist seems more appropriate.

3. Rowntree was the anonymous author of the 'urban' report of Lloyd George's Land Enquiry Committee, published on the eve of the First World War, which is a classic statement of liberal-interventionist views on housing provision.

4. It should be noted that many commentators and politicians in the 1970s and 1980s have been guardians of this tradition in the way in which they suggest that living standards have risen to levels where general state intervention into the housing sphere is no longer required. Frequently, of course, such statements are associated with the view that state-subsidised rental housing should be phased out or put on a free-market footing.

5. See Harloe and Martens (1983) for a detailed survey of the comparative literature.

6. See Ball (1986) for a survey of housing analysis within the neo-classical economics tradition.

7. See Ball (1983) for greater consideration of this point.

8. Basing views on inequality solely in terms of income does not adequately encompass differences created through gender and race (Watson, 1986 and Gilroy, 1987). Within the liberal-interventionist perspective, such inequalities would be confronted by identifying and trying to overcome discrimination in the market or classifying 'special needs' groups and devising housing programmes for them.

REFERENCES

Aaron, H. (1972) *Shelter and Subsidies*, Brookings Institute, Washington DC

Abrams, C. (1965) *The City as Frontier*, Harper and Row, New York

Ball, M. (1983) *Housing Policy and Economic Power*, Methuen, London

—— (1985) 'Coming to terms with owner occupation', *Capital and Class*, *24*, 15–44

—— (1986a) 'Housing analysis: time for a theoretical refocus?', *Housing Studies*, *1*(3), 147–65

—— (1986b) 'The built environment and the urban question', *Society and Space*, *4*, 447–64

—— (1988) *Construction Rebuilt? Economic Change in the British Construction Industry*, Routledge and Kegan Paul, forthcoming

Ball, M., Martens, M. and Harloe, M. (1986) 'Mortgage finance and owner occupation in Britain and West Germany', *Progress in Planning*, *26*(3), 189–260

Bullock, N. and Read, J. (1985) *The Movement for Housing Reform in Germany and France 1840–1914*, Cambridge University Press, Cambridge

Burnett, J. (1978) *A Social History of Housing 1815–1970*, David and Charles, Newton Abbot

Burns, L. and Grebler, L. (1977) *The Housing of Nations*, Macmillan, Basingstoke

Cutler, A., Smith, J. and Williams, K. (1986) *Keynes, Beveridge and Beyond*, Routledge and Kegan Paul, London

Dickens, P., Duncan, S., Goodwin, M. and Gray, F. (1985) *Housing, States and Localities*, Methuen, London

DOE (1977) *Housing Policy Review: Technical Volume Part III*, HMSO, London

Donnison, D. (1967) *The Government of Housing*, Penguin Books, Harmondsworth

Donnison, D. and Ungerson, C. (1982) *Housing Policy*, Penguin Books, Harmondsworth

Duclaud-Williams, R. (1978) *The Politics of Housing in Britain and France*, Heinemann Educational Books, London

Fuerst, J. (ed.) (1974) *Public Housing in Europe and America*, Croom Helm, London

Gilroy, P. (1987) *There Ain't No Black in the Union Jack*, Hutchinson, London

Hallett, G. (1977) *Housing and Land Policies in West Germany and Britain*, Macmillan, Basingstoke

Harloe, M. (1985) *Private Rented Housing in America and Europe*, Croom Helm, London

Harloe, M. and Martens, M. (1983) 'Comparative housing research', *Journal of Social Policy*, *13*, 255–77

Headey, B. (1978) *Housing Policy in the Developed Economy*, Croom Helm, London

Kemeny, J. (1981) *The Myth of Homeownership*, Routledge and Kegan Paul, London

Le Grand, J. (1982) *The Strategy of Equality*, Allen and Unwin, London

Lukes, S. (1974) *Power: a Radical View*, Macmillan, London

Mandelker, D. (1973) *Housing Subsidies in the United States and England*, Bobbs-Merrill, Indianapolis

McGuire, C. (1981) *International Housing Policies*, Lexington Books, Lexington

Merrett, S. (1979) *State Housing in Britain*, Routledge and Kegan Paul, London

Muth, R. (1969) *Cities and Housing*, Chicago University Press, Chicago

Odling-Smee, J. (1975) 'The impact of the fiscal system on different tenure systems', in *Housing Finance*, Institute of Fiscal Studies, publication no 12, London

Robinson, R. (1979) *Housing Economics and Public Policy*, Macmillan, London

Roistacher, E. (1986) 'The rise of competitive mortgage markets in Britain and the US', mimeo

Sutcliffe, A. (1981) *Towards the Planned City*, Basil Blackwell, Oxford

Swenarton, M. (1981) *Homes for Heroes*, Heinemann, London

Watson, S. (1986) *Housing and Homelessness*, Routledge and Kegan Paul, London

Westergaard, J. and Resler, H. (1975) *Class in a Capitalist Society*, Heinemann Educational Books, London

2

The Changing Role of Social Rented Housing

Michael Harloe

INTRODUCTION

Social rented housing has only been of major significance in a relatively few capitalist countries: elsewhere it is limited to a very minor role or hardly exists at all. Given that social housing is, in some respects, a form of provision which cuts across the dominant feature of housing in these societies — namely that it is a commodity, sold at the market price — its limited development is not surprising. Indeed, what needs to be explained is why it has sometimes developed on a significant scale.

Although the historical origins of social rented housing lie in the nineteenth century and are strongly linked to middle-class philanthropy and workers' movements, its major growth has occurred since 1945. This was neither the product of philanthropy nor simply a consequence of the rise of reforming social democracy. Essentially, large-scale state support for social rented housing was closely linked to various economic and political problems caused by the wartime destruction of productive capacity and the built environment and the needs generated by post-war economic growth and restructuring. But the particular combination of circumstances which gave rise to the post-war growth of this housing has now ended.

The collapse of post-war prosperity has had profound consequences for capitalist housing provision. But, even before this collapse occurred, there had been a considerable erosion in the status of and prospects for social rented housing. This decline has accelerated in the past decade, although it takes rather different forms and is more acute in some countries than others — because of the specific political, social and economic

41

circumstances in which social housing has developed in each country. In some countries this housing is already, or may soon become, a residual form of provision for politically, socially and economically marginal households. Elsewhere, this residualising process is limited to certain parts of the stock. Conventionally, such changes are seen as the consequence of a decline in the need or demand for such a form of housing. A decade ago this might have seemed a plausible explanation but in the 1980s the need for decent and affordable rental housing is growing as the limitations of the market-based tenures become more evident.

This chapter will examine the post-war history and current situation of social rented housing, showing how its changing fortunes have not been a simple product of changing consumer or even political preferences but of wider and more complex changes in social relations. In a single chapter we can only focus on some of the key developments and cross-national variations and have to omit much detail. But some aspects of the varying definition and organisation of social rented housing are too important to be ignored. These are discussed next.

THE CONSTITUTION OF SOCIAL RENTED HOUSING

It is easier to provide an approximate rather than a universally applicable general definition of social rented housing. It is certainly *not* a form of provision which is non-capitalist, either in terms of its immediate production or of its significance for the reproduction of capitalist social relations. But it can be differentiated from other forms of housing in three major respects:

1. It is provided by landlords at a price which is not principally determined by considerations of profit. These landlords are usually formally limited to 'non-profit' or 'limited-profit' status insofar as their social housing activities are concerned. Historically, rents have usually been below the levels charged on the open market for similar accommodation, although this may no longer always be so.

2. It is administratively allocated according to some conception of 'need' (although often not to those in objectively the worst housing conditions). Ability to pay can be important but, in contrast to private market provision, is usually not the dominant determinant of allocation.

3. While political decision-making has an important influence on all aspects of capitalist housing provision, as do market forces, the quantity, quality and terms of provision of social rented housing are more directly and sharply affected by the former than the latter, relative to other forms of provision. Government control over social rented housing is extensive and has increased as it became a central feature of state housing policies.

Even these broad features are subject to considerable cross-national variation. A useful starting point is to consider the varying nature of the landlords who provide social rented housing. Table 2.1 sets these out for the six countries which are discussed in this chapter: Britain, the USA, the Netherlands, Denmark, France and West Germany. In all six countries there have been periods when some housing has been directly provided by central or, more normally, local government. However, the more usual pattern is for provision by various other bodies. Often these have close, although sometimes conflict-ridden, links with local government. Only in Britain is most social rented housing provided by local authorities.

One important aspect of provision which the table does not make clear relates to the permanency of social rented housing. In most countries there have been controls on the disposal of social rented housing to the private market. Often this has not been completely ruled out in theory, but in practice has been discouraged or prevented. The main exception concerns West Germany, where social subsidies have been available to private firms and individuals wishing to provide social rented housing, and the USA. In Germany the law has always provided for the reversion of these properties to the private market some years after the receipt of social subsidies ceases. Much of this stock is now in fact reverting to the private sector. A rather similar situation exists in the USA although disposals are on a very small scale so far. In the other countries, most notably in Britain where there have been large-scale sales since 1980, sales are now being encouraged or at least seriously contemplated by governments and/or some social landlords.

An important aspect of the differing institutional structures of social rented housing provision concerns the relative autonomy of social landlords in respect to political control. In the four mainland European countries examined here there has often been considerable resistance to attempts by central and/or

Table 2.1: Principal Social Housing Landlords

Britain

Local authorities — 400 locally elected district and metropolitan councils have responsibility for a range of local services including housing. Apart from developing and managing social rented housing (and very occasionally housing for sale), they have a wide range of other housing powers and duties relating to private housing. Social housing capital development is financed by local government borrowing, mainly on the private market. Debt charges and running costs are met from central government subsidies, rents and local taxes. For many years councils were not allowed to make a 'profit' on their rented housing, now they are. This does not have to be used for housing purposes. Over the past 20 years central controls over local housing authorities have increased, the process has accelerated considerably since the mid-1970s. In recent years there has been considerable activity by about 2,500 non-profit housing associations — grant-aided and regulated by government — but they still only manage a small proportion of the rented stock. The average number of properties managed by councils is about 12,000, by housing associations 150 (1985 figures).

USA

Public housing authorities — public housing is developed and managed by about 2,800 public housing authorities (PHAs). Most are legally autonomous public corporate bodies created by local government in accordance with state enabling legislation, and run by commissioners. Though formally politically independent, they are often strongly influenced by local politics. Funding is by tax-exempt bond issues. Originally federal subsidies were only available for debt servicing, operating costs had to be met from the rents. But federal operating and modernisation subsidies are now provided. Any 'profit' on rents goes to reduce the federal liability. Detailed regulations for PHA operations are made by the federal government but apparently there has been a good deal of local autonomy. The average PHA holding is about 450 units (many are not run by professional staff) but 6 per cent of PHAs manage 65 per cent of all public housing (1979 figures).

The Netherlands

Historically, both *municipalities* (elected local authorities) and *housing corporations* have provided social housing ('Housing Act' dwellings). But since the 1960s the corporations have become the main social landlords, in recent years they have also been allowed to build other rented as well as owner-occupied housing. They can also now make 'profits' but these have to be reinvested in their housing activities. Corporations are subject to government controls and local authority regulation. There are strong

Table 2.1: Principal Social Housing Landlords (*continued*)

links between the corporations and the major political/religious groupings as well and there are two influential national federations, one linked to the labour movement and the other to the 'confessional' parties. They have taken two legal forms: membership associations and foundations (with a managing board and no members), but now the former form is favoured and the foundations have been converting to associations. Corporations are financed by rent income, loans and subsidies from central and local government (often the latter channels funds from the former) and, recently, by some private market borrowing. Over the years there has been a struggle by the corporations to maintain some independence, especially from local government. At the moment they seem to be losing some autonomy. There are about 900 corporations with an average holding of 1,400 units (1979 figures) — they usually only operate in one municipality.

Denmark

Housing associations — these non-profit bodies control about 85 per cent of the social rented stock (the rest is state/municipally owned). The associations can only be active in building and managing social rented housing. There are three types of association: (i) co-operatives; (ii) independent; and (iii) guarantee. In 1978 there were about 210 of (i), controlling 44 per cent of the stock; 260 of (ii), controlling 45 per cent; and 28 of (iii), controlling 11 per cent. Housing associations of type (i) have boards elected directly or indirectly by the residents; in the case of type (ii) local government appoints the majority of members, the rest being elected by the residents; in the case of type (iii) local government, the guarantors and the residents each elect members. There are also estate-based tenants' organisations which have some powers, but mainly make representations to the main boards. In recent years there has been tenant pressure for further devolution of decision-making from the central boards and management bureaucracies. Associations are funded by grants and subsidies from local and (mainly) central government but most development capital is obtained by selling index-linked bonds on the private market. Most associations are members of a national federation which has had strong links with the labour movement. Associations are subject to central and local government regulation and controls and their position in this respect is rather similar to that of the corporations in the Netherlands. The average holding of the associations in 1978 was about 600 units.

France

HLM organisations — there is no local authority control of social housing, it is mainly owned by various forms of these organisations (Habitations à

45

Table 2.1: Principal Social Housing Landlords (*continued*)

Loyer Modéré), which also build government-subsidised housing for sale. The two main types are Offices Publics d'HLM (OP) which are created on the initiative of one or more units of local government and Sociétiés Anonymes d'HLM (SA) which are established by the private subscription of capital and divide into various sub-types, including co-operatives. OP are non-profit making, have local authority, government and other public bodies participating in their management, and build mainly for rent. SA can make limited profits, are not under such direct public control and have mainly built for sale. HLMs are also involved in the purchase and rehabilitation of private housing. They are not necessarily limited in operation to a single locality. There is an influential national federation. HLMs are controlled and regulated by central government from which they obtain loans and grants. Other income comes from rents, the local authorities and a pay-roll tax on employers. Despite the extensive central controls, HLMs have often resisted certain policies with which they disagreed. There are about 1,200 HLMs, with an average holding of about 1,900 units, but the average for OPs alone is higher (1984 figures).

West Germany

The situation is extremely complex. Social rented housing can be provided by *'non-profit' organisations*, *private individuals* or *companies*, provided that they accept the general rules regarding rent, tenant eligibility, building standards etc. for such housing. The 'non-profits' are managed by local authorities, commercial/private enterprises, groups of individuals, unions, central government and the churches, there are especially strong links with the local authorities. The 'non-profits' take various forms: (i) housing societies (about 600 with about two-thirds of the non-profit stock, average holding 3,700 units — mostly they are limited liability companies); (ii) co-operatives (about 1,200 with one-third of the non-profit stock, average holding about 900 units); (iii) a small number which take other legal forms including nine state-based development agencies (1978 figures). 'Non-profits' dividends are limited to 4 per cent. Co-operatives are membership-based and generally rather small scale. The management of social housing organisations is often highly bureaucratised and centralised especially the other bodies listed above which are mainly the creation of the public sector (local authorities, states, etc.). Some have been involved in a wide range of other housing activities, including for profit housing, urban renewal, and other development, both in Germany and abroad (but many only operate in a single locality, especially those tied to a local authority). The largest social housing organisation, Neue Heimat, owned by the trade unions was extensively involved in such activities. It collapsed due to mismanagement and corruption and is now being broken up and sold off. The scandals surrounding NH have done much to discredit social housing organisations as a whole. There is an influential national federation. They are subject to extensive federal/state/local controls and regulation and receive finance

Table 2.1: Principal Socal Housing Landlords (*continued*)

from all these sources but most development capital comes from the private market. About half the post-war output of social housing has been provided by the 'non-profits' but about 25 per cent of their stock is in the non-socially subsidised sectors of the housing market, in all they control about 14 per cent of the total housing stock (1984 figures).

local government to control how these landlords allocate or manage other aspects of their housing. In the USA, where public housing authorities are created by local government, and in Britain, where the local authorities are themselves the land-lords, conflict and resistance to political direction focuses on central government. However, these institutional differences themselves arise out of the distinctive national political and economic histories of social housing provision, these are reviewed in the next sections.

THE GROWTH OF SOCIAL HOUSING BETWEEN THE WARS

As Table 2.2 shows, social rented housing, even in the five European countries, which are among the small group of capitalist countries where it has major significance, is by no means *the* dominant tenure. In the Netherlands and Britain it is the largest rental tenure. In France, Denmark and West Germany more rental housing is provided by private landlords (although this share has been in long-term decline, see Harloe, 1985). The USA is an example of that group of countries where it is of far less significance (although in some older and larger urban housing markets it accounts for up to 10 per cent of the stock).

These differences derive from the historical circumstances which surrounded the development of social rented housing. In the five European countries there was some growth of social rented housing after 1918. This was in response to the deep crisis faced by these nations immediately after the First World War. In most cases the eventual reversion to more settled economic and social conditions, with the resurgence of the private housing market, led to the ending or curtailment of government support for social housing (Harloe, 1985, pp. 27–38). In some countries, for example Denmark, there was

Table 2.2: Social Rented Housing as a Percentage of the Stock around 1980

	Britain	Nether-lands	Denmark	Germany	USA	France
Social rent	31	43	20	18	2	13
Private rent	11	13	26	45	32	40
Owner-occupied	58	44	54	37	66	47

Sources: Britain — 1981 Population Census;
Netherlands — Flynn, 1986 (data is for 1981);
Denmark — 1980 Housing Census;
West Germany — 1978 1% National Housing Survey;
USA — 1980 Population Census;
France — 1978 National Housing Enquiry.

renewed activity in the Depression years of the 1930s when social housing construction was used as a means of fighting unemployment. In Britain the need to modernise the urban structure, and therefore to clear slums, provided the main motive for social house building in this period. In the USA slum clearance and the reduction of unemployment — rather than any concern with meeting housing needs *per se* — also provided the main rationale for the first public housing legislation in the 1930s.

So the inter-war growth of social housing, even when — as in Denmark and Britain — it was partially sponsored by social democratic governing parties, was strongly influenced by broad considerations relating to the effective and continuing functioning of the capitalist economic and social order and of the capitalist built environment. For these reasons social housing received some support, for limited periods, from non-socialist politicians. The form this housing took and the terms upon which it was provided were strongly influenced by these considerations. Typically, this housing was not provided for the poorest strata of the working class but for skilled manual and white-collar workers — groups who were politically better organised and more important in relation to the economy than the poor. In this context it is interesting to note that in Britain, where much of the housing built in the 1930s *was* for poorer households displaced by slum clearance, it was constructed to lower standards than that built for the 'core' working class in the 1920s (Merrett, 1979, pp. 54–62).

THE POST-WAR EXPANSION OF SOCIAL HOUSING

A far larger expansion of social housing occurred after 1945. But it was driven by causes which were not so dissimilar to those present in the earlier period. Certainly the influence of social democratic parties and the labour movement, with an ideological rather than a purely contingent commitment to social housing, was significant, to varying degrees, in the European countries. But the requirements of economic reconstruction and development, the destruction of private housing markets and, particularly in the early years, the management of potentially explosive social tensions in the aftermath of war, led even those governments which had no ideological commitment to social housing to assist its development. This commitment was most limited in the USA, where the economy and the private housing market recovered very rapidly and where the main rationale for public housing soon became its use as an aid to profitable private-sector urban renewal. From the 1950s this housing was increasingly restricted to housing the permanent poor, often in poor-quality and heavily stigmatised 'welfare' housing (Bratt, 1986).

In Europe the task of post-war reconstruction was much greater than in the USA. Private capital and housing markets were in no position to provide the required accommodation, not just for the poor (they had never done this well), but also for much of the better-off working and middle classes. Moreover, there were acute housing shortages, because of wartime destruction and, especially in the mainland European countries, because of the new requirements of economic development. Unlike Britain, these countries have only completed their transition to fully urban-based economies and societies since the war. The completion of this transition was a major political objective. It involved some profound social, geographical and economic changes. Industrialisation, urbanisation and population growth generated massive new housing demands. The new industries had to be built up, partly by the expansion of domestic markets but crucially by the development of exports.

There was a need to sustain internationally competitive economies and hence to control wages, prices and consumption investment.

So, although some housing investment was an economic and political necessity, it had to be closely controlled and provided at costs which did not encourage rapid wage inflation. Private building was not enough or sufficiently cheap to meet these requirements. So subsidies and controls over the levels and standards of output and the price of rental housing were instituted. The impact of these subsidies and controls on the production and distribution of social and private rented housing varied but in all the five European countries social housing became a key element in housing provision.

In Britain these economic considerations were of less import-ance from the mid-1950s, when the economy prospered and Conservative governments encouraged the rapid development of owner occupation — attempting to restrict social housing to the same role as in the 1930s, as an aid to slum clearance and urban renewal (and, as before, the quality of the housing built for this purpose was lower than that of the 'general needs' housing built immediately after the war (Merrett, 1979, pp. 246–54)).

In the four other European countries the link between the growth of social housing and economic development was constituted in rather different ways (Haywood, 1984; Harloe and Martens, 1985; Magri, 1977; Marcuse, 1984). Likewise, the politics of social rented housing differed. For example, the influence of social democratic parties on social housing policies was strongest in the Netherlands and Denmark, although limited by the need to govern in coalition. In West Germany, where Christian Democrat governments held power until the late 1960s, there was a strong commitment to an early return to the private market in housing and attempts to disengage the state from its involvement in social rented housing from the mid-1950s onwards (this attitude also helps to explain why social subsidies were provided for owner-occupied and rental housing and, within rental housing, were not limited to legally defined non-profit landlords). A further political complication was, however, that this Christian Democratic Party (and similar groupings in the Netherlands) were not classic conservative parties but 'centrist' parties, containing a labourist/social reformist wing which appealed to a working-class electoral constituency and which often supported the growth of social rented housing in terms not so dissimilar from those advanced by the social democratic parties. Also the German federal system of government meant that the Länder (states) had major housing powers; in some of these areas Social Democrat governments strongly supported social housing.

To summarise, despite the variation in the ideological basis of support for social rented housing in Europe, there were strong reasons in practice why governments of differing political persuasions supported its growth. In the United States not only was the ideological climate hostile to social housing but there were less compelling economic or social reasons for it to be expanded. However, even here some got built, mainly to rehouse low-income groups who could not be served by the private market but. whose occupation of inner-city slums obstructed profitable urban renewal. In Britain the link between urban renewal and public housing was also strong, especially from the late 1950s. But, in contrast to the United States, there was also a political commitment to this housing by Labour local councils and, in the 1940s and less determinedly in the 1960s, by Labour governments too.

THE TENANTS OF SOCIAL RENTED HOUSING

In mainland Europe (and to a lesser extent in Britain), as in the inter-war period, much of the new social housing was not built to house those at the bottom of the income distribution. Such groups continued to concentrate in the private rented sector (which lost many relatively better-off households to social rented housing and later to owner occupation (Harloe, 1985)). The assumption in the Netherlands, West Germany and Denmark was that building should be aimed at the mass, middle-income demand, providing better quality housing than the private sector at rents which were affordable by such groups. The stock which was vacated would then filter down to the less well-off. Even today, when governmental support tends to concentrate on stimulating owner occupation rather than social rented housing, such arguments are still heard in these countries — despite the proven limitations of the filtering process. In France there were similar assumptions but here the link between the allocation of social housing and the requirements of expanding industry for skilled manual and white-collar workers was particularly close (Magri, 1977). Indeed, much new social housing was built expressly for such industries and, in exchange for compulsory contributions which they made to its construction, many employers directly nominated workers to this stock.

Even when there was no direct link between labour market requirements and access to social housing, aspects of the institutional structures and finances of the social housing organisations tended to sustain the focus on middle-income groups. Subsidies were limited, so financial viability required a certain level of rents. These were normally above what could be afforded by those on the lowest incomes, especially as individual rent allowance schemes barely existed before the late 1960s. Cross-subsidising the rents of newer properties by charging higher rents on older stock than would be justified by its historic costs ('rent pooling') had existed as a legal possibility for British housing authorities since 1935, in the 1950s the government began to press for it to be used to reduce the rents of new properties, thus allowing the state to economise on subsidies (Malpass, 1985, pp. 151–80).

In the rest of Europe such a possibility was often prevented by law. Moreover, the average stock of each social landlord was far smaller than in Britain (see Table 2.1 for more recent averages) and most had been built since 1945, so the benefits to be gained from cross-subsidy would have been very limited in most cases. Also, in many cases these units were occupied by relatively well-off households, who strongly resisted any attempts to raise their rents in order to divert subsidies to assist new building when, later, this was attempted. The semi-autonomous nature of most social landlords facilitated this. Moreover, even when the management of these organisations was not influenced by tenant pressure, there was no sense in allocating housing to groups which might not be able to pay the rents and which, in other ways, could create far more problems for these organisations than their existing constituency (see, for example, the conflict which occurred between the HLM landlords and the government in France (Duclaud-Williams, 1978, pp. 130–8)). And, even in Britain many local authorities resisted pooling and their allocation procedures tended to favour certain sectors of the working class and avoid many of those in the worst housing situation, although the link to slum clearance and the early development of working-class owner occupation began to change the income and social composition of local authority housing from the 1950s onwards (Lansley, 1979, pp. 161–4; Murie, 1983, pp. 187–94).

THE CHANGING PATTERN OF SOCIAL HOUSING CONSTRUCTION

Figure 2.1 presents details of the output of all housing and social rented housing and Figure 2.2 the share of the latter in the former for the six countries (the rental data for West Germany is for the 'first subsidy scheme', a small proportion of these completions were for owner occupation. But it excludes completions under the 'second subsidy scheme' which was mainly used for owner occupation, although a small proportion was also for rental occupation). It shows that there were sharp increases in building in the four mainland European countries after the period of relative austerity which accompanied economic reconstruction in the early part of the post-war period. Output peaked between the mid-1960s and the mid-1970s, since then there have been sharp falls in output as a consequence of the recession (in the USA there has been extreme instability of output with cycles of far greater amplitude than hitherto).

Except in Britain, the USA and West Germany, where the output of social housing has been in long-term decline since the 1950s, the output of *social* housing also peaked in the 1965–75 period. Data for the *share* of social housing in total output shows a very different picture: in five of the six countries, despite some fluctuations, this has been in long-term decline since the 1950s. The exception is France where the share rose sharply until the late 1960s and then fell.

A more detailed examination of developments in each country shows the following patterns.

Denmark

In the 1950s when resources for housing were very limited and the private market was still recovering, reliance on the social sector was high. In the 1960s, with more resources available for

Figure 2.1: Output of Social Rented and All Housing

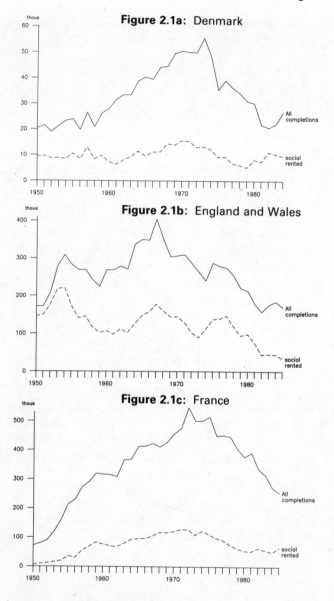

Figure 2.1a: Denmark

Figure 2.1b: England and Wales

Figure 2.1c: France

Sources: Danmarks Statistik;
CSO Annual Abstract of Statistics;
Ministère de l'Urbanisme et du Logement: Statistiques de la Construction;

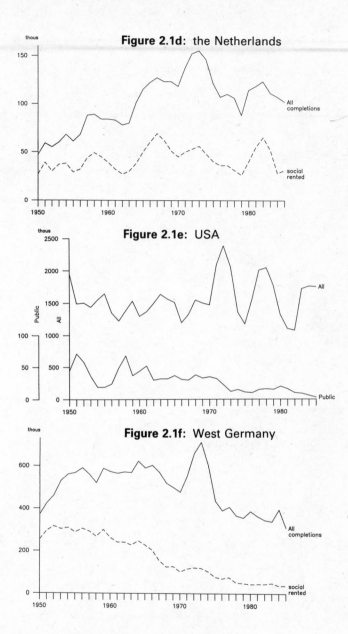

Figure 2.1d: the Netherlands

Figure 2.1e: USA

Figure 2.1f: West Germany

Centraal Bureau voor de Statistiek;
Statistical Abstract of the United States;
Statistisches Bundesamt.

Figure 2.2: Social Rented Housing — Share of Total Output

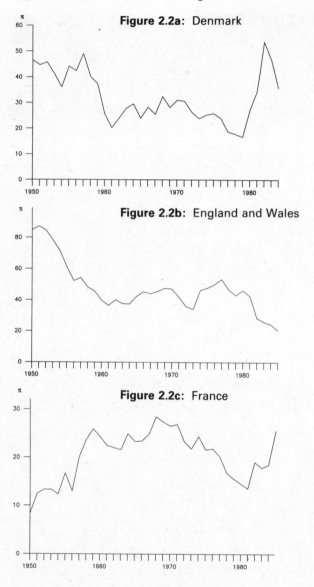

Figure 2.2a: Denmark

Figure 2.2b: England and Wales

Figure 2.2c: France

Sources: Danmarks Statistik;
CSO Annual Abstract of Statistics;
Ministère de l'Urbanisme et du Logement: Statistiques de la Construction;

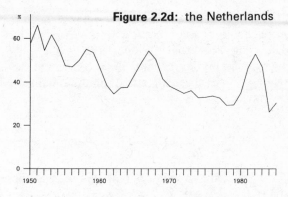

Figure 2.2d: the Netherlands

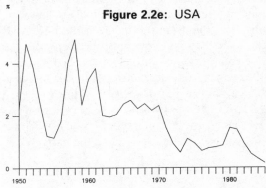

Figure 2.2e: USA

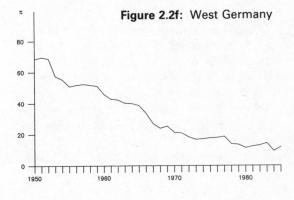

Figure 2.2f: West Germany

Centraal Bureau voor de Statistiek;
Statistical Abstract of the United States;
Statistisches Bundesamt.

housing, output rose in both the private and social sectors, but, increasingly, production took place in the private sector, so the share of social housing fell. From the mid-1970s to the mid-1980s the house-building market collapsed and for a time the government increased the share of social housing built to counter unemployment.

Britain

In this country the sequence of changes noted above and the replacement of the social sector by the private sector as the leading house-builder occurred from the mid-1950s onwards, the only interruptions in this trend occurred in the late 1960s and early 1970s when Labour governments were elected pledging to increase total production, including social housing. Note, however, the very modest degree to which this involved an actual increase in the share of social building on each occasion. Since the late 1970s the Conservative government has reduced the share and absolute numbers of social house building to their lowest peacetime levels since the early 1920s.

France

Because of the priority placed on industrial investment and the large amount of money paid for the rebuilding of war-damaged housing, new building remained at a very low level well into the 1950s. It then climbed steeply and virtually continuously. At first support for social building was limited but, with the growth of income and the intense drive to modernise the economy after De Gaulle came to power in 1958, rather more funding was available and the share of social housing grew. But, as elsewhere, the revival of the private market meant that this was only a temporary phase and it soon began to fall again.

The Netherlands

In many ways the pattern has been rather similar to that in Denmark, including in the most recent period when there was a temporary increase in the share of social construction for broader economic and social reasons. Interestingly, the peak in social housing output in the 1960s occurred under a centre-right government which made increased social subsidies available for a temporary period in order to try and eliminate the persistent absolute housing shortage. If this could be achieved it planned to dismantle housing controls, drastically reduce investment in social housing and let the private market take over.

The USA

Social housing has never been more than an insignificant proportion of total output but has declined to new lows under the Reagan presidency which aims to eliminate public housing construction. Subsidised low-income housing *was* expanded under the Democratic administrations of the 1960s but it mostly took the form of assistance to the private sector which was ideologically more acceptable.

West Germany

Like Britain both the share and the totals of social rented housing have declined since the 1950s as even the Social Democrats when in government have encouraged the private market to become the major force in housing provision. Like elsewhere there was a temporary increase in social building in the early 1980s to combat unemployment but the government has now announced that no further federal government subsidies are to be available for social rented construction. As in the Netherlands, France and the USA (in the 1960s) direct subsidies have been used to stimulate private-sector building (as well as the tax subsidies which exist — universally for owner occupation and sometimes for private rental housing — in all six countries).

THE LIMITED STATE COMMITMENT TO SOCIAL HOUSING

Thus high levels of social house building have occurred when the private market has been unable to supply sufficient output. Over the whole post-war period the most striking development has been the expansion of the private housing market, especially building for owner occupation. Although social democratic governments have often put a relatively higher priority on social construction, this priority has declined over time, nor has it always been the case that major expansions of such construction have been initiated by socialist governments. Very recently there were increases in social housing construction in West Germany, the Netherlands and Denmark. In each case these were initiated by centre-right governments as purely temporary measures, in the longer term all these governments were even more determined than their predecessors to limit social housing and rely on the private market. Even the socialist government which ruled France from 1981–6 did not sustain its plan to expand social house building for more than a year or -two.

There are several other aspects of this limited commitment to social housing which have implications for its current position. The first concerns the standards and cost of the accommodation which was built. In the 1950s, given the restrictions on housing investment, units were usually modest in size and facilities. But later there were substantial increases in space standards and in facilities, especially in the European countries. Both these quality improvements and the accelerating inflation in construction and financing costs, which occurred from the 1960s onwards, meant sharp increases in the costs of new social housing. This tended to make it even less accessible to lower-income households, and intensified the wish of governments to find ways of reducing their budgetary commitments to it. However, despite the quality increase, as measured by conventional indicators of space and amenities, there was a worsening of other aspects of housing quality at this time. Much social rented housing was provided in high-density, often high-rise industrially built estates. Many of these were located on the urban periphery, where land was cheap, but where access to urban services and employment markets was poor. By the late 1970s some were beginning to suffer from physical deterioration and acute social problems (Pearsall, 1984; Kennedy, 1984; Kristensen, 1986; Van Kempen, 1986; Cantle, 1986).

In fact, this concern with the budgetary costs of social housing was evident from the start of its post-war growth, although it intensified later. In the early 1950s social housing was normally financed, wholly or partly, with cheap state loans.

UN reports on housing in Europe show that even at this time there was concern about the heavy commitments that governments were accumulating (Economic Commission for Europe 1954, 1958). So, as capital markets revived, there was a trend away from the provision of cheap state loans towards reliance on private capital supplied at market interest rates, with subsidies to reduce the cost of debt repayments. Normally, this was a more costly means of financing than the previous systems. Private capital (obtained via tax subsidised bonds) had always been the means of financing US public housing but between the mid-1950s and the mid-1960s all the European countries, except the Netherlands, ended or greatly reduced state loans for social housing.

By the 1960s there began to be determined efforts to reduce the subsidy commitments. A particular target was the growing gap between the rents of the newer and more expensive units and the older stock (Economic Commission for Europe, 1980, pp. 49–53). A related issue was the long-term undertaking to subsidise every unit. Inflation, which resulted in increasingly heavy subsidies for each new unit produced, also meant that money incomes grew (and real incomes were rising too). So the existing tenants, many of whom (except in the USA) were in middle- rather than very low-income groups, benefitted from rising incomes and rents, linked to historic costs, which were falling. At the same time the rents of new housing were becoming ever less affordable by many lower-income households which required this accommodation — unless deeper subsidies were provided.

Increasingly, governments tried to raise the rents of older housing and limit subsidies to the first few years after construction. These changes brought about a further development — schemes of individual rent allowances, introduced to aid the minority (so it was assumed) of low-income households whose housing costs would be raised to unsupportable levels by the new regimes of higher rents and limited (normally degressive i.e. annually reducing) subsidies. Small-scale allowance schemes already existed in several countries (notably France) but between the early 1960s and the mid-1970s they became a central feature of social housing subsidies in all five European countries (Howenstine, 1983). At first they were intended to supplement degressive construction subsidies but increasingly, as new construction has fallen and rents have continued to rise, they have become a major means of subsidising social housing and a rapidly growing element in housing public expenditure.

In the USA there was a different situation. As we have already noted, public housing was restricted to the very poor (until the 1960s households were evicted if their income rose above the very low limits for admission — this was one of several ways of ensuring that public housing did not become a serious competitor to the private landlord). By the 1960s there were two broad types of public housing project. Especially in smaller communities there were projects which housed a high concentration of low-income white elderly households. In the major urban areas the projects were increasingly occupied by black (mainly female-headed) households dependent on welfare payments. As in Europe, many of the projects built in the 1950s and 1960s were in large high-rise blocks. Unlike the European stock they often had a very poor standard of amenities and space (again, partly so that they should not compete with the private market). Soon the interlinked processes of physical deterioration and social malfunctioning, which later became evident in many large social housing estates in Europe, began to develop. The problems were made worse by the very poor standards of management and the social and political stigmatisation of public housing (Kolodny, 1979; Struyk, 1980; Bratt, 1986).

These developments eventually resulted in a financial crisis for many of the larger public housing authorities. The financing basis for public housing was that the federal government paid the interest and amortisation on the bonds with which it was financed and rents met the operating costs (there was also limited assistance from the partial remission of property taxes). But the intensifying low-income character of the projects together with rapidly increasing operating costs (the product of inflation plus the costly problems which were arising in this stock) meant that authorities were faced with the stark choice of raising rents to levels which were far beyond the means of many low-income households, or going bankrupt. The choice was resolved in 1969 when Congress decided that rents should not exceed 25 per cent of tenant incomes. This forced the government to provide operating subsidies (and later modernisation subsidies). These escalated and, increasingly, the politics of public housing centred on the attempts of the government to control their growth.

THE NATIONAL POLITICS OF SOCIAL HOUSING

As we have already noted, the revival of private capital and housing markets, together with the impact of inflation on housing costs and public expenditure, stimulated persistent attempts to reduce state support for social rented housing.

These were first evident in Britain and the USA — the two countries which had vigorous private (especially home-ownership) markets and conservative governments in the 1950s. In the USA even the limited programme of public housing agreed in the late 1940s was not carried out (Bratt, 1986). In Britain the local authorities were forced back to the private market for loan capital, housing subsidies were restricted to use in connection with slum clearance and a few other special purposes, controls on private building were lifted and the nationalisation of land development values was repealed (for a detailed discussion see Merrett, 1979). In fact council house building continued on a substantial scale into the 1960s, it was during this period that most of the high-rise, industrially built estates were constructed in inner cities and on the urban periphery. There was no direct intervention in rent setting at this time, although the changes noted above did put upward pressure on them and, as noted already, government began to force local authorities to pool rents as a means of avoiding the need for increased central subsidies.

In the early 1960s Labour returned to power committed to expanding housing output. By now the party had shifted towards a much greater degree of support for owner occupation. By the mid-1970s Labour regarded owner occupation as the 'normal' tenure for most households, with council housing playing a supplementary role. But in the 1960s there was still a wish to expand council housing. However, costs were rising and the old system of flat-rate annual subsidies was insufficient to stimulate increased production. So a new interest subsidy system linked to strict cost controls was introduced. The subsequent boom in output only lasted for a short period before the economic crisis of the late 1960s forced deep public expenditure cuts.

To a considerable extent the pattern of the 1950s and 1960s recurred in later years. Between 1970 and 1974 a Conservative government renewed the effort to reduce council housing to a minimal role — subsidies and output were cut and rents were sharply increased, removing from the local authorities their power to set these and linking them to rent levels in the private rented sector. At the same time a national rent allowance scheme began. So there was a shift from general support for the expansion of social housing to the limited provision of consumer subsidies. In the mid-1970s Labour returned, repealed some of the most ideologically objectionable aspects of this legislation and, for a short period, before the economic crisis returned in an even more severe form than in the 1960s, output rose. But the general direction that housing policy had been taking was not reversed and the scene was set for the radical attack on social housing which has occurred since 1979.

Developments in the rest of Europe have been less extreme than in Britain or the USA. We have already noted that economic recovery and the development of the private housing market took longer to achieve in these countries. Also the politics of housing provision was not — for many years at least — so strongly biased in favour of owner occupation. But the aim of reducing support for social rented housing in favour of the private market has been evident. The main elements in this strategy have already been referred to. They are: (i) rent harmonisation — relating market-oriented rents to variations in housing quality, breaking the link with historic costs. This involves increasing the rents of older property, so reducing subsidies; (ii) limiting subsidies for new building — normally by degressive means, i.e. reducing subsidies over time as, it is assumed, tenants' incomes, and hence their ability to pay, increase; (iii) introducing rent allowances to target assistance on lower-income households.

In Denmark the 'rent gap' had become an important issue by the mid-1960s, when there was still an overall housing shortage but new social housing was standing empty because of its high rents (Haywood, 1984; Harloe, 1985, pp. 133–5). In 1966 a Housing Pact between the Social Democrats and the main non-socialist parties resulted in phased rent increases in the older stock plus additional degressive subsidies for new building (and the imposition of controls on the amount of social house building). The aim was to move all rents to market levels (aiding low-income families with housing allowances) by the mid-1970s. The policy failed. Inflation was much higher than predicted and the sharp rent rises were a political disaster for the Social Democrats. Rents in the newer property stayed at high levels in relation to incomes and by the early 1970s there was again new empty housing which those who needed it could not afford. Despite the increases, the rent gap persisted.

The unpopularity of the 1966 measures was an important factor causing the Social Democrats to lose power in the late 1960s. They returned briefly in the early 1970s with a programme which would have somewhat improved the position of social housing. There followed a Liberal minority government and a new Housing Pact in 1974. This reduced new building and further raised the rents of older housing to provide some cross-subsidy. Again the Social Democrats, which had been a party to this pact, suffered politically as sharp rent rises occurred both in the older stock and, because of degressive subsidies, in the newer housing too.

By the end of the 1970s the phenomenon of empty new housing together with unmet housing needs had reappeared. By this time too, as in Britain, there had been a shift in the attitude of the Social Democrats towards owner occupation, from hostility towards accommodation and then encouragement. This occurred as workers began to buy their own houses, moving from city centres to suburbia and there was an erosion of support for the party. In fact, throughout the 1970s there were efforts, supported by most of the major political parties, to limit the role of social housing and to target it more narrowly on lower-income households (for example in 1972 the quota for social housing was cut by 50 per cent and space standards lowered — by the Social Democrats). At the same time there was a boom in home-ownership which received widespread political support. In 1980 a new attempt was made to reduce the high rents of new housing and economise on subsidies with the introduction of index-linked loans for social housing construction, so reducing the burden of early loan repayments (Ministry of Housing, 1984). In addition, since the mid-1970s rent increases have been linked to increases in wages or prices and there has been a rapid growth of expenditure on rent allowances, as growing numbers of tenants have suffered stagnating or even declining incomes because of the recession.

Despite some important differences, there are certain similarities between these Danish developments and what has occurred in the Netherlands (Priemus, 1981; Harloe and Martens, 1985). After the temporary expansion of social housing under centre-right governments in the mid-1960s, the policy objective was to reduce subsidies and, by raising the rents in the older stock, to induce better-off tenants to move out into owner occupation. The vacant units could then house lower-income tenants, aided, where necessary, by rent allowances. But sharp rises in rents in 1972–3 led to widespread protest and, as in Denmark, were a factor in the subsequent defeat of the centre-right government. However, the new centre-left government did not abandon the policy direction followed by its predecessor, it merely modified it. A new rent harmonisation scheme was more gradual in impact — relating rents to building costs and to quality standards. Subsidy for new building was to be reduced with the introduction in 1975 of a new and more complicated system of degressive subsidies. This 'dynamic cost price' scheme — like the Danish index loans — reduces initial housing payments, raising these over time as, it is assumed, incomes and rent-paying ability increases (for a full discussion see Priemus, 1981). In terms of its initial objectives the scheme has been a failure. As in Denmark there has been a rapid escalation of rent allowances (initially it was assumed few tenants would require these) and various additional subsidies have been needed to make the rents of new housing affordable — even with these rents have risen sharply.

Once again, these developments occurred against the background of a boom in owner occupation which was aided by direct subsidies and supported by all the major political parties. As we have already noted, the growth of social housing had been supported not just by the Social Democrats but also by the key power broker in the Dutch political system — the Christian Democrats. But as the pressures and opportunities for a return to the private market grew there was a considerable consensus on this development and for the measures to redefine the role of social housing more narrowly. As in Denmark, there was notable resistance to some aspects of these policies, especially from the existing tenants of social rented housing, but while this has restrained the direction taken by policy it has not reversed it.

The Dutch pattern of consensual support for major programmes of social housing to meet mass moderate- and middle-income demand in conditions of housing shortage and austerity, later giving way — as the private market recovered — to a new consensus, promoting owner occupation and seeking to reduce the role of social housing has similarly occurred in West Germany (Marcuse, 1984; Wollmann, 1984). However, for several reasons, including their domination of government up to the late 1960s, the limited and temporary nature of the German Christian Democrats' support for social housing was clear from the 1950s onwards — as Figure 2.1 shows. As early as the mid-1950s measures were taken to encourage the use of social subsidies for owner occupation and by 1960 — considerably earlier than in the Netherlands — the government declared that the post-war housing crisis was virtually over. It then embarked on measures to rid the housing market of controls and open it up to private enterprise.

The policies adopted were similar to those elsewhere. Private-sector rent controls were abandoned, rents were raised and limited rent allowances introduced (although large-scale protest at the hardship caused led to the restoration of weaker controls when the Social Democrats gained power in the early 1970s). Interestingly though, discussions at this time in the ruling party about the wholesale return to the private sector of social rented housing led, instead, to some strengthening of the law preventing non-profit organisations (but not private landlords) disposing of this stock. Pressure from the labourist wing of the Christian Democrats probably accounted for this. However, social subsidies were reduced and they were increasingly used for owner occupation. Although some aspects of these policies, especially rent decontrol, were opposed by the Social Democrat Party, it too went through the transformation which its counterparts underwent elsewhere and increasingly supported measures to open up the private market in housing. A major step in this direction was taken in the period of Social Democrat/Christian Democrat government in 1967, when a second major social subsidy system was enacted. This involved the limited and degressive subsidisation of privately obtained construction loans. Although formally available for social rented construction, it was aimed at encouraging middle-income owner occupation. In the 1970s an increasing proportion of social housing construction (which continued to fall as a proportion of total output) was subsidised in this way. Later the system of degressive subsidies was applied to all new social housing.

As British Labour governments had done, the Social Democrats came to power (in coalition with the Free Democrats) in 1969 determined to increase building in the social and the private sectors. As in Britain too, the boom was short-lived and was ended by a recession in 1973. Meanwhile, the sharply rising cost of new house-building greatly increased the level of subsidies required to keep rents at reasonable levels and, despite the extension of rent allowances, there were empty new units accompanying unmet low-income housing needs. In Germany, unlike Denmark or the Netherlands, until very recently there has been successful opposition to any proposals to harmonise rents. This, together with the impact of degressive subsidies, led to an increasing rent gap and a persistent problem of affordability barring access by lower-income households to newer units. The large number of middle-income tenants, paying relatively low rents for older social housing, has been an important electoral constituency for the major parties and the social housing organisations have anyway resisted a shift in their role towards lower-income provision. However, despite the political difficulties (until recently at least) which prevented a radical reorientation of the role of social housing, governments have vied with each other to increase subsidies for home-ownership and tried to limit support for social rented housing. There has also been increasing criticism, from Social Democrats and Conservatives, about the continuing middle-income bias of social housing and this has been added to by events such as the financial scandals which have wrecked the largest non-profit social housing organisation, Neue Heimat.

As Figure 2.1 shows, the post-war expansion of social rented housing in France occurred later than elsewhere and, as a proportion of total output, never reached the levels achieved in the other five European countries studied here. The exclusion of the Left from government until the 1980s, when it took office in an era of deepening economic crisis and pressure on public expenditure, meant that housing policy was determined by successive centre/right wing governments. Housing policy, as much else besides, was moulded by an alliance between large-scale, modernising capital and the state technocracy. This is why the connection between the expansion of social housing and economic development objectives was so close for many years (Magri, 1977). At the same time there were strong links between the labour movement and some of the social housing organisations, so there was also resistance to centrally deter-mined policies. However, throughout much of the post-war period — despite arguments concerning exactly which house-holds should gain access to social housing — a good deal was allocated to middle-income groups: junior white-collar workers and the skilled working class (Duclaud-Williams, 1978, pp. 130–8). Not all social housing organisations had strong links with the labour movement but even those that did concentrated on a 'core' sector of organised labour — not groups such as the unskilled and the growing number of low-paid 'guest' workers.

However, within this overall pattern there did develop a variety of different subsidies for, and standards of, social rented housing. There began to be a need, for example, for lower-income housing for households relocated from the commercial urban renewal activities of the 1960s and 1970s and from the *bidonvilles* (shanty towns) occupied by foreign workers, especially in the area round Paris and near other major cities. This cheap housing was built to low standards and much of it became heavily stigmatised (there are clear parallels with US developments here) (Pearsall, 1984). Thus, more deliberately than elsewhere in Europe, the social rented sector in France has reproduced the same sort of segregation, based on income and social status, which is found in the private market.

Although the shift to the private market and owner occupation encountered numerous obstacles from the late 1960s onwards, building within the social sector was increasingly for owner occupation. Subsidy and rent developments were rather similar to those elsewhere. Changes in the mid-1960s reduced the assistance given to social rented housing and led to sharp rent increases. Cost inflation and quality improvements led to rents for new units which made them less and less accessible to lower-income households (despite some further development in rent allowances). As the better-off households increasingly opted for owner occupation, the phenomenon of vacant new social rented housing — especially on the less well-located peripheral estates — began to arise. As a result, by the mid-1970s many social housing organisations had serious financial problems.

The reorientation of policy away from social housing was accelerated by a major reform of housing finance in 1977. This aimed to promote home-ownership, limit social rented housing subsidies and target them on low-income households which, it was assumed, would be the major client group for this form of housing in future. Rent rises were to be linked to increases in construction costs, degressive subsidies would limit the extent and duration of state support for new units and a more

69

extensive system of rent allowances would ensure that only low-income households were protected from the sharp increase in rents that this new regime entailed. At the same time the government abandoned the policy of subsidising various forms of poorer-quality social rented housing and set a rather high standard for new units. An overall objective was to peg the level of direct state support for housing at its 1977 level. Given the new subsidies for owner occupation, this meant less resources for social rented housing.

The fate of this reform is interesting. It left rents in the pre-1977 stock on a historic cost basis, although the long-term aim had been complete rent harmonisation. But rents of new units paid by middle-income households were sharply increased while the new housing allowance for lower-income groups enabled them, for the first time, to afford this housing. But this strategy, of inducing middle-income households to leave social rented housing and shifting its role towards housing low-income groups, was strongly opposed by the social housing organisations. They already faced serious problems on some estates, where there were substantial concentrations of such households, and were reluctant to lose their middle-income tenants. For these reasons (plus the increasing costs of building to the high standards required) social rented house building collapsed. As the rents of new units rose, they were less and less attractive, compared with owner occupation, to middle-income households. So, as more lower-income groups moved in (despite their wishes, the landlords had no option but to admit some), there was a rapid rise in the take-up and costs of housing allowances and increasingly heavy construction subsidies for each new unit built.

Extensive reference has been made to the introduction of rent allowances in the 1960s and early 1970s. There are some general features of these allowances which were, as we have seen, a key element in governmental attempts to change the role of social rented housing. Of course, each scheme differs in detail but there are some major limitations of most of them (for detailed discussions see Harloe, 1985, pp. 201–11; Economic Commission for Europe, 1980). They are:

1. The question of take-up. In some countries, such as the Netherlands and Denmark, there appears to be little social stigma attached to claiming such benefits. They are regarded as a part of the welfare state to which all those eligible are entitled.

However, in West Germany — where there has been a strong ideology of self-help and self-reliance — there is little doubt that stigma is attached to the claiming of benefits, so far fewer households than are eligible apply for allowances. This reduces accessibility of social housing and increases the payments' burden for many existing tenants. More generally, in all countries there are many households who are eligible for allowances but which do not claim them — often they are put off by complex regulations or by the lack of any realisation that they are entitled to claim.

2. Most schemes require all tenants to make at least a minimum rent payment. Often this may be more than low-income households can afford if other vital expenditure is not to be cut. Minimum payments or calculations concerning what proportion of income tenants can 'afford' to pay are rarely based on careful studies of budgetary requirements — they are normally decided on grounds of political or financial expediency (an example is the recent decision of the Reagan administration to increase the proportion of income that public housing tenants can 'afford' to pay from 25 to 30 per cent (Hartman, 1986)).

3. Most schemes have rules restricting the 'over-consumption' of housing, requiring for example, that the space occupied is closely matched to family size. Moreover, some countries have put upper limits on the rent levels which can be subsidised. This has been a severe problem in Germany where the rents of new social housing have often been above this level, so forcing lower-income households to meet the top 'slice' of the rent out of their own pockets.

4. A final point concerns whether housing allowances can substitute for production subsidies and bring about investment in new and improved housing. In Europe, governments have recognised that allowances are limited in this respect and have continued to provide some subsidies for new building and the improvement of existing housing. In the USA the issue was put to practical test in the 1970s in the course of a large-scale experimental housing allowance scheme and in a separate system of rent subsidies for new and existing private rented housing. The outcome was negative (Hartman, 1986). In the existing stock most households refused to move to standard quality accommodation when this was made the condition for the receipt of allowances. Some new building occurred, but only when the government entered into long-term contracts to

subsidise rents, so making the subsidies little different in practice from conventional construction-related assistance.

As we have stressed, the growth of housing allowances has to be seen in the broader context of attempts to change the role of social rented housing, to target it on low-income households and to reduce overall support for this tenure with lower levels of building, degressive construction subsidies and rent levels linked to current market costs. Governments introduced these changes at a time of economic growth when most sections of the population had rising real incomes. The belief was that, as income growth continued, the state obligation to social housing could be reduced. But this has not proved to be the case. Investment in social housing has been increasingly restrained but costs have continued to rise at a time when tenants' incomes have stagnated or even fallen. The public expenditure costs of housing allowances have risen sharply, as have the numbers of claimants. Despite the aim of shifting the focus of the sector so that it concentrated on housing those excluded from access to the market, this has not been fully achieved. The residualisation of social housing is more advanced in Britain than elsewhere in Europe (and it occurred many years ago in the USA for the reasons which have been described). Yet, as Forrest and Murie (1986) and others have noted, the growing mass of the marginalised population is not exclusively concentrated in this tenure, nor is the whole of the council stock solely occupied by this group. And in the other European countries there have been several important factors which have meant that, while the trend towards a residualisation of social rented housing is evident in some parts of the stock, at the moment it is also limited in extent. These factors include:

1. The still restricted extent to which owner occupation has been opened up to moderate income groups, compared to the USA and Britain. Moreover, despite the rapid expansion of owner occupation in the mainland European countries in the 1970s, for reasons described elsewhere in this book, this development has suffered a serious reverse recently. The collapse of the private market also occurred in Britain and the USA but to a lesser extent (and ownership was anyway on a higher level before the collapse).

2. The resistance from social housing organisations to a redefinition of their role. It is of course impossible to separate out as reasons for this resistance the formally semi-autonomous

constitution of these organisations from the fact that they have remained a significant source of middle-income housing and, as such, have been a political force to be reckoned with.

3. A politics of housing which is less marked by hostility to social rented housing than is the case in the USA or in Britain and where governments have found in recent times that opposition from tenants to their policies can be politically costly.

THE CURRENT SITUATION

We have traced how a major shift in the politics of housing provision occurred in the 1960s and 1970s, involving an increasing emphasis on owner occupation and the attempted withdrawal of support for social rented housing. Despite the collapse of private house building in the late 1970s and temporary increases in social housing investment in some countries, plus the resistance to this change already discussed, the general policy objective has not altered. In fact there has been an increased desire by all governments to reduce public expenditure on housing. Given the level of assistance for owner occupation, it is perhaps surprising that this has not been reduced. But the political costs of such cuts, as well as their possible serious impact on financial markets and the house-building industry, have restrained governments. Also the reductions in social housing investment have mainly been carried through in the most recent period by right-wing governments with a more radical commitment than hitherto to reducing social housing to a limited role.

At the same time the social housing organisations have faced increasing difficulties because of conditions in some parts of their stock. We have already noted the serious financial, physical and social problems which arose in US public housing from the 1960s onwards and which later began to occur in Europe. As middle-income households began to filter into owner occupation some social rented housing began to suffer from high vacancy rates. This often created severe financial problems for social housing organisations. So, despite their un-willingness, they were forced to house an increasing proportion of lower-income households, including groups such as ethnic minorities, one-parent families and other households which they had often tried to avoid accommodating. Allocation practices were often discriminatory, concentrating such households in housing estates which were, for reasons of cost, location or physical condition, becoming unacceptable to their 'traditional' tenants. However, alongside these new tenants there continued to live those long-term tenants who had been unable to move into owner occupation and who were often severely affected by recession and unemployment. Typically, such households were white, skilled manual or service workers and nationals of the country concerned (and had often voted for the Left in the past). But, faced with new tenants who, by virtue of their colour, culture or domestic arrangements, were 'different', there has often been a growth of social conflict. In addition, as the faults of much of the system building of the past decades emerged, all this has occurred in a deteriorating environment (which was often never very attractive anyway). The result has been a complex interaction between physical deterioration, poverty and growing social tensions.

Many social housing organisations have been forced to devote the reducing resources which they receive to attempting to alleviate such conditions. More broadly, there is a growing need to renovate much of their housing stock, not just the system building but earlier housing which is ageing. While all governments have begun to recognise these needs, resources are not available on the required scale. Regarding the 'problem estates', a variety of innovative schemes are being tried. These usually combine physical renovation (often to minimal standards) and attempts to involve tenants in the running of their housing. The motivations behind the latter aim are mixed. There is a belief that increased participation will encourage the social solidarity now lacking in such areas. There is also some response to tenant criticism of remote, inefficient and bureaucratic housing management. But there is also a hope that the landlords' responsibilities can be reduced and those of the tenants increased. In the USA there has been a highly publicised series of projects in which full tenant management has occurred. But, despite some successes, the idea has been slow to spread and there is evidence that tenants often want better housing services from their landlords, not to take over from them (for survey results on this point, see Struyk, 1980, pp. 131–2; on the preconditions necessary for successful tenant management see Rigby, 1982).

A more detailed picture of the situation can be obtained by highlighting some of the more important recent developments in each country.

USA

The Reagan administration wants to disengage itself from directly subsidised housing as soon as possible (Hartman, 1986; Bratt, 1986). It has tried to end all new public housing construction and, despite some Congressional resistance, is now in sight of achieving this. It has also reduced operating subsidies and increased rent/income ratios. It has tried to ensure that only very low-income households are admitted to public housing (reversing earlier measures which attempted to widen slightly the range of those eligible for admission, hence increasing the rent-paying capacity in this tenure and easing public housing authorities' financial problems). At the same time it continued — for a limited period only — an earlier policy of providing, on a rather haphazard basis, substantial subsidies for the modernisation of the stock. The objective is to bring the stock up to a level where operating subsidies can be limited and rents can be tied to those charged for equivalent private-sector housing. It has encouraged public housing authorities to dispose of as much of the stock as is possible, by demolition (to make way for more profitable private-sector land uses) or by sale to the private housing market or to sitting tenants. However, given the inability of the private market to house those displaced by such losses and the fact that, because of their very low incomes, few tenants could afford to buy their units, there have, so far, been severe limits to the scope for sales. At the same time, while public housing has few enthusiastic supporters, as poverty has grown there has been an increase in the demand for it from those who would previously have relied on the private sector and a recognition by some politicians that a limited public housing sector — as residual provision for the poor — should be retained.

Britain

While developments in the USA have simply reinforced the role of public housing which has evolved over the post-war years, the changes which have occurred in this country since the

75

advent of a Conservative government in 1979 mark a far more dramatic acceleration in the trend towards the residualisation of social housing (Forrest and Murie, 1986; Malpass, 1986). There has been a co-ordinated series of policies with this objective in view. Construction subsidies have been sharply reduced and new building decimated. In the early 1980s rents were increased far faster than the increase in either earnings or building costs — so that many authorities now receive no general subsidies at all and some are making 'profits' on their social housing. The escalating cost of housing allowances has been trimmed by changes in its regulations which have reduced eligibility and increased rent/income ratios. Apart from the desire to reduce public expenditure, these changes are intended to encourage as many tenants as possible to buy the properties that they occupy or to move into private housing. From 1980 the government has offered large sales discounts to tenants who are prepared to buy and forced the local authorities to sell to them. As the volume of sales has tailed off (given the low incomes of council tenants, many could not afford to buy, even with discounts, especially as the housing allowance scheme only covers rental housing), these discounts have been increased so some tenants can now buy at only 30 per cent of the market value. As the limits of this privatisation of the stock have become clear, the government has begun to encourage and provide subsidies for whole estates to be sold off to property developers — for improvement and resale for owner occupation (or, less frequently, for private renting). In 1986 legal rights which tenants had to resist such moves were removed. As a result of these developments the social rented sector has declined both as a proportion of the housing stock and numerically. But, with continued large-scale unemployment and the increased difficulty of gaining access to private housing, the unmet demand for social rented housing (as measured, for example, by waiting lists and homelessness statistics) is increasing. By 1986 even the official watchdog over local government expenditure was referring to such problems and to the 'crisis' of council housing (Audit Commission, 1986).

Denmark

In 1982 a new centre-right government introduced austerity measures, including substantial reductions in public expenditure. There had been a small increase in social house building under the previous government, for the reasons already described, but the new government reduced production and diverted some subsidies to the renovation of the existing stock. Some in the governing coalition wanted to encourage social housing sales but there was still sufficient support for the tenure to make this politically unacceptable. The government also aimed to reduce the cost of rent allowances. In the 1970s there had been a growth in supplementary allowances, provided by the local authorities because of the limitations of the government scheme. These had often been crucial in enabling lower-income households to gain access to new social housing. But in the early 1980s, under increasing financial pressure, many local authorities ended such assistance. In addition, some local authorities were increasing their control over who moved into social housing. Some areas with high proportions of social housing believed that 'problem' households were being diverted to their areas from municipalities which had restricted social house building (Kristensen, 1984). In particular, as elsewhere, there was resistance to the housing of foreign workers. More generally, there was a growing recognition of the problems of certain parts of the social housing stock. As described earlier, as the better-off tenants moved out of social housing in the 1970s, the vacancies had often been filled by low-income households, for example those nominated by welfare agencies. Rent arrears escalated and this, together with accelerating physical decay, caused a financial crisis for many social landlords. They faced a difficult situation. If they again became selective in their choice of tenants, they would risk increasing the amount of vacant property and incur even worse financial problems. In fact, in some areas where the municipalities did use their powers to exclude lower-income households, those social housing organisations with property which had become unlettable except to such households (who had no other choice of accommodation) were placed in great financial difficulty.

The Netherlands

As in Denmark, the Social Democrats lost power in 1982 and were succeeded by a centre-right government, committed to austerity policies and wishing to reduce support for social rented housing (Harloe and Martens, 1985; Flynn, 1986; Van Weesep, 1986). However, the free-market sector could not provide more than a trickle of new (and very expensive) housing after a disastrous collapse in the late 1970s. There was also pressure from many local authorities for the government to modify its plans and allow for more social house building (backed by evidence that an increased proportion of households now wanted to rent rather than to buy). At the same time, the failure of the dynamic cost-subsidy system to allow the government to withdraw from its support for the newer housing stock resulted in a build-up of massive future public expenditure commitments. The cost of rent allowances was rapidly escalating, despite some reductions in its provisions, and the government wanted to make further economies by forcing landlords to allocate the older and cheaper stock to lower-income households. Similar problems to those experienced elsewhere were found on some of the large housing estates and there was conflict between the local authorities, which had a limited duty to secure housing for some lower-income households in the greatest need. Some social housing organisations were reluctant to accommodate such households, particularly if they were foreign workers. As in Denmark, there had been some discussion of selling off social housing. This faced strong political resistance but some sales may occur because of the lack of other sources of funding for new investment, especially in improvement and repairs. Despite the counter-pressures, the government still wanted to encourage the shift out of social housing by middle-income groups and refocus on lower-income accommodation (even though most of this owner-occupied housing was also directly subsidised). Thus rents were deliberately increased faster than construction costs. As in other countries (for example, Germany, Britain and Denmark) there were reductions in the standards of new building in an attempt to ensure that what was built was within the means of lower-income households with the lowest feasible subsidies.

West Germany

In 1983 the Social Democratic government lost power to a Christian Democrat/Free Democrat coalition. Even before this, influenced by the Free Democrats with whom they were then in coalition, the Social Democrats reduced social housing assistance (Wollmann, 1984; Kreibich, 1986). In 1981 the rents of the older housing stock were increased. This had the effect of reducing the time during which social housing subsidies were received by this stock and bringing forward the point when its owners (if they were not non-profit associations) were free to sell or let it on the private market. At first the new government increased social housing subsidies but, as noted already, from 1986 no further federal support was available for new social rented housing. All further construction is now dependent on the limited funds available from the states and local authorities. The costs and standards of new social housing were reduced but the rents of the more expensive units built in the 1970s had now reached levels which encouraged better-off tenants to move out and become owner-occupiers. Overall, rents rose much faster than tenants' incomes, so most newer housing could only be afforded by relatively better-off households or by those whose rent was paid by the welfare authorities. This mix of households led to the growth of social tensions in some areas. Meanwhile, many families required but could not afford social housing (waiting lists and the number of homeless households were rising). The social housing organisations resisted the redefinition of their role as housers of low-income households. But, as in the Netherlands, some local authorities tried to gain more control over allocation policies in order to force landlords to respond to these needs. Increasing problems occurred on some of their estates where there were high concentrations of lower-income households (especially 'guest' workers). Although the ability of non-profit landlords to sell off their properties was restricted, as in the Netherlands, some of them were contemplating doing this to finance the increasing need for repairs and renovation of their existing stock. Overall, the government wanted substantially to reduce the size of the social rented sector and it was estimated that by 1995, with the termination of subsidies on much of this stock and the inducements which were being provided for the early repayment of housing loans, the sector will have shrunk by 50 per cent. The plan to limit social rented housing to a residual role was clear, even though there was resistance to this policy.

France

Despite the return of a Socialist government in 1981 with a commitment to expanding social house-building, it soon reverted to austerity measures and there was no fundamental change of direction in policies (Galarza, 1986). The comparative development of rents and owner-occupier costs, influenced by the relative provision of subsidies for these two sectors, continued to encourage all who could afford it to become owner-occupiers. Despite the social housing organisations' strong resistance to accommodating low-income households, there were increasing concentrations of these households in some parts of their stock, especially on the high-rise peripheral estates. In France, more than in other European countries reviewed here, there has been a very serious growth of inter-group and, especially, inter-racial tensions and violence on some of these estates. Pilot projects have attempted to reverse deteriorating physical and social conditions by a mixture of community work, social services provision and physical investment but results have not been very encouraging (UNFOHLM, 1981). Many social housing organisations have become increasingly concerned with managing and renovating their existing stock rather than new building. There are serious conflicts between the social housing organisations, the local authorities and central government. As in Denmark (but unlike the situation in Germany and the Netherlands), the local authorities have resisted government attempts to change the role of social housing. In some cases they have tried to restrict the admission of low-income households and encouraged them to move to other localities. Even left-wing local authorities, which have housed many such households, have become more restrictive. In general, as social housing has increasingly been seen as low-income housing, especially for non-French households, there has been a reduction in political and popular support for the tenure.

These brief reviews of developments in each country illustrate the point made earlier — that governments are persisting in trying to reduce their commitment to social rented housing. One common feature of these policies is an attempt to devolve greater responsibility for lower-income housing provision to the local level (see, for example, Flynn, 1986; Struyk et al., 1983, pp. 79–95; Harloe and Paris, 1985, pp. 85–90; Galarza, 1986). But local resources are very limited, even when localities are, in principle, prepared to do more. In some countries there are also attempts to devolve responsibilities from social landlords to the tenants and/or to break up the stock of existing social housing organisations into smaller holdings (see, for example, Kennedy, 1984; Cronberg, 1986; Audit Commission, 1986). All these varied attempts are presented in positive terms. Decentralisation will, it is claimed, enable a more effective and flexible response to be made to local needs by those who really understand them. Encouraging tenant participation and even the take-over of management responsibilities is presented as an innovative response to the (justly) criticised defects of bureaucratised and insensitive social housing management. But in order to achieve desirable goals, such as increased tenant control or local flexibility of response, there needs to be an increase in funding, especially in an era when the capacity of many tenants to bear high housing costs is declining. And this is *not* what is occurring. Moreover, along with the attempt to withdraw from responsibility for meeting lower-income housing needs, there has also been an *increase* in some aspects of central control. As we have seen, there have been increasing restrictions on the level and standards of new building and rents and, in general, attempts to restrict social housing to a more limited role. Local government has also tried to increase control over tenant allocations and new building plans.

THE CONTRADICTIONS OF SOCIAL RENTED HOUSING

There has been an erosion of much of the political, social and economic rationale which underpinned the post-war expansion of social housing. Even in those European countries where it has a much bigger role than in the USA, by the end of the 1970s there were signs that, despite the resistance of many tenants, social housing managers and some politicians, it was being reshaped to become housing for those low-income households which, even with extensive subsidisation, could not afford private market housing. It was also beginning, to varying degrees, to develop some further characteristics which had long been present in the USA. Some parts of the stock were becoming socially stigmatised, suffering from severe physical deterioration and were a focus for social conflict. Most of the changes which have occurred in the 1980s, the advent of austerity policies and right-wing governments ideologically committed to the private sector, have simply served to accelerate these trends. Nevertheless, the policies now being pursued are increasingly contradictory and their eventual outcome is by no means certain — it will depend on the balance of economic and political forces and their future development in each country.

The central contradiction is the pursuit of a strategy of reducing social housing to a more limited, lower-income role and relying increasingly on the private sector for housing most people at a time when the market is not able to provide all the required housing at reasonable standards and an affordable cost. The demand for social housing is rising as fewer new, elderly or unemployed households can afford the private alternatives. Obviously, governments can try to ignore these needs or provide further subsidies to underpin the private sector. In practice there has been a mixture of both responses. But it seems reasonable to suggest that, eventually, there must be a political price to pay for the growth of unmet needs, especially as these begin to affect households which have provided the core support for major political parties. Yet the option of increasing subsidies for the private market means that the objective of reducing state expenditure is thwarted. Moreover, although this is rarely recognised, such subsidies are usually more expensive and less efficient than support for non-profit social housing.

This central contradiction has further contradictory consequences. Raising rents and reducing general subsidies in order to economise on public expenditure and encourage the better-off tenants to become owner-occupiers, *increase* the dependency of the remaining, increasingly low-income sector on income-related subsidies if escalating housing stress is to be avoided. Apart from the diminishing returns, in terms of public expenditure savings, gained by raising rents (higher rents but higher rent allowances), the capacity of the existing tenants to pay, through their rents, for the growing costs of dealing with physical decay and the more general pathology of 'problem' estates is reduced by policies which narrow the income range of those accommodated in the sector. Moreover, although there is no simple or necessary connection between concentrations of low-income households and the intensity of the physical and other problems of some areas of social housing, there is some correlation between these characteristics. In fact, several governments have stressed that a partial solution to these problems is to *avoid* the further build-up of areas which are solely occupied by lower-income groups. Yet these *social* objectives are in conflict with the consequences of the rent and subsidy policies which have been adopted and the wider *politics* of housing provision which underlie them. The experience of the only country which has so far adopted major measures to privatise sections of the social housing sector suggests that this accentuates the concentration of low-income households which are confined to poor-quality housing. In Britain, council house sales have been concentrated in the better parts of the stock — single houses rather than high density flats — and have creamed off many of the better-off tenants, together with their higher rent-paying capacity (Forrest and Murie, 1986). So an increasing proportion of the remaining social housing offers poor living conditions and suffers from costly defects. The opportunities to move within the social housing sector from these less desirable properties to the better parts of the stock is reduced and popular perceptions of the stigmatised and problem-ridden nature of this tenure are reinforced.

These contradictions are becoming increasingly evident. How they are resolved, or moved on to a new phase, depends, first, on broader economic developments. If unemployment falls and private housing again becomes more accessible to those who are now excluded from it, the transformation of social rented housing, accompanied by the further growth of the private market, may continue. Even if this does not occur there may well be developments within the private market, for example, increased subsidisation of home-ownership or private renting, further reductions in standards, the growth of sharing etc., which will limit the resurgence of demand for social rented housing.

Also the distinctive politics of housing in each country will continue to affect the prospects for social rented housing. In the USA public housing will surely continue to play a residual role. In Europe the most determined effort to reduce it to such a role has occurred in Britain but there are also strong indications that this may be its future in France and Germany. But in the Netherlands in particular (where social renting is a much larger tenure than in any of the other five countries) and in Denmark, access to owner occupation has been hit especially hard in the recession, social housing retains considerable political support and, above all, considerable popular support as acceptable housing for middle-income households.

Now that the economic benefits and affordability of owner occupation have sharply declined, the question of whether social housing as a whole will be reduced elsewhere, as in the USA, to a severely limited, stigmatised and welfare-oriented role is still open — although the developments of such features in parts of the stock seem to be firmly established in Europe too.

REFERENCES

Audit Commission for Local Authorities in England and Wales (1986) *Managing the Crisis in Council Housing*, HMSO, London

Bratt, R. (1986) 'Public housing: the controversy and the contribution' in R. Bratt, C. Hartman and A. Meyerson (eds), *Critical Perspectives on Housing*, Temple University Press, Philadelphia

Cantle, T. (1986) 'The deterioration of public sector housing' in P. Malpass (ed.), *The Housing Crisis*, Croom Helm, London, 57–85

Cronberg, T. (1986) 'Tenants' involvement in the management of social housing' *Scandinavian Journal of Housing and Planning Research 3*(2), 65–87

Duclaud-Williams, R. (1978) *The Politics of Housing in Britain and France*, Heinemann Educational Books, London

Economic Commission for Europe (1954) *European Housing Progress and Policies in 1953*, United Nations, Geneva

—— (1958) *The Financing of Housing in Europe*, United Nations, Geneva

—— (1980) *Major Trends in Housing Policy in EEC Countries*, United Nations, New York

Flynn, R. (1986) 'Cutback contradictions in Dutch housing policy' *Journal of Social Policy, 15*(2), 223–36

Forrest, R. and Murie, A. (1986) 'Marginalisation and subsidised individualism: the sale of council houses in the restructuring of the British welfare state', *International Journal of Urban and Regional Research, 10*(1), 46–66

Galarza, M. (1986) 'Housing and the crisis: rehabilitation policies in France', paper presented to the International Conference on Housing Research, Gavle, Sweden (mimeo)

Harloe, M. (1985) *Private Rented Housing in the United States and Europe*, Croom Helm, London and Sydney

Harloe, M. and Martens, M. (1985) 'The restructuring of housing provision in Britain and the Netherlands', *Environment and Planning A, 17*, 1063–87

Harloe, M. and Paris, C. (1985) 'The decollectivisation of consumption: housing and local government finance in England and Wales 1979–81' in I. Szelenyi (ed.), *Cities in Recession*, Sage, London and Beverly Hills, 70–98

Hartman, C. (1986) 'Housing policies under the Reagan administration' in R. Bratt, C. Hartman and A. Meyerson (eds), *Critical Perspectives on Housing*, Temple University Press, Philadelphia

Haywood, I. (1984) 'Denmark' in M. Wynn (ed.), *Housing in Europe*, Croom Helm, London

Howenstine, E. (1983) *Attacking Housing Costs: Foreign Policies and Problems*, Center for Urban Policy Research, Rutgers NJ

Kennedy, D. (1984) 'West Germany' in M. Wynn (ed.) *Housing in Europe*, Croom Helm, London and Canberra

Kolodny, R. (1979) *Exploring New Strategies for Improving Public Housing Management*, US Department of Housing and Urban Development, Washington DC

Kreibich, V. (1986) 'The end of social housing in the Federal Republic of Germany? The case of Hanover', *Espaces, Populations, Sociétiés*, 85–96

Kristensen, H. (1986) 'Danish post-war public housing in trouble', Danish Building Research Institute

Lansley, S. (1979) *Housing and Public Policy*, Croom Helm, London

Magri, S. (1977) *Logement et Reproduction de L'Exploitation*, CSU, Paris

Malpass, P. (1985) *The Development of Public Housing Policy in Britain*, PhD thesis, University of Bristol

—— (1986) 'From complacency to crisis' in P. Malpass (ed.), *The Housing Crisis*, Croom Helm, London, 1–23

Marcuse, P. (1982) 'Determinants of state housing policies: West Germany and the United States' in N. and S. Fainstein (eds), *Urban Policy Under Capitalism*, Sage, London and Beverly Hills

Martens, M. (1985) 'Owner-occupation in Europe: post-war developments and current dilemmas', *Environment and Planning A, 17*, 605–24

Merrett, S. (1979) *State Housing in Britain*, Routledge and Kegan Paul, London

Ministry of Housing (1984) *Financing of Housing in Denmark*, Ministry of Housing, Copenhagen

Pearsall, J. (1984) 'France' in M. Wynn (ed.), *Housing in Europe*, Croom Helm, London

Priemus, H. (1981) 'Rent and subsidy policy in the Netherlands during the seventies', *Urban Law and Policy, 4*, 299–355

Rigby, R. (1982) *The Resident as Resource: A Public Housing Management Demonstration in Jersey City*, State of New Jersey, Trenton

Struyk, R. (1980) *A New System for Public Housing*, The Urban Institute, Washington DC

Struyk, R., Mayer, N. and Tuccillo, J. (1983) *Federal Housing Policy at President Reagan's Mid Term*, The Urban Institute, Washington DC

UNFOHLM (1981) *'Vivre Ensemble dans la Cité* , UNFOHLM, Paris

Van Kempen, E. (1986) 'High rise housing estates and the concentration of poverty', *The Netherlands Journal of Housing and Environmental Research, 1*(1), 5–26

Van Weesep, J. (1986) 'Dutch housing: recent developments and policy issues', *Housing Studies, 1*(1), 61–6

Wollmann, H. (1984) 'Housing policies in West Germany: between state intervention and the market mechanism' in K. von Beyme, and M. Schmidt (eds), *Policy Making in the Federal Republic of Germany*, Sage, London and Beverly Hills

3

Owner-occupied Housing:
a Tenure in Transition

Maartje Martens

INTRODUCTION

Recent interest in the study of owner-occupied housing derives from the significance of the sector in meeting current housing needs for most households. After years of policies cutting back on social housing provision and with the decline of private rental sectors, most households now opt for individual home-ownership through choice or necessity. At the same time, many of the features related to owner occupation that had been taken for granted in the post-war era, are now being questioned. To mention only a few examples, government financial support for owner-occupied housing provision is being reviewed in many countries, particularly where it concerns subsidies related to income tax deductions for home-owners. Even if there are no immediate changes, such discussions reduce confidence in the fortunes of the sector. Recent experiences in several countries, in addition, have shown that house price inflation is not endemic to the sector. House prices can fall, with major effects for the owner-occupied market as well as for individual home-owners. Elsewhere, price differences between regions are increasing, affecting the rate of mobility within national housing markets. It seems that the context of owner-occupied housing markets is changing rapidly everywhere.

Interest in the study of owner-occupied housing markets only evolved in recent years. Before, attention focused on social housing sectors and state housing policies. As such attitudes to research prevailed in most Western countries, a presentation of a cross-national comparison of owner-occupied housing markets on the basis of existing research is very difficult. Despite growing interest in the study of owner-occupied housing, understanding of what is constituted by this form of provision is still very limited. Research in this area, in fact, has suffered from much of the same problems as earlier housing studies focusing primarily on state policies (see Chapter 1 for a detailed critique). Recent surveys of owner-occupied housing markets tend to emphasise distributional aspects and are concerned with two issues in particular: (i) the effects of state subsidies to owner occupation and (ii) the accessibility of the sector for differing types of household.

The main issues which policy-orientated studies focus on when looking at owner-occupied housing relate to the question of whether existing forms of subsidy contribute *effectively* to the expansion of the tenure. The problem is seen of particular relevance when state housing policies aim to expand home-ownership to lower-income households. A related issue concerns the *state expenditure effects* of present subsidy arrangements for owner occupation. The costs of income-tax-related subsidies, in particular, have risen considerably in recent years with governments having little ability to control them. The upward trend arises from the terms on which tax-relief subsidies are given, in the face of long-term house price inflation and rises in interest rates. Finally, a major issue in policy-orientated studies of owner-occupied housing concerns the *equity* of the distribution of subsidies. Discussions in this context centre on the regressive, income-distributional effects of mortgage interest rate tax relief and on inequalities in the subsidies given to the different housing tenures.

Proposals to reduce the distributional inequalities of housing subsidies, to reduce state expenditure on mortgage tax-relief subsidies or to target subsidies more effectively towards expanding the tenure are often taken up by politicians. But, although these issues are of major importance, too much prominence is given to the role of the state in determining the way the owner-occupied housing market operates. As will be shown in this chapter, state support for owner occupation has become an integral part of that market, but it also constitutes only one aspect of the social relations of housing provision in the tenure. In order to understand the dynamics of the owner-occupied housing market or, indeed, the effects of state housing policies on the sector, it is imperative to consider the operations of all the major institutions and agencies linked to this market and the relationships between them. The dynamics of the growth of owner-occupied housing markets are determined by a set of social relations of provision which are specific to each country. The approach includes the study of the contemporary agencies involved in the provision of owner-occupied housing as, for instance, the construction industry, the agencies which control the housing development process, and the mortgage finance industry.

The second theme for research into owner-occupied housing concerns the study of who the home-owners are. Issues addressed in this context relate to whether the tenure has made society more 'democratic' by allowing a wider access to housing and wealth by lower-income households, ethnic minorities and households headed by women. Related questions raised in this context are whether home-ownership changes peoples' voting behaviour and, more generally, how (or whether) the 'property owning democracy' affects class, race and gender relations in society. Others deal with the problem of tenure, class and political consciousness in more sophisticated ways, by not assuming a direct mediation between tenure, class and political practices (see Pratt, 1986; Preteceille, 1986).

Even though the issues raised in these sociological studies are of major interest, most of them are subject to one major problem: distributional- and consumption-orientated housing research generally regards owner occupation as a unified housing market. Even when owner-occupiers are differentiated according to social category and class position, little significance can be given to the social meaning of owner occupation, if the different ways in which home-ownership is acquired (or provided) are not taken into account. Otherwise, tenure classification refers only to the formal ownership rights attached to the house occupied by a household.

This chapter will argue that there are substantial differences in the constitution of owner-occupied housing markets, not only between countries and in different periods of time, but also within national contexts where different forms of owner-occupied housing provision co-exist. The consequences for individuals of home-ownership, therefore, do not only depend on the social or class position of the members of the household concerned, but also on how access to the sector is achieved and how their housing situation is maintained. Within any socio-economic category, there are, for example, major differences between home-owners who bought their houses years ago, or just recently.

Rather than dealing with the issue of social stratification, this chapter aims to highlight differences in owner-occupied housing provision between six advanced capitalist countries: Britain, France, West Germany, the Netherlands, Denmark and the USA.[1] The aim is to outline, in a comparative way, general frameworks and trends without providing a comprehensive overview and explanation of owner-occupied housing markets and the state policies associated with them. To summarise, owner-occupied housing markets differ between countries in terms of (i) the historical periods in which they expanded; (ii) the social relations that have emerged around owner-occupied housing markets at national levels; and (iii) the political support that has developed for the tenure.

Historical differences in the expansion of owner occupation will be dealt with first, followed by a description of the varying forms of political support for the tenure. An analysis of the major forms of owner-occupied housing provision in each of the countries is then undertaken, including an outline of the differing role of the existing housing stock in this market. The remainder of the chapter will focus on several interrelated issues affecting all national housing markets at the moment: namely, a long-term decline of owner-occupied housing output, market instability, increased mortgage debt and house price inflation (and sometimes deflation). Together these characteristics indicate that owner-occupied housing markets may have entered a severe structural crisis.

THE OVERALL SIGNIFICANCE OF OWNER OCCUPATION

One indicator for the importance of individual home-ownership is its growth within the existing housing stock, as shown in Figure 3.1 for the post-war era. The differing rates of growth and the variations in the percentage share of the tenure in each country's housing stock indicate that one cannot assume a similar dynamic of development. The USA has the highest rate of owner occupation and has maintained this position throughout the post-war years, unlike Britain, which started with the lowest proportion of home-owners in 1948 and then showed the most rapid expansion. The low initial level of owner occupation in Britain in comparison to the other countries indicates the importance of urban/rural divisions for the tenure. Britain's population was already fully urbanised by the Second World War, whereas in most other countries urbanisation processes did not reach completion until later. In addition, all the countries considered here, except for Britain, had large agricultural sectors and well-populated rural areas, with owner occupation as part of the forms of land ownership. This includes the USA and explains the high rate of owner occupation there, already 47 per cent of all households at the turn of the century, compared to less than 10 per cent in Britain.

Figure 3.1: Owner-occupied Housing: Share of Stock in Great Britain, Denmark, France, the Netherlands, West Germany and the USA

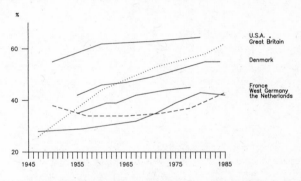

Sources: Britain: *The Social Survey,* 1949; Donnison, 1967; DoE, 1977, *Census,* 1981; *Housing and Construction Statistics,* 1985.
Denmark: Danmarks Statistik.
France: Topalov, 1981.
The Netherlands: van der Schaar, 1979; Dijkhuis-Potgieser, 1982; Buijs et al., 1987.
West Germany: Statistisches Bundesamt.
USA: *Statistical Abstract of the United States.*

Differing landownership relations and rates of urbanisation provide some explanation for home-ownership rates at the time of the Second World War, but subsequent developments also differ between countries. The rate of owner occupation declined in West Germany and growth was only slow in the Netherlands until the late 1960s, which indicates that the expansion of owner occupation as an urban tenure is a relatively recent phenomenon in these two countries.

Figure 3.2: Housing Completions

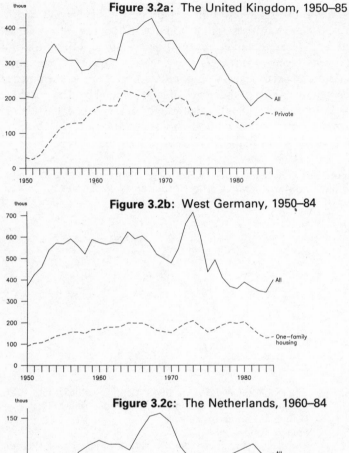

Figure 3.2a: The United Kingdom, 1950–85

Figure 3.2b: West Germany, 1950–84

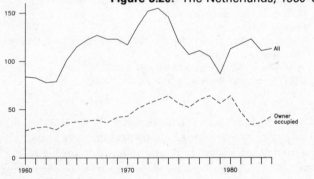

Figure 3.2c: The Netherlands, 1960–84

Sources: Central Statistical Office, *Annual Abstract of Statistics*;
Statistisches Bundesamt;
Centraal Bureau voor de Statistiek;

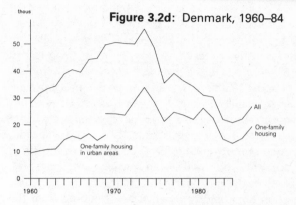

Figure 3.2d: Denmark, 1960–84

All

One-family housing

One-family housing in urban areas

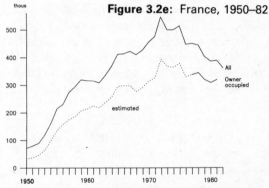

Figure 3.2e: France, 1950–82

All

Owner occupied

estimated

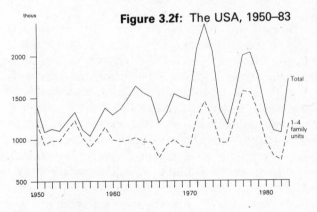

Figure 3.2f: The USA, 1950–83

Total

1–4 family units

Danmarks Statistik;
Topalov, 1983;
Statistical Abstract of the United States.

More information about the rate of expansion of home-ownership can be derived from house-building data. In all countries, owner occupation has become the dominant house-building sector (see Figure 3.2), but this position was reached in different time periods for each country.[2] In Britain, it had already taken place at the time of the speculative house-building boom of the 1930s and the associated decline of private renting. Similarly, in the USA in the 1930s, house building for owner occupation became more prominent, although private renting continued to remain significant. During the decade, however, housing output remained low compared to the 1920s and it was not until the 1940s that owner-occupied house building expanded dramatically. In France and Denmark, owner occupation dominated private house building from the late 1950s and early 1960s onwards; whereas in West Germany and the Netherlands, such expansion only occurred in the 1970s. Historical differences in the growth of owner-occupied house building are obviously reflected in its current share in the housing stock, although the sale of rented housing to home-owners has contributed significantly to the tenure's growth at certain time periods.

The decline in the share of home-ownership in West Germany and its slow growth in the Netherlands are explained by the importance of rented house building until the early 1970s. As discussed in Chapter 2, contributing factors were massive housing shortages caused by the devastation of large parts of the housing stock during the Second World War. The shortage, combined with rapid economic growth, expanding urbanisation and greater household formation in the decades following the war led to state policies which prioritised subsidies to low- and middle-income rental housing in both the social and private sectors. Subsidies were targeted at rental house building because, combined with policies to control rent costs, it enabled greater governmental control over inflation and wage costs. Housing policies were directly linked to economic policies aimed at improving the international competitiveness of national industries. Rental house building in West Germany and the Netherlands was only sustained through the extensive produc-tion subsidies allocated to it, whereas owner occupation had taken over the role of private renting as the main provider of housing via the market since the 1950s in the other countries. As shall be shown next, the development of a mass market for owner occupation was always strongly supported in post-war state housing policies.

STATE SUPPORT FOR THE PROMOTION
OF OWNER OCCUPATION

Differences in the timing of the expansion of owner occupation are reflected in a similar variety of forms of state support for the sector. This section will only focus on the main long-term types of state intervention, whereas later some of the more recent policy developments will be mentioned. The discussion of forms of state support will concentrate on initiatives to facilitate access to the tenure. Other important issues, like planning and building regulations, the provision of infrastructural services and regulation of the conditions of market exchange will be ignored here.

Given the high costs of private housing provision, a key determinant in the development of a mass market for owner occupation has been the creation of conditions which enable individual households to buy their homes. Improving households' access to the tenure has been a central concern of state housing policies. Three areas of public intervention are important here and the significance of each varies between countries. First, governments have intervened in financial markets to facilitate the availability of long-term loans to house-buyers. This has been particularly important in countries where the relevant financial sector had previously collapsed, as was the case in the USA during the 1930s, or where there was no tradition within the banking system of providing long-term loans, as was true for post-war France, and to a certain extent the USA in the 1920s. Second, production subsidies have been important in a number of countries. In both the Netherlands and France, the expansion of owner-occupied housing markets relied heavily on the availability of housing at prices below the costs of pure market provision. Finally, various types of income-tax-relief subsidy have substantially reduced the costs of borrowing for home-owners, although many of these incentives were not explicitly introduced as housing-policy instruments.

Belying the USA's free-market image, owner occupation there has perhaps enjoyed more government backing than in any of the other countries included in this survey. Federal support centres on the mortgage market and originated during the great Depression of the 1930s. One of the knock-on effects of the banking crisis of the early 1930s was a virtual standstill in the housing market. Housing starts fell from 900,000 in 1924 to only 93,000 in 1933, a year when 49 per cent of the $20 billion outstanding mortgage debt was in default (Fish, 1979). The high default rate was exacerbated by the practice of the banking system of providing short-term mortgage loans, usually of three or five years, because of which a large number of housing loans had to be renewed each year. When borrowers wanted to renew loans in the early 1930s, banks had no money and instead demanded repayment of the debts. When borrowers could not repay (partially because banks refused them access to their savings deposits for similar reasons), the properties were repossessed and often sold for less than the price they were mortgaged at (ibid.). Losses on the sales of repossessed houses further contributed to the crisis in financial markets and led to a collapse of the construction industry.

Reviving the housing market and creating jobs in the building industry to relieve high unemployment became the principal aims of federal policies during the 1930s. But rather than subsidising house building, a restructuring of financial markets was envisaged as the most appropriate strategy to boost the housing market. Financial acts under the New Deal created specialised housing finance institutions, whose operation was separated from capital markets and which enjoyed substantial federal regulatory backing (see Chapter 4 for more details). The new housing finance system provided for easily available cheap, long-term, fixed-interest-rate loans, which proved to be the key to a massive expansion of suburban, single-family house building in the decades following the Second World War. Particularly important in facilitating the growth of home-ownership in the USA was the mortgage insurance provision of the 1934 National Housing Act. Mortgage loans insured by the Federal Housing Administration (FHA) allow for low down payment ratios and were explicitly introduced as an instrument to revive the construction industry. FHA was joined by a new insurance scheme (the Veterans Administration (VA)) ten years later. The two programmes provided assistance for about 40 per cent of private housing starts during the 1940s, the decade which marks the start of a major expansion of owner-occupied house building in the USA. The mortgage insurance schemes continued to remain a significant federal instrument in assisting house building. During the late 1960s, for example, the FHA scheme was extended to mobile homes and to moderate-income building and improvement schemes in decaying inner urban areas.

Structural problems limiting the issue of long-term loans to assist individual house-buyers have continued to be key features of the French banking system. By the mid-1960s, state intervention was regarded as necessary to support further development of the owner-occupied housing market. A secondary mortgage market was created in 1967, allowing banks to sell bonds on the money market if liquidity shortages limited their mortgage-lending activities. The French secondary mortgage market, however, did not achieve much real significance. More important for the actual development of mortgage lending was the successful introduction of state-subsidised savings' schemes. The large pool of personal savings that resulted has enabled banks to issue long-term mortgage loans (in a similar way to the savings banks' matching of short-term borrowing with long-term lending; see Chapter 4). Moreover, it has made housing finance extremely profitable for banks, as cheap funds could be used for mortgage lending, enabling them to achieve a wide interest-rate margin. State subsidies for personal savings schemes, in other words, have not been reflected in lower mortgage-interest rates, but rather in increased supply of long-term loans available to house-buyers.

The development of a mortgage market, was also a major precondition for the emergence of a mass market for home-ownership in the other countries, but generally it did not require state intervention on similar scales to that in France and the USA. Pre-existing specialised housing finance institutions managed to adapt sufficiently well to the loan requirements of the growing owner-occupied market and government policies simply continued to support the special housing-finance circuits for these lenders for most of the post-war period (see Chapter 4). Subsidised savings schemes, however, were introduced in West Germany. But unlike France, the schemes were linked to just one type of mortgage lender, the *Bausparkasse*, which only offers second loans above those secured for the first 60 per cent of the house prices. Although the subsidised savings scheme was promoted to facilitate higher mortgage to house price ratios, it did not substantially transform the housing finance system.

Government guarantees on mortgage loans were also introduced in the Netherlands and have been of major importance in promoting home-ownership, particularly at the lower-income end of the housing market. The administration of the Dutch mortgage-guarantee scheme, however, was far less complicated than for the FHA and VA loans in the USA. There were no limitations on the volume of guarantees that could be issued each year in the Netherlands nor restrictions on the type of mortgage loan insured. In the absence of specialised mortgage-lending institutions of major significance, the guarantee scheme did help to draw sufficient funds into mortgage lending.

Subsidies to owner-occupied house building have been important in France, the Netherlands and, to a somewhat lesser extent, in West Germany. Production subsidies have been especially important in France, where several subsidy schemes co-existed for most of the post-war period and helped finance a significant proportion of owner-occupied house building. As mentioned earlier, rental house building prevailed in governmental subsidy policies in West Germany and the Netherlands. So it was not until 1966 that the West German Housing Act was modified by the introduction of an additional subsidy scheme, aimed at supporting building for owner occupation. Although social rented housing could also be built under the new scheme, the form in which the assistance was given was more favourable to home-owners. Subsidies to owner-occupied house building existed in the Netherlands from the late 1950s onwards, but building programmes under the scheme were severely restricted until the second half of the 1960s. Earlier it was feared that if speculative house building developed, the government would lose control over housing costs and output levels and that building resources would be diverted from the rented sectors; issues which have been key elements of Dutch post-war economic policies (Harloe and Martens, 1985).

Production subsidies for owner-occupied house building generally take the form of capital grants or premiums, either lump sums or with payments spread over a number of years, or of below market interest payments for mortgage loans (or even a combination of the two, as occurred in France). Subsidies were usually linked to stipulations fixing limits on the overall investment costs, on house sizes and standards and on the incomes of eligible house-buyers. Subsidies were aimed at the lower-income end of the owner-occupied housing market and usually, subsidised owner-occupied house building is included in social housing statistics. Although the subsidies are actually given to households, they can be referred to as production subsidies, because they are linked to newly built projects, rather than for the purchase of existing housing, and they in effect sustained builders' profits by allowing higher rates of housing sales under conditions of rising production costs.

A third form of state support for owner-occupied housing is income tax relief, which has been significant in all six countries. Generally, such taxation policies were not introduced as explicit instruments to encourage home-ownership, but rather to provide general fiscal relief on personal borrowing. In Britain, for example, interest payments on all personal borrowing were exempt from taxation until 1969, when the relief was abolished with the exception of housing loans. Similarly in the USA, personal income tax deductions allowable for interest and property tax payments were introduced early this century and have remained unchanged since. Apart from the USA, unlimited reliefs on mortgage interest payments also exist for home-owners in Denmark and the Netherlands. In Britain, there is a maximum loan amount on which interest is deductable which, however, has been adjusted in response to house price inflation. In France interest-rate deductions are more restricted, as these are limited to 25 per cent of interest costs, payable up to a maximum sum.

The West German fiscal scheme for home-ownership is very different. It is based on the ability to offset taxable income by allowances for accelerated depreciation of the nominal value of the house. For taxation purposes, a house is regarded as an investment good on which a depreciation allowance can be claimed. The scheme treats rental and owner-occupied housing similarly, although it is more favourable to rental housing, contributing to the continuing significance of private rental house building by personal investors in West Germany. The tax scheme also accounts for the popularity of the so-called two-family house, whereby maximum use is made of the income-tax-deduction scheme, by an owner living in one part of the house, whilst renting out the other. After the tax benefits of the accelerated depreciation scheme lapse the two houses are often joined together. Another feature of the West German tax allowance scheme is that, until 1977, it only applied to newly built housing.

In some of the countries, income tax reliefs are partially offset by taxes on imputed rental income. This happens in West Germany, Denmark and the Netherlands. The tax is, however, unimportant as the notional rental value is very low. Such a taxation scheme also existed in Britain, but was abolished by the Conservative government in 1963. Again, the origins of the tax scheme were unrelated to owner occupation, being part of a system of taxing real property primarily aimed at private landlordism.

Another major fiscal incentive helping to shape owner-occupied housing markets is tax exemptions on capital gains made on house sales by individual home-owners. The exemption exists in all six countries. Only in West Germany and Denmark is an exception made when the house is sold within two years of purchase, with a more restrictive five-year period in France. In the USA, on the other hand, tax exemption on capital gains is unlimited, provided purchase is made of a house of similar quality and standard. Deferral of capital gains tax was introduced in 1951 with the explicit aim of promoting geographical mobility for owner-occupiers and of enabling households to trade up within the housing market (HUD, 1973).

Although in some cases certain tax exemptions have consciously been introduced in support of owner-occupied markets, the fiscal treatment of home-owners usually derives from policies related either to private landlords or general income tax policies, which have subsequently been maintained. The impact of favourable fiscal treatment for owner-occupiers has become far more important in recent years with the expansion of owner occupation, post-war house price inflation, the rise in interest rates and with a widening of the income tax net. At the same time, tax exemption schemes have also become more difficult to change as these shelter owner-occupiers from some of the effects of high house prices and rising mortgage interest rates. Fiscal subsidies to owner-occupiers, in other words, have not only become costly for the state, but have in many ways also become an integral part of the structure of owner-occupied housing markets.

Politically, tax-relief subsidies are easier to maintain than production subsidies to housing as the cost effect is not shown as an expenditure in national budgets. Such accounting conventions help to shape political commitments by governments to the expansion of individual home-ownership at the expense of providing support for social rented housing. The commitment has also been influenced by the high levels of owner-occupied output during the long post-war house-building boom, as happened in all six countries and lasted until the 1970s (and the late 1960s for Britain). High house-building levels were seen as 'natural' within advanced capitalist economies, rather than the product of peculiar circumstances, such as high levels of economic growth, rising real incomes and careful state orchestration. The perceived 'naturalness' of the post-war house-building boom, and the growth of owner occupation in particular, have been foundations for policy arguments aimed at withdrawing production subsidies from the social housing sectors.

With the end of the post-war house-building boom, total output in all six countries declined substantially. The main cause of the decline was the collapse of rental house building. Owner occupation became proportionally more significant in house building during the 1970s as a result, even though output levels in this sector have by no means been able to compensate for the overall decline in house building. In Britain, France and Denmark there has been a long-term decline in owner-occupied house building since the late 1960s/early 1970s, while in West Germany and the Netherlands output in the sector remained stable through the 1970s, until a decline set in in the 1980s. Only in the USA was there a rising trend in owner-occupied house building until the late 1970s (see Figure 3.2). Developments in owner-occupied house building have varied between the six countries throughout the post-war period, but one feature that has become a general characteristic is the emergence of increasingly sharp fluctuations in house-building rates. So, despite extensive (and increasingly expensive) governmental support to the tenure, developments in the owner-occupied markets seem increasingly difficult to control, indicating the limitations of the policy prescriptions devised in earlier post-war years. In order to analyse recent developments more carefully, the main forms of housing provision in owner occupation need to be examined.

FORMS OF OWNER-OCCUPIED HOUSING PROVISION

Forms of provision of owner-occupied housing are defined here by the relations between those who initiate and control house building and the other institutions and agencies that are part of the development process. The latter can include builders, financial institutions, landowners, housing consumers and the state. Any of these participants can, in fact, act as the developer or promoter controlling the development process. I shall focus on the most significant types of agency initiating and controlling owner-occupied housing provision, without giving a detailed account of their social relations with the other participants.[3] Such additional detail is difficult to present, because of the limitations of existing housing research mentioned earlier. Apart from the primacy given to state policies in most housing studies, difficulties also arise when trying to use national surveys of, say, the building industry or the financial sector. Such surveys tend to aggregate data relating to distinctly different structures of provision.

Variations in statistical categories between countries (frequently referred to as a major headache in comparative research), do often highlight cross-national differences in housing provision structures (although not always satisfactorily for our purposes). In Britain, for instance, private house building is regarded synonymous with owner occupation in housing statistics, and speculative house-builders with the type of institution that initiates and controls owner-occupied house building. But in the Netherlands, West Germany and France, private house building is dominated by contractors, rather than speculative builders, which points to traditionally different power relations between builders and developers and, of course, the fact that the two are institutionally separate. Speculative house-builders, as simultaneously builders and developers, are in a European context a specifically British phenomenon and their existence relates to the particular social conditions at the time period when owner occupation initially expanded (Ball, 1983). Speculative house-builders are also important in the USA, where they are referred to as merchant builders, but have never been the sole providers of owner-occupied housing. US statistics, however, do not distinguish house building for sale as a separate category, so its overall significance is difficult to establish. Instead, use can be made of information provided by the National Association of Home Builders (NAHB), which analyses a builder's main type of investment.

The dominance of contractors in house building in most European countries reflects the prominence of others in the initiation of housing development. Initiators are in these cases usually public, social — limited profit — or private institutions, or indeed private persons who may decide to build rented or owner-occupied housing. House-building statistics in these countries, therefore, tend to distinguish types of developer rather than tenures. Such developers or promoters are the initiators of house building, but use various forms of contractors to undertake the actual building work. They provide land and finance and oversee the house-building process. Builders may also at times perform the role of promotion, but such speculative roles for builders cannot be regarded as a major type of production system. They are quantitatively insignificant with builders only one of the many professional institutions involved in speculative housing developments. Moreover, such speculative activities are secondary to their main activities as contractors.

There are, however, differences in housing promotion for owner occupation and private renting. Modern promoters of rented house building generally opt for a long-term investment and let the housing themselves. In West Germany, for instance, where rental housing constitutes the main part of post-war house building, the largest type of housing promoter is limited-profit housing corporations. These housing corporations build both social and private, rented and owner-occupied housing. Unlike rental housing, promotion of owner-occupied housing necessitates immediate sales to individual house-buyers and a short-term return on investment is expected. With the expansion of owner-occupied house building for sale, new forms of housing promotion arose alongside those linked to rental house building (even though the two types of promotion can be incorporated in the activities of one firm).

In France, the new type of promoter of owner-occupied housing has been described as *promoteurs immobiliers privées*, who from the mid-1950s onwards introduced speculative housing development as a new 'profession' (Topalov, 1974; 1980). A similar expansion occurred in the Netherlands from the beginning of the 1970s, with the growth of the *projektontwikkelaar*, who integrates all development aspects of house building, from land purchase, financing, to sales to individual house-buyers. They may also build housing, but this is only a minor part of their activities, even when they are building firms (Dreimuller, 1980).

The French *promoteurs immobiliers privées* and Dutch *projektontwikkelaars* both disappeared in the housing market slumps of the early 1980s, or rather have diverted investments away from house building for sale. Their 'disappearance' shows that speculative housing developments in most European countries have had no tendency towards being dominated either by large housing promoters or the house-building industry itself. In most countries in Europe, centralisation of housing-related capital has been directed more towards the financing of housing production than the producers themselves. In fact, a wide range of professionals and institutions (including banks and builders) entered speculative house building during housing market booms as little own capital was needed. They are geared towards quick turnover and are backed by large financial institutions, which readily offer short-term building loans, regarding housing development as a secure and profitable investment.

The picture is very different in Britain or the USA, where a number of speculative house-builders or merchant builders have developed into giant housing producers with major market shares. Apart from the volume builders, numerous small- and medium-sized speculative builders have continued to exist, particularly in the USA. Unlike the European promoters of owner-occupied housing, speculative builders had from the start made house building and selling integral parts of their operations. When the conditions for a mass market for owner occupation were created, during the 1930s in Britain and in the USA from the 1940s onwards, economies of scale could be achieved by combining land development and house building (see also Ball, 1983 for Britain). Land holding and centralisation within the speculative building industry can be seen as strategies adapted to market cycles which historically have been endemic to house building. Many smaller firms disappear during housing market slumps and stage comebacks during up-turns. Land holding allows large builders to release land for house building when demand rises, whereas capital investments in building are kept low during market down-turns.

Speculative house building in Britain has remained largely institutionally separated from the financial industry. This is different in the USA, where many of the large builders that have arisen from the merger and acquisition boom of the late 1960s, developed skilful financing techniques, plus land-banking and aggressive marketing strategies, as ways to expand their market shares. Each one of the ten leading house-builders created at least one mortgage banking subsidiary during the early 1970s. Initially the mortgage banks were set up to facilitate housing sales, but they eventually also proved to be a major source of earnings during housing market slumps (Schlesinger and Erlich, 1986).

One other major form of housing provision, which is only significant in the USA, is the industrial production of mobile homes. It consists of a highly concentrated industry, characterised by factory-based, production-line fabrication techniques. Distribution of the homes generally occurs via a large number of non-exclusive mobile home dealers and buyers use specially designated, landscaped sites, for which rents are paid.

The mobile home industry expanded dramatically during the post-war years. From near insignificance in the 1950s it grew to produce one-third of all new single-family housing in 1972, its peak year of production (HUD, 1973). The sector mainly caters for the lower end of the owner-occupied housing market. Mobile homes are not subject to building regulations and their quality tends to be much below traditionally built housing, even though their size and standards, and the quality of the services provided in the so-called parks where they are stationed, have improved over the years. Industrial production methods have helped to reduce the real costs of the units, but this has been counteracted by the extremely high financing costs of mobile homes (ibid.). Ordinary mortgage loans are not available to buyers, because these homes have a short technical life expectancy and cannot be considered as 'real estate' anyway. Instead, buyers are subjected to similar loan conditions as when they buy consumer durables. Government guaranteed FHA and VA loans have also been made available to this sector, but again, at about double the interest rates charged for ordinary mortgage loans.

The final form of owner-occupied housing provision that will be mentioned here is usually referred to as self-building, commissioned house building or custom building. The main characteristic of self-building is that private persons build for their own use and not for sale on the market, as is the case for all previously mentioned provision forms. Thus the development process is initiated and controlled by the future owner-occupiers, using land which they themselves acquired. Individuals buy a plot of land and then commission an architect and a contractor (usually local ones) to design and build the house. In many cases self-help is also contributed by the future occupier at several stages of the development to reduce expenses. Self-building is traditionally associated with detached housing, designed to the taste and requirements of the client and usually built in rural areas. It is in many ways a pre-capitalist, non-market, form of housing provision and accounts for the high early home-ownership rate of several countries mentioned in the previous section.

A recent innovation in commissioned house building is what can be called catalogue building. Here, an industrially-fabricated house is chosen from a catalogue and assembled on a site which is already owned by the future occupier. Catalogue house building has been expanding in France during the 1970s, from 17 per cent in 1970–73 to 25 per cent in 1975–8 of all new houses sold (and over the same period from 28 per cent to 40 per cent of all commissioned house building; Topalov, 1981). Catalogue building has also developed in West Germany, but on a less significant scale. During the 1970s production remained at a

Figure 3.3: Housing Approvals for Sale and Personal Use in France, 1960–81

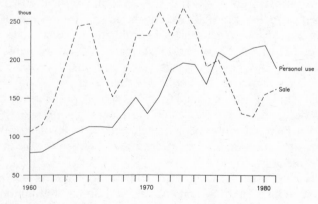

Source: Topalov, 1983.

level of 12 per cent of building permissions given to one-family housing (Knechtel, 1983).

Commissioned house building exists in all countries, but is particularly significant in France, West Germany and the USA. It is less affected by general cycles of economic activity, because it is not provided for a market where a buyer has to be found at completion. The land acquisition and building process, in addition, can be spread over longer time periods, proceeding when financial circumstances permit.

From house-building data it appears that commissioned house building in France increased significantly during the 1960s and 1970s, in both relative and absolute terms. Its output shows a continuous growth and it even exceeded the number of houses built for sale by private promoters in the second half of the 1970s (Figure 3.3). A structural change in French owner-occupied house building is further marked by a significant reduction in multi-family house building after 1983, which paralleled the decline of private housing promoters.

Self-building dominated one-family owner-occupied house building in West Germany throughout the post-war period (Figure 3.4). But some qualifications need to be made for the data provided here. The category 'private households' also includes individual persons who invest in private rented house building, a provision structure favoured by fiscal policies. The long-term fall in output for 'private households' is likely to

Figure 3.4: Private Housing Completions in West Germany, 1960–82

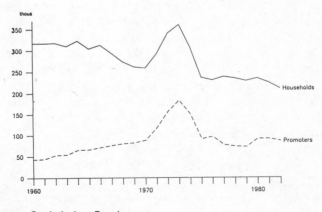

Source: Statistisches Bundesamt.

107

reflect the decline of the private rental sector. Further analysis of the data shows that by 1980 about three-quarters of all owner-occupied single-family housing was provided by home-owners themselves (Martens, 1985).

The significance of self-building in the USA is more difficult to deduce from the available statistical information, as house-building data do not distinguish building 'for sale' or 'for own use' or between types of investors/clients. But surveys on the structure of the construction industry carried out by the National Association of Home Builders (NAHB) give some indication of the structural changes that have taken place in recent years. These surveys indicate that builders who have custom home building as their main area of operation have remained stable within the industry at about one-quarter of all home-builders. The number of builders that concentrate activities on single-family house building for sale, however, decreased substantially from the mid-1970s onwards, whilst house building in this sector continued to expand during the 1970s. Speculative single-family house building has shifted geographically towards the 1970s' economic growth areas in the south and west of the country. The shift also occurred in the mobile homes industry and most of the large mobile home manufacturers to date can be found in the south of the USA.

To summarise, various forms of owner-occupied provision exist. Defined by the type of institution or agency that initiates and controls the housing development process, forms of owner-occupied housing provision include speculative house-builders in Britain and the USA; speculative housing developers or promoters, which have been significant in most other European countries and consist of a range of institutions or professionals, which either diversified into speculative housing development, or took it up as a new 'profession'; the mobile home industry as the provider of industrially produced homes (rather than houses) for lower-income households in the USA; and finally, the commissioning of house building by private persons for their own use has continued to exist as a major form of owner-occupied housing provision in many countries.

The importance of each of these provision forms has changed over time and between regions within a country. For example, the shift in the geographical location of speculative house building activities towards the new economic growth areas did not only occur in the USA during the 1970s, but has also been noticeable, although more recently, in West Germany and Britain. There have also been shifts in building activities away from suburban expansion towards a growing significance of home-ownership within existing urban locations. The shift includes a new emphasis on owner-occupied house building in multi-family, rather than single-family, units and also on conversions of existing buildings for sale to owner-occupiers. The expansion of owner occupation as an urban tenure, however, was accompanied by changes in the significance of the existing housing stock in defining the structure of owner-occupied housing markets which, until then, had mainly been defined by house-building activities.

THE ROLE OF THE EXISTING HOUSING STOCK IN OWNER-OCCUPIED MARKETS

One feature that has become a general characteristic of owner-occupied housing markets is the emergence of short-term fluctuations in housing output. Volatility in house-building levels has been a general characteristic of private housing markets for a much longer period of time, but fluctuations have tended to become sharper and shorter-lived in recent years. One major contributing factor is a growing importance of existing home-owners in housing market transactions.

The role of the existing housing stock in housing market activities is perhaps best illustrated by Britain, where less than 15 per cent of annual sales are represented by newly built housing (Ball, 1983; Ball et al., 1986). The large number of existing dwellings offered for sale mainly represent sales by existing owner-occupiers. High levels of house price inflation during the 1970s and 1980s encouraged many existing home-owners to trade-up within the sector, as it allowed them to improve their housing situation for similar long-term costs. With general price inflation, the real value of the initial mortgage debt is eroded, while rising house prices enable existing owners to realise money gains. When existing home-owners trade up, the new purchase will, of course be commensurately more expensive, but if there are high levels of general inflation, households can expect that their housing costs will soon subsequently fall again in real terms.

As activities in the British owner-occupied housing market

became dominated by transactions by existing home-owners, chains of sales became common with more purchases and sales needing to be matched. Market volatility further increased as the level of new building came to depend on house price inflation. Because of a general rise in real construction costs, house prices have to increase at a faster rate than general inflation to sustain house building. House price inflation also affects the type of housing built, because money gains made by existing home-owners had made these households the most profitable category to build for. For this reason, there has been a long-term trend towards building up-market housing in Britain. During housing market slumps transactions slow down significantly as existing home-owners delay housing sales when lower money gains are expected. House-building activities are reduced substantially as a result, particularly in the up-market sector.

In the mid-1970s, transactions within the existing housing stock started to affect the Dutch owner-occupied housing market in a similar way to Britain's, but under very different conditions. Owner occupation has dominated private house building in Britain since the 1930s and over 60 per cent of all households are now home-owners, so that new house building only counts for a small proportion of the existing stock. In the Netherlands owner-occupied house building only started to become significant after the late 1960s and output levels quickly reached a plateau in the following decade.

Sales from the rented housing stock became a significant feature of the Dutch owner-occupied housing market, particularly during the second half of the 1970s. Policies to decontrol rented housing led to a rapid rise in sales by private landlords to owner-occupiers or to property developers who resold to owner-occupiers. From 1975 onwards, prices of existing owner-occupied housing started to rise at much faster rates than prices of newly-built units, which more or less followed the general rate of inflation. (Unfortunately, no Dutch house price data exist for the period between 1974 and 1976, but in 1977, the penultimate year of the house price boom, house prices went up by 32 per cent in nominal terms and 25 per cent in real terms; see Figure 3.7b; page 120.)

House price inflation within the existing stock is partially explained as a 'delayed reaction'. Prices of houses bought from private landlords were initially very low, partially because landlords disposed of a large number of units at the same time or offered them to sitting tenants at below market prices. The low price of ex-rental housing was also a consequence of Dutch post-war rent control policies, which meant that the capitalisation of actual rental values resulted in a price much below free market prices. Many landlords were more interested in disposing of their properties than in maximising profits from sales (although profits certainly were made too). House price inflation within the existing stock, therefore, reflected a process of bringing the prices of ex-rental housing up to the general level of market prices. Such rapid price rises encouraged existing home-owners to realise money gains and to trade up, in a similar way as in Britain. The inflationary process was heightened by state policies encouraging home-ownership and the extension of government guarantees on mortgage loans to existing housing, which allowed mortgage loans of up to 100 per cent of the purchase price.

As with the housing market booms in Britain, new Dutch house building in the years of the boom became dominated by up-market housing aimed at higher income groups and traders-up. The building sector for middle-income first-time buyers, for whom production subsidies are provided by the state, was cutback through reductions of subsidy conditions (reflecting the consistent counter-cyclical Keynesian-style policy pursued by successive post-war Dutch governments towards the construction industry). Even so, the up-market sector continued to remain significant (see Figure 3.5). In this way, housing policies in the Netherlands helped to create two distinct sectors of owner-occupied house building: one aimed at first-time buyers, the other at existing home-owners trading up within the sector.

The spectacular boom in owner occupation in the Netherlands during the second half of the 1970s was only short-lived and came to an end in 1978, when house price inflation within the existing stock started to slow down. The possibility of making money gains reduced for existing owners, particularly after house prices started to fall substantially (see Figure 3.7b; page 120). The up-market house-building sector almost totally collapsed as a result (see Figure 3.5). The collapse was accelerated by the effects of the early 1980s economic recession with its high real interest rates, rapidly rising unemployment and declining real incomes.

The sectors most seriously affected by falling house prices

Figure 3.5: Owner-occupied Housing Completions in the Netherlands, 1960–84

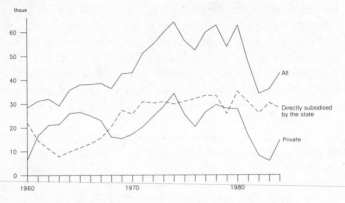

Source: Centraal Bureau voor de Statistiek, 1960–84.

were luxury housing and the older housing in working-class inner-city areas. In these sectors, house prices declined by as much as half after the late 1970s. House prices only started to keep up with inflation again after 1982 and mainly at the cheaper end of the market. Owner-occupied house building was only viable by returning to the market for first-time buyers with increased support from direct state subsidies. Housing market transactions have continued at a low level as the possibility of realising money gains is still very limited while losses are more likely. The up-market sector has now also turned to building for first-time buyers and since 1983 special land cost subsidies have been allocated to support their development. Relatively few houses are built now by the Dutch private sector without any form of direct state subsidy. Housing policies have continued to create a highly segmented supply — delimited by tenure, promoter and subsidy — all of which are competing for similar types of effective demand during the current housing market slump. Housing offered to the market by existing home-owners only adds to the competition for would-be buyers.

In Denmark, West Germany and France, owner-occupied house building has remained orientated towards first-time buyers. In Denmark, sales by existing owners are of little significance, at least until very recently. Until 1982, such sales accounted for only about 12 per cent of all loans annually issued by mortgage credit institutions. The same is true for West Germany where, according to a sample survey amongst home-owners who bought between 1969 and 1982, only 7 per cent were previous owner-occupiers (Weissbarth and Hundt, 1983).

Owner-occupied housing markets dominated by first-time buyers do not necessarily imply that sales within the existing stock are unimportant. In France, for example, around 45 per cent of all annual sales are of existing property, a share, however, that has hardly increased since the 1950s. Such transactions are particularly significant in large towns and especially in the Paris region (Topalov, 1981). The second-hand market in France is divided into two sectors. One is of low quality and functions as a market for lower-income households who may eventually improve their properties. The other sector is of a comparable standard to new housing and acts as an alternative for those whose incomes are too high to be eligible for state-supported new housing (ibid.). The existing housing stock fills some of the gaps in a very segmented market for new housing. Segmentation in the French housing market, therefore, implies that sales of second-hand dwellings are not necessarily in direct competition with new housing. The secondary effects of an existing housing stock in an integrated market are similarly absent. There is no downward pressure on the purchase prices of new housing during market slumps, nor encouragement of the expansion of new house building during periods of rising house prices.

The type of owner-occupied housing market described for Denmark, West Germany and France contrasts strongly with the type of market in Britain and the Netherlands. The latter two can be classified as unified markets, where both new and existing dwellings compete for would-be purchasers and the transactions of the large number of houses and households already in the tenure influence activities in new housing construction. Moreover, market sub-sectors are linked together through transactions by existing home-owners, including trading-up and down, home improvements and inter-regional moves. As a result, all parts of the national owner-occupied housing market are linked by common market forces (Ball et al., 1986).

In contrast, owner-occupied markets which are dominated by first-time buyers consist of a variety of sub-markets, differentiated by region or housing sector. Fragmentation is encouraged by the low rate of mobility of existing home-owners. Second-hand sales are limited to stock transfers from rented sectors, or sales by dissolved households, job movers or by those in financial difficulty. New house building meets localised demand and stock transfers concern particular sub-markets, as was illustrated in the case of France.

State policies and conditions linked to mortgage lending have helped to create the distinct types of owner-occupied housing provision in the respective countries. With the exception of Britain and the Netherlands, mortgage finance for buying a second-hand dwelling is less favourable than for new housing. In Denmark, for instance, buyers of existing housing until 1982 could only obtain a loan up to 40 per cent of the purchase price and, in West Germany, tax depreciation allowances did not exist for second-hand dwellings until 1977. In France, no form of state loan or state-supported loan was available for purchases within the housing stock; whereas most sales of new housing are helped by publicly supported finance. Only the most expensive forms of credit are available to buyers of second-hand housing, which helps to explain the segmentation of the French housing market into the sub-markets mentioned above.

Sales of existing housing have become much more important in West Germany since 1977, when tax depreciation subsidies were extended to the sector. The increase in transactions of existing dwellings resulted from a rise in sales of previously rented housing to owner-occupiers, usually accompanied by gentrification processes in certain inner-urban areas, rather than an increase in the mobility of existing home-owners. So, like in France, stock sales seem to represent a different market segment. But the liberation of mortgage lending conditions for existing housing in Denmark had a different effect. Sales by existing owner-occupiers soared from 1982 onwards, a development, which was further encouraged by rapidly rising house prices.

The US owner-occupied housing market seems to combine the characteristics of both a unified and a segmented market, both regionally and within a metropolitan area. By 1984 only about 18 per cent of all transactions were sales of newly-built housing, which indicates that, as in Britain, existing home-owners dominate housing market transactions. Yet, due to the sheer size of the country, a vast number of regional sub-markets have continued to exist, as indicated by differences in house price changes. Major geographical shifts in employment growth enhanced the evolution of the regional differences in the USA, but also at the same time they help to link housing markets of different parts of the country.

The south and west of the USA (the so-called Sunbelt) experienced massive growth during the 1970s in terms of job creation, particularly in the defence and energy sectors, and a net inflow of population (Tabb, 1984). Suburban expansion was the main characteristic of spatial transformation of cities in these regions and there house building continued to dominate housing market transactions. Substantial inter-regional migration movements towards the Sunbelt meant, however, that not all of the new housing was sold to first-time buyers, but also to movers from the economically depressed regions. In this way, migration movements tend to link up housing markets in different US regions. Within the context of the Sunbelt area, market fragmentation persists because additional house building during the 1970s was mainly encouraged by demand fuelled by rapid job creation and immigration, rather than by demand generated through house price inflation in the existing housing stock. Within the Sunbelt region, sales by existing owners did not compete with new housing construction. Segmentation in the US house-building market also arises through the sectoral division between mobile homes, providing shelter for those in low-paid jobs, and traditionally built units housing the better paid.

House price studies in the 1970s showed a high degree of segmentation in US urban housing markets, particularly in the large cities (see Harvey and Chaterjee, 1974 and Straszheim, 1975). But a reordering of such market hierarchies has taken place in the 1980s. The recent transformation of the older large cities along the US east and west coasts increased the importance of the existing housing stock in defining the characteristics of local owner-occupied housing markets. Inner-city areas had largely been abandoned by the white middle class during the 1960s and were mainly inhabited by a much poorer black population. Federal funds were allocated during the 1970s to improve inner-city areas. But rather than improving the housing situation of the inner-city poor, the use of federal funds and loan guarantees by property developers, backed by financial interests and (sometimes corrupt) city officials, gave rise to rapid processes of gentrification. Condominiums, owner-occupied housing units in multi-family buildings, emerged as a new, urban housing sector during the 1970s. The sector includes both new construction and conversions of existing, previously rental, buildings and responds to the demand of the white middle class for re-migration to inner-city locations. The growth of service industries during the 1980s and a concomitant creation of well-paid jobs, helped to intensify processes of inner-city gentrification. High levels of house price inflation during the 1980s encouraged existing home-owners to trade up, giving rise to the emergence of owner-occupied housing markets dominated by movers and traders-up in the big cities during the 1980s — a gentrification process that is still taking place.

HOUSEHOLD CHARACTERISTICS OF OWNER-OCCUPIERS

Different types of housing market are reflected in household characteristics of the owner-occupiers. Immobility in markets dominated by first-time buyers means that buying a house is a purchase for life. This is particularly true for households which acquire their homes via self-building, which is the dominant form of owner-occupied housing provision in West Germany and France, and which also is significant in the USA. As self-built houses are designed for the specific needs of the occupiers, they are unlikely to move after the purchase has been made unless they have to. But a low rate of mobility generally implies waiting periods before the big purchase is made, especially as often time is needed to save for down-payments. Down-payment requirements, in turn, reflect the mode of operation of national mortgage finance institutions. In most countries, typically about 20 to 30 per cent of the house price is advanced by the future home-owner with the remaining sum mortgaged. A major exception is West Germany, where about 50 per cent of the purchase price tends to be contributed by the house-buyer in the form of savings or self-help. The latter again stresses the prominence of commissioned house building in that country. Subsidised savings schemes, which exist in both France and West Germany also lead to a tradition of waiting periods before houses are bought. So first-time buyers generally do not constitute newly formed households, but older households with previous housing careers. The situation is, again, most striking in West Germany, where first-time buyers tend to be 35 years or older (Martens, 1985).

Unified owner-occupied housing markets have different household characteristics. Here, newly formed households are not expected to remain outside the owner-occupied sector until sufficient money has been saved. Instead, households are likely to make a number of purchases during their lifetimes. First-time buyers are often newly formed households, who expect to improve their housing quality a few years after their purchase. The high rate of mobility within unified owner-occupied markets is well illustrated by Britain, where the average life of a building society mortgage is very short, for example, only four years in 1983.

The existence of strong rental sectors facilitates relatively late entry to owner occupation, whereas the much reduced rental housing stock in Britain forces many newly formed households into home-ownership. So, although owner occupation on average tends to represent higher-income households than non-owners everywhere, in countries where the rate of home-ownership is very high, as in the USA and Britain, the tenure represents a much broader section of the population than where rental sectors remain significant in accommodating middle-income households. High home-ownership ratios reflect a relatively high proportion of young and lower-income house-

Figure 3.6: Mortgage Debt as a Percentage of House Prices in Great Britain, 1969–85

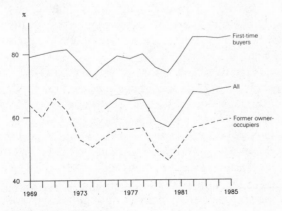

Source: BSA Bulletin 1987, January.

117

holds in the tenure. Access to owner occupation for these households is not only facilitated by the process of trading up, as was illustrated for Britain. Sub-markets of low quality housing may provide similar functions in fragmented housing markets, as was illustrated by the mobile-home sector in the USA and for parts of the old inner-city housing stock in France and other countries like Britain (Topalov, 1981; Byrne, 1986).

The expansion of owner occupation towards younger and lower-income households has in all countries been facilitated by an increased role of mortgage debt in financing purchase. Mortgage to house price ratios are especially high for first-time buyers and, therefore, in housing markets dominated by first-time buyers. The high debt ratios for first-time buyers are illustrated for Britain in Figure 3.6, where they are compared with those of former owner-occupiers. The fall in average mortgage to house price ratios for former owner-occupiers in Britain during the 1970s indicates the significance of the money gains made in housing sales, rather than a reduction in mortgage to income ratios. The dominance of existing owners in British housing market transactions led average mortgage to house price ratios to decline during the 1970s, although debt ratios of first-time buyers remained stable. In Denmark and West Germany, where first-time buyers dominate market transactions, average debt ratios rose significantly during the same decade. In West Germany the ratio rose from 46 per cent in the period 1969–72 to 57 per cent in the period 1977–80, and in Denmark, it rose from 71 per cent in 1965 to 88 per cent in 1980 (Weissbarth and Hundt, 1983; Vestergaard, 1982). The Dutch government mortgage guarantee scheme has already been mentioned. It allows for very high mortgage to house price ratios and use of the scheme rose substantially during the 1970s housing market boom.

The average debt to house price ratio of new West German home-owners may seem low in comparison to other countries, but international surveys show that house prices in West Germany are exceptionally high. House price to income ratios in most countries usually vary between 3 and 4, but the ratio is nearly double that in West Germany (Köster and Mezler, 1979). In a recent survey (Nationwide, 1987), house prices are expressed as the number of hours average earners have to work to pay for average houses offered in national markets. Again, for most European countries about 8,000 to 10,000 working

118

hours are required, whereas this is 20,000 for West Germany. So, although German households may have lower mortgage to house price ratios, their mortgage debt to income ratios compare with home-owners elsewhere.

HOUSE PRICE INFLATION AND HOUSING MARKET INSTABILITY

High levels of house price inflation have been characteristic of owner-occupied housing markets in all countries since the Second World War. As the cost of providing housing has continued to increase, because of upward pressures on the costs of land, building and finance, long-term house price inflation has become necessary to sustain housing output. The rate of house price increases, however, is ultimately limited by the ability of households to buy these houses. But high post-war levels of general inflation and the growth of personal income and frequent excess demand for housing have all facilitated the long-term house-building boom, which for most countries lasted into the 1970s. Growth has been cyclical, rather than continuous, and post-war fluctuations in house building have tended to coincide with rates of house price changes and with general cycles of national and, increasingly, international economies (see Chapter 5).

Table 3.1: Average House Price Changes in West Germany, 1972–83

	Estimated annual house price change, one-family housing (%)	Annual rate of change of retail prices (%)
1972–5	5–8	5.5–7.0
1977	8–10	3.7
1978	10–15	2.7
1979	>30	4.1
1980	16	5.5
1981	−5	5.9
1982	−5	5.3
1983	−7	3.0

Note: No accurate national data either for new or for second-hand house prices are available for West Germany. The data given in this table are based on an unweighted crude averaging of local data provided by estate agents.

Source: Martens 1985.

Figure 3.7a: Owner-occupied House Price Changes in Britain (percentage per year), 1957–85

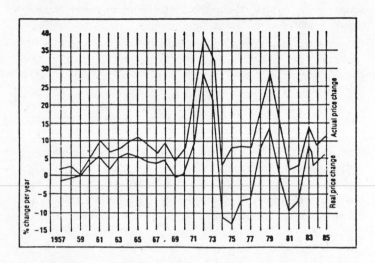

Source: Ball (1986), *Homeownership: A Suitable Case for Reform*, Shelter, London.

Figure 3.7b: House Price Changes of All Owner-occupied Dwellings Sold in the Netherlands (percentage per year), 1966–84

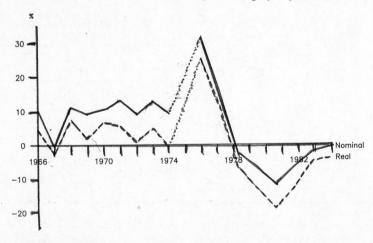

Source: Centraal Bureau voor de Statistiek, 1966–81; Dijkhuis-Potgieser (1985), 1982–4.

Not all countries produce national house price data. Such information is particularly poor for France and West Germany, where no systematic surveys have been undertaken (Martens, 1985). This reflects the fragmented nature of housing markets in these countries and hence the existence of a vast number of regional sub-markets. The house price data that are available are presented in Figure 3.7 and Table 3.1. For most countries the data represent changes in the prices of new housing as it has dominated housing market transactions for most of the post-war period. Exceptions are Britain during the 1970s and the Netherlands during the second half of that decade, where the development towards unified housing markets and the prominence of existing owner-occupiers in market activities are reflected in much higher rates of nominal house price rises during up-turns in housing markets than appeared in previous periods. Similar developments have occurred in the most recent housing market boom in Denmark.

Figure 3.7c: House Price Changes of One-family Housing in Denmark (percentage per year), 1966–84

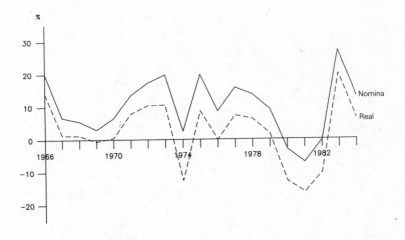

Source: Danmarks Statistik.

Nominal house price rises in all countries were much higher during the 1970s than in earlier decades. In real terms though, house prices fell at times, as for example in the mid-1970s in Britain and Denmark, but rises have generally been rapid during periods of housing market boom. Despite higher rates of inflation for much of the 1970s, house-building levels have, as a long-term trend, generally either stagnated or declined. Falling rates of house building in Denmark have been explained by the increasing unaffordability of house purchase for most households. House prices had already risen so high, that after housing expenditure and tax deductions, real incomes were in 1977 35 per cent below the 1971 level (Vestergaard, 1982). Similarly, real house prices continued to increase in France after 1975, but not at a sufficient rate to meet the rise in the costs of building and finance (Topalov, 1985). Housing output declined as a result. Unprecedented levels of house price inflation during the 1970s in Britain could not stem a long-term fall in the rate of house building. The decline here is even more striking because rising house prices reflect money gains of existing home-owners, which are contributed to the purchase of new housing in addition to mortgage payments from earnings. Whereas in Denmark and France declining house-building levels mainly relate to the reduced affordability of new housing directly paid out of income. The major house price boom during the late 1970s in the Netherlands also could not stimulate a rise in house building. Instead, and similarly in West Germany, output levels remained more or less stable throughout the decade. Only in the USA did owner-occupied house building expand, because of a sharp rise in housing demand in its Sunbelt region.

General high rates of inflation, another characteristic of the 1970s, gave impetus to the expansion of owner occupation. The growth of the tenure was not necessarily met through new building, but also by sales of rental housing from the existing stock. High levels of inflation made home-ownership an increasingly attractive proposition for many households, as their real incomes rose significantly, while the real costs of the initial mortgage debt eroded substantially within a few years. Inflationary trends, combined with increasingly aggressive marketing strategies by mortgage lending institutions and state policies aimed at promoting the tenure, encouraged more households to become home-owners and to take on much higher debt burdens than they would have done in earlier decades. So during the 1970s, mortgage debt became increasingly significant in facilitating expansion of owner occupation.

Higher mortgage house price ratios allow more households to become home-owners as shorter saving periods are required. Reduced down-payment requirements also make home-ownership more feasible in an era of rising house prices. But at the same time, high debt ratios make home-owners much more vulnerable to changes in interest rates, as the costs of buying a house fluctuate with interest rates.

The housing market booms of the late 1970s were in all countries followed by a major market down-turn during the early 1980s and the consequences were substantial. Housing production was at a low level everywhere and in the Netherlands, Denmark and West Germany house prices fell in both real and, for the first time since the war, in nominal terms too (Figure 3.7). A major crisis in the world economy contributed to cause the housing market slump, as it was associated with sharply rising unemployment, stagnating real incomes and extremely high levels of nominal and real interest rates. Interest rates were particularly high in Denmark, where they increased from about 10 per cent in 1970 to nearly 22 per cent in 1982. The effects of high interest rates were partially offset by the high marginal tax rate, allowing substantial income tax deductions for owner-occupiers with large mortgages. But, as the tax incentive was significant only for higher-income households, high interest rates combined with rising house prices substantially reduced demand for owner-occupied housing for the middle-income groups in the early 1980s. By 1982, housebuilding rates fell to only about one-third of owner-occupied units produced in the previous peak production year of 1973. So, as in the Netherlands (but for somewhat different reasons), Danish private house building virtually collapsed during the early 1980s. Elsewhere, the decline was less devastating, but still substantial.

The effects of the sharp rise in interest rates were also noticeable in West Germany, where the income-tax-relief scheme for home-owners does not allow for interest rate deductions but only for relief based on an accelerated depreciation of the house's price. By the late 1970s most housing loans had variable (or short-term fixed) interest rates so households were badly hit by market rates of interest, which nearly doubled between the late 1970s and early 1980s. German home-owners who bought during this period therefore experienced large increases in their housing costs. Mortgage defaults and forced sales grew substantially as a result. But in many cases the auction prices received did not cover the original mortgage costs, leaving many previous home-owners with outstanding debts (Brambing et al., 1983). An interest-relief tax-deduction scheme was introduced as a temporary measure by the West Germany government in 1982, but the workings of the scheme did not give much relief to the housing costs of existing home-owners.

In the USA, the extent of the down-turn in the early 1980s housing market varied sharply between regions. Developments were particularly devastating in three types of region: in the boom areas of the 1970s (the southern Sunbelt), following a crisis in the energy and mining industries; the 'Farmbelt' area of the Mid West, after it was hit by the agricultural crisis; and in regions of the Mid West with significant employment in the automobile industry. Rising rates of unemployment helped to reduce the number of new housing starts substantially in these regions and an increasing number of houses were offered for sale by existing owners who wished to leave the area or could not afford the mortgage anymore. These houses, however, were often sold for much below their initial prices (if they could be sold at all). The geography of housing investment activities has again shifted in the USA, this time towards those parts of the north-east and west, where the service and high-tech industries are expanding rapidly. The slump in the Sunbelt continued into the mid-1980s, and is still particularly significant in oil towns like Houston.

By the mid-1980s, regional disparities in owner-occupied housing markets were also becoming significant in West Germany and Britain, reflecting geographical changes in economic growth and employment. In West Germany housing production has shifted towards the south of the country and in Britain to the south and west. As in the USA, these shifts are reflected in greater regional disparities in house prices.

Generally, the mid-1980s saw a revival of owner-occupied markets and house building, although this still remains limited for the Netherlands. But in some countries, such as Britain, owner-occupied house building by 1987 had reached levels achieved in the speculative booms of the early 1970s. Forecasting future developments of owner-occupied markets is difficult, but there are strong indications that current high building levels cannot be sustained. Housing costs in the late 1980s are significantly higher in most countries than they were in the previous decade. In the USA, for example, the percentage of households meeting the qualification requirements for a fixed-rate mortgage and a median-priced new single-family house had fallen from 80 to 40 per cent between the early 1970s and early 1980s (FRBNY, 1984/5). Inflation is low and no longer erodes the nominal value of mortgage debt, while real interest rates are very high, rather than negative as they were for much of the 1970s. The future of owner-occupied markets therefore seems perilous everywhere, especially if the world economy experiences another down-turn.

CONCLUSION

The survey of owner-occupied housing markets in Western Europe and the USA indicates that the tenure is in transition. Bolstered by rising real incomes and major state intervention, home-ownership had become the main housing tenure by the 1980s in all the countries considered. Its role within housing provision, however, varies between countries. Variations include the relative significance of the tenure, its forms of provision and the ways state support is given to the tenure.

The type of market that is constituted by owner occupation and the role of existing home-owners and second-hand dwellings in market transactions also differ between countries. Existing home-owners became more important in market transactions with the growth of the tenure. This has been particularly true in those countries where sales by existing owner-occupiers helped to create unified markets, as occurred in Britain and the Netherlands during the early and late 1970s respectively and in Denmark and in some US cities during the mid-1980s. A dominance of existing home-owners in market activities in unified markets has contributed to a greater instability of owner-occupied markets, as house-building activities have come to depend on the input of money gains realised by sales from existing owners in addition to purchasing power from salaries and wages. So, house prices have to rise at a much higher pace than the general rate of inflation for house building to expand. Conversely, when house price inflation slows down, market activities are substantially reduced. House price falls in unified markets may even lead, as we have seen in the Netherlands, to a serious, prolonged market crisis. The situation is different in countries where owner-occupied markets remain fragmented. There, falling house prices, aided by reductions in the standard and quality of new housing, may actually contribute to a revival of house building, as buying a house again becomes affordable for larger sections of the population. It is, however, yet to be seen whether the recent sharpening of the divide between regions of economic growth and decline, occurring in many countries and paralleled by similar differences in house price developments, will lead to greater fragmentation (or regionalisation) of previously unified markets.

Owner occupation has not only become more significant, but the tenure is also changing in other ways. There are pressures on key institutions associated with its provision, particularly those related to mortgage finance and house building, as Chapters 4 and 5 will show. Involvement by the state, despite frequent rhetoric to the contrary, has grown, especially via lost tax revenues caused by the various forms of income tax deduction associated with owner occupation. In addition, production subsidies were extended during the housing market down-turn of the early 1980s in the countries where that subsidy was already significant. And such subsidies were newly introduced in Denmark for 'co-operative housing', a new sector aimed at middle-income first-time buyers. So, state subsidies have not only become more important, but also remain a necessity for expanding owner occupation; both in periods of housing market booms when income tax subsidies shelter home-owners from some of the effects of rising house prices and interest rates, and during down-turns in the market when production subsidies gain significance in boosting owner-occupied house building.

More worrying is the increasing number of households which have entered home-ownership in the last decade that are highly vulnerable to adverse shifts in the delicate balance of housing affordability. Housing costs have risen substantially in the 1980s and low rates of inflation and high real interest rates make home-ownership an expensive purchase in the longer term. The current high costs of owner occupation are also reflected in the very high number of mortgage defaults and repossessions in all countries concerned here, irrespective of whether the housing market is booming or in decline.

NOTES

1. This paper is a much extended and revised version of an earlier publication, which analysed post-war developments in owner-occupied housing markets in the five European countries surveyed here (Martens, 1985).

2. There are problems with assessing the amount of owner-occupied house building from the statistical information available for some countries. In Denmark, West Germany and the USA, single-family housing has been used to define owner occupation. It is, however, not possible to use this category for France, where, especially in urban areas, large-scale multi-family housing projects have been built for sale to individual home-owners throughout the post-war period. Housing completions in owner occupation in France could be assessed by adding house-building categories indicating the destination for which the dwellings are produced (sale, personal use and second homes). Unfortunately, until 1977 such data only existed for housing approvals. Data for 1950–77 have, therefore, been estimated by using completions of all private housing for this period, which have then been adjusted to the owner-occupied house-building data available for the 1977 to 1981 period. Dutch house-building statistics indicate tenures, whereas for Britain completions in the private sector can be regarded as synonymous with owner occupation (see also Martens, 1985).

3. In the brief description of structures of owner-occupied housing provision it is inevitable to cover some of the material described in greater depth in Chapters 4 and 5. These chapters, however, concentrate on explaining the changes taking place to the institutions associated with mortgage finance and house building.

REFERENCES

Ball, M. (1983) *Housing Policy and Economic Power. The Political Economy of Owner Occupation*, Methuen, London

Ball, M., Martens, M. and Harloe, M. (1986) 'Mortgage Finance and Owner Occupation in Britain and West Germany', *Progress in Planning, 26*(3), 187–260

Byrne, D. (1986), 'Housing and Class in the Inner City', in P. Malpass (ed.), *The Housing Crisis*, Croom Helm, Beckenham, 151–73

Dijkhuis-Potgieser, H.I.E. (1982) '*Trends op de Woningmarkt 1976– 1981, Nationaal Rayon Onderzoek 1976–1981*', Instituut Foss, Oegstgeest (NL)

Donnison, D.V. (1967) *The Government of Housing*, Penguin Books, Harmondsworth, Middlesex

Dreimuller, A.P. (1980) '*Taak en Plaats van de Projektontwikkelaar in het Bouwprocess*', Report 20, EIB, Amsterdam

Fish, G.S. (1979) 'Housing Policy during the Great Depression', in

G.S. Fish (ed.), *The Story of Housing*, Macmillan, New York and London

FRBNY (Federal Reserve Bank of New York) (1984/5), *Quarterly Review*, Winter

Harloe, M. and Martens, M. (1985) 'The Restructuring of Housing Provision in Britain and the Netherlands', *Environment and Planning A, 17*, 1063–1087

Harvey, D. and Chatterjee, L. (1974) 'Absolute Rent and the Restructuring of Space by Financial Institutions', *Antipode 6*, 22–36

HUD (Department of Housing and Urban Development) (1973) *Housing in the Seventies* (Draft Report), HUD, Washington DC

Knechtel, E. (1983) 'Marktdaten zum Fertigteilbau 1965–1982', Bundesgemeinschaft Fertigteilbau, Hamburg

Köster, J. and Mezler, J. (1979) 'Wohnungseigentumsquote, Bestimmungsgründe der Wohnungseigentumsquote in den Ländern Belgien, Dänemark, Frankreich, Grossbritannien, USA, Bundes Republik Deutschland', Schriftenreihe Wohnungsmarkt und Wohnungspolitik 07.005, Der Bundesminister für Raumordnung und Städtebau, Bonn

Martens, M. (1985) 'Owner Occupied Housing in Europe: Postwar Developments and Current Dilemmas', *Environment and Planning A, 17*, 605–24

Nationwide Building Society (1987) 'House prices in Europe', *Nationwide Building Society Background Bulletin*, January

Pratt, G. (1986) 'Against Reductionism: the Relations of Consumption as a mode of Social Structures', *IJURR 10*(3), 377–400

Preteceille, E. (1986) 'Collective Consumption, Urban Segregation, and Social Classes', *Environment and Planning D: Society and Space 4*, 145–54

Straszheim, M. (1975) *An Econometric Analysis of the Urban Housing Market*, NBER, New York

Schlesinger, T. and Erlich, M. (1986) 'Housing: the Industry Capitalism didn't forget', in R.G. Bratt, C.W. Hartman and A. Meyerson, *Critical Perspectives on Housing*, Temple University Press, Philadelphia

Tabb, W.K. (1984) 'Urban development and regional restructuring, an Overview' in L. Sawers and W.K. Tabb (eds), *Sunbelt/Snowbelt*, Oxford University Press, New York and Oxford

Topalov, C. (1974) *Les Promoteurs Immobiliers*, Mouton, Paris

—— (1980) 'Transformation des systèmes de production du logement et politiques étatiques en France (1950–1980)', paper presented at the conference la Casa e la Sinistra Europa, Venice

—— (1981) 'Tous Propriétaires! Propriété du Logement et Classes Sociales en France depuis 1950', Centre de Sociologie Urbaine, Paris

—— (1983) 'Report on Social and Owner Occupied Housing in France', unpublished manuscript

Vestergaard, H. (1982) 'Report on Social and Owner Occupied Housing in Denmark', unpublished manuscript

Weissbarth, R. and Hundt, B. (1983) 'Die Eigentumsbildung im

Wohnungsbau', Schriftenreihe Wohnungsmarkt und Wohnungspolitik 07.014, Der Bundesminister für Raumordnung, Bauwesen
und Städtebau, Bonn

4

The Revolution in Mortgage Finance

Maartje Martens

INTRODUCTION

Mortgages developed as a form of long-term finance for individual home-ownership with the emergence of mass markets for owner-occupied house building. As was shown in the previous chapter, the timing of the growth of urban home-ownership differs substantially between countries. In the USA and Britain, the inter-war period marked the advent of mass home-ownership, whereas in most European countries it developed during the post-war era. Owner occupation did exist before then, but mainly in the form of scattered, self-built housing developments in rural areas.

Similarly, the growth of specialised mortgage finance institutions is linked to the expansion of a mass market of standardised housing for sale. That market could only develop with the existence of specialised mortgage lenders, facilitating house purchases by individual home-owners. Although some mortgage finance institutions, as we know them now, were created as late as the 1930s, most derive from institutions that were set up in earlier centuries. For instance, the building society movement in Britain and the savings and loans associations (s&ls) in the USA developed during the eighteenth and nineteenth centuries respectively. Yet in both cases their current institutional structure and market significance were established during the inter-war period, as home-ownership became a mass phenomenon.

The history of the mortgage banks, which are major providers of housing loans in most European countries, is somewhat different. Their contemporary structure had already developed during the second half of the nineteenth century, when mortgage banks played a major role in financing rapid urbanisation. Mortgage banks traditionally funded rented house building and urban infrastructural developments. The switch to owner occupation only occurred in the post-war period.

Recent changes in the traditional institutional structure of mortgage finance in many advanced capitalist countries have been amongst the most dramatic transformations in housing provision. Protected specialised financial circuits that dominated housing finance for long periods are disappearing in many countries. The changes are taking place in an era of increased competition between financial institutions, deregulation of financial markets and increasingly unstable housing markets. This chapter summarises and discusses the main developments leading to this 'mortgage finance revolution' and evaluates its likely consequences for housing markets and consumers.

Before dealing with recent developments, a description is given of the major types of specialised mortgage lenders in each of the countries we are dealing with.[1] A historical perspective shows that the implementation of protected and regulated housing finance systems in many cases resulted from earlier failures in financial and housing markets. Post-war inflation created optimism amongst policy-makers, investors and consumers alike, that house price rises are eternal and mortgage defaults a risk for consumers only. Such optimism is unfounded as past and current examples from a number of countries show.

MORTGAGE FINANCE INSTITUTIONS: TYPES AND SIGNIFICANCE

Two basic types of institution specialise in long-term housing loans in the countries included in our survey. The difference between them focuses fundamentally on the characteristics of their financial circuits. The first type of specialised mortgage lender uses personal sector liquid assets, further referred to as retail or personal savings, to fund housing loans and dominates mortgage finance in the USA and Britain (as well as in most other English-speaking countries). It can be referred to as savings banking, which may be limited to lending for housing only or include wider activities. The second type of institution is

131

found in most European countries (but not Britain) and taps funds from the wholesale money market via the issuing of mortgage bonds. These are called mortgage banks.

The distinct income sources of these institutions influence the type of financial market in which they operate and the terms and conditions of the mortgage loans they offer. The savings banking type operates in the personal sector and traditionally has been comparatively sheltered from fluctuations in capital markets. Savings banks work on the principle of borrowing short-term 'liquid' retail savings and lending longer-term loans. To respond to short-term fluctuations in interest rates, savings banks tend traditionally to offer variable interest rate loans. This has always been the case with the British building societies (as with savings banks in most countries), but the exception to interest rate variability are the savings and loan associations (s&ls) or other Thrift institutions in the USA, for reasons that shall be explained below.

The situation is very different for mortgage banks, which buy their funds wholesale on capital markets, or more specifically, the bond market. The long-term fixed interest rate debt papers (mortgage bonds) they issue, in principle reflect the time profiles and the interest rate structure of the mortgages they lend.

Further differences exist between the two types of mortgage finance institutions, for instance regarding the housing market sectors in which they traditionally specialise. Other variations occur between countries with similar types of housing finance institutions. The following section first describes the savings banking scheme in more detail for Britain and the USA, followed by a description of the specialised types of institutions that dominate mortgage lending in West Germany, the Netherlands and Denmark.

The Savings Banking System

The origin of the savings banking scheme for funding housing loans goes back to the start of the building society movement in eighteenth-century Britain. The first were terminating societies, regularly subscribed to by a small number of members, until enough money was accumulated to build houses for each of them. Such initiatives for providing housing, based on thrift and co-operation, expanded amongst the middle class and the regularly employed working class. Even though their overall significance in house building remained limited at the time, the growth of the building society movement was linked to processes of industrialisation and the growth of wage-earning classes and signified the need for personal savings and loans for obtaining home-ownership. British immigrants introduced the building society concept to the USA, where they are referred to as the Thrift industry, which comprises savings and loan associations and mutual savings banks (Ornstein, 1985).

As the building societies and the Thrift industry expanded, many were converted from a terminating to a permanent basis. In both countries, this transformation occurred around the mid-nineteenth century and signified a major change as the link between investors and borrowers was broken. Individuals could deposit their savings without necessarily wanting to buy a house and the savings associations and societies could diversify their investments by lending to house-builders and private landlords. But, in the main, the associations continued to raise retail funds from moderate-income households and to lend to individual house-buyers.

Although the origins of the British building societies and the Thrift industry in the USA are quite similar, their current structures are very different. The legal framework for building societies was first established in its modern form by the Building Societies Act of 1874. Adjustments, however, were made in subsequent decades, following society failures through reckless speculation, which reduced public confidence in the sector as a whole. An act of 1894 tightened supervision by the Registrar of Friendly Societies and lending was restricted to first mortgages only (Cleary, 1965). Further adjustments were made at the end of the 1930s, after building societies had experienced 20 years of rapid expansion with the emergence of mass home-ownership in Britain and low returns on competing investments. Building societies complemented the activities of speculative house-builders through facilitating large-scale house purchase amongst the skilled working and middle classes. Building societies and builders developed practices which required only small down payments by house-buyers. These so-called builder's pools led to malpractices in mortgage lending and eventually to a new act in 1939 (see Craig, 1986 for a detailed account). Rather than just outlining the structure of building societies, the act defined, for the first time in some detail, practices relating to lending security and property valuation and also aimed to distinguish between the interests of builders and lenders (Cleary, 1965).

Another major development during the 1930s concerned the formation of a building societies' interest-rate-fixing cartel following intense competition between them. The cartel only became effective at the end of the decade, when demand for mortgages was faltering, but it was subsequently maintained until the early 1980s. Interest rate levels in the cartel generally allowed for a sufficient inflow of funds to building societies, plus an adequate interest rate margin between borrowing and lending for most of them. A strong inflow of funds was further secured by tax advantages given to the societies and their investors, which helped the societies to expand their share of the retail savings market. The ascendance of building societies in mortgage lending was established during the inter-war period, a position that was to improve after the war in an era of non-price competition between them.

Compared to the building societies, the American Thrift industry relied far less on self regulation. As in Britain, the modern structure of the Thrift industry was established in the 1930s, but the circumstances differ substantially. Savings and loans associations grew rapidly during the 1920s, but the Wall Street crash of 1929, and the subsequent run on savings deposits, caused massive failures amongst Thrifts, which in addition had to cope with large-scale defaults on housing loans during the Depression. In response to these problems, measures were taken in a number of acts under the New Deal, making the housing finance industry in the USA possibly the most regulated in the world. The new regulations, meant to prevent similar banking failures in the future, can be summarised as follows:

i) A segregation was created between the various sectors of the financial industry. Commercial banking became separated from investment banking, and investment banks were not allowed to accept deposits or to make loans. To insulate housing finance from capital markets, Thrifts became legally required to invest in housing loans and received tax exemptions for doing so. Both commercial banks and Thrifts were barred from having branches in more than one state (Florida, 1986).

ii) The Thrift industry was subordinated to a special chartering and regulatory body, the Federal Home Loan Bank Board (FHLBB), which also has supervisory authority over the Federal Home Loan Bank (FHLB). The FHLB was established as a central bank for the savings and loan industry (equivalent to the Federal Reserve System for commercial banks) to advance extra funds to its member organisations when these were needed (Ornstein, 1985).

iii) All federally regulated financial institutions were required to insure their deposits. For the s&ls, the Federal Savings and Loan Insurance Corporation (FSLIC), also supervised by the FHLBB, fulfilled this function and to a lesser extent also the Federal Deposit Insurance (FDIC), which was mainly set up to insure deposits with commercial banks.

iv) Interest rate ceilings on savings deposits were imposed. The measure aimed to reduce competition for such funds and thus encourage more prudent lending practices. Regulation Q, which set interest rate ceilings on deposit accounts, gave Thrifts a quarter percentage differential above commercial banks' lending rates.

v) A secondary market for mortgages was established via the creation of the Federal National Mortgage Association (FNMA, usually referred to as Fannie Mae), which could buy mortgages from the portfolios of s&ls which were in need of extra funds.

vi) Finally, a mortgage insurance scheme was introduced through the Federal Housing Administration (FHA). After the war the scheme was joined by a guarantee scheme under the Veterans Administration (VA). The main advantage of the FHA and VA loans is that they require only small deposits from house-buyers and the scheme was aimed at encouraging house building. Another aspect of these loans is that they introduced a new type of mortgage, the fixed interest rate, self-amortising annuity loan. The fixed interest rate loan also developed as the standard instrument for what is called conventional, i.e. non FHA & VA, loans.

Thus the fixed rate loan, refinanced by relatively cheap funds resulting from interest rate ceilings on retail deposits, made individual home-ownership an increasingly attractive proposition. FHA and VA loans, in particular, helped to fuel the post-war house-building boom in standardised housing in large-scale suburban developments (Checkoway, 1980). Although Thrifts

135

were not the only participants on the housing market, they remained the main mortgage lending institutions after the war and expanded their asset volume considerably. Although the largest American Thrifts have more assets than the largest British building societies, the Thrift industry is much more dispersed, because of the inter-state banking laws: with 3,350 Thrift institutions, in 1984 and the largest five taking up nine per cent of the total asset volume, whereas building societies numbered 206 institutions, with the largest five taking a 55 per cent market share (see HM Treasury, 1984 and National Council of Savings Institutions, 1985).

Finally, the West German *Bausparkassen* should be mentioned as another specialised mortgage lender within the savings banking scheme. Unlike British building societies and American Thrifts, *Bausparkassen* have always maintained the link between investors and borrowers, but in a way which differs from the terminating societies mentioned earlier. Loans are only allocated to contract savers and the size of a loan depends on the amount saved and the duration of the savings contract (usually about seven to ten years), *Bausparkassen* operate fixed low-interest savings and loan schemes. Contract savings are subsidised by the state and have therefore been competitive. The low interest loan costs, however, are offset by their high amortisation rate (seven per cent). Loans are repaid rapidly relative to other mortgages, which in terms of annual outgoings makes them at least as expensive as other forms of finance. The high amortisation rate thus limits the *Bausparkassen* to funding second mortgages as their loans are too expensive to repay full housing loans.

Bausparkassen were founded from the mid-1920s onwards to encourage collective savings schemes for house building. Their foundation was a response to a period of hyper-inflation, which was followed by a currency revaluation in 1923, and had led to a massive destruction of savings. Their role in funding second mortgages grew in the 1930s when deflation led mortgage banks to restrict lending limits to 40 per cent of house prices. *Bausparkassen* expanded substantially after the Second World War, with a 20 per cent market share of all outstanding housing loans by 1970. Their expansion was strongly linked to owner-occupied one-family house building.

The Mortgage Banking Scheme

The origins of mortgage bonds go back to eighteenth-century Prussia, when agriculture was destroyed after a war with Austria (1756–63) and large landowners were unable to finance recovery (Pleyer and Bellinger, 1981). To overcome the problem, landowners formed associations, which issued collectively guaranteed debt papers (bonds) to their individual members. These bonds were secured by landed property and enabled landowners to raise long-term funds on capital markets. The mortgage bond scheme subsequently expanded rapidly to other European countries.

With the creation of the Crédit Foncier de France (CFF) in 1852, the mortgage bond issuing system was transformed into what are now known as mortgage banks. Rather than just facilitating borrowing for their members, mortgage banks act as financial intermediaries between borrowers and investors. But, like their predecessors, they specialise in raising long-term funds with debt papers secured by real estate. Such mortgage banking institutions were founded in West Germany and the Netherlands (as well as in many other European countries) from the 1860s onwards.[2]

The Danish mortgage credit institutions (MCIs) differ somewhat from the mortgage banks. Most contemporary MCIs developed out of the agricultural co-operative movement during the second half of the nineteenth century. They did not function as banking intermediaries, but were based on similar principles to the original Prussian scheme, with mutual associations of borrowers who provided mortgage bonds for their members, farmers or house-buyers. Only as late as 1980 were MCIs fully transformed into a 'cash loan' system, whereby borrowers were given loans directly, rather than in the form of bonds, which they could sell individually to raise finance. But MCIs remain mutual organisations (except for one founded after the war), with members collectively guaranteeing all the bonds issued.

Mortgage banks in West Germany and the Netherlands were originally privately owned stockholding companies. Most Dutch mortgage banks used to be independent, although the first one to be founded was owned by the co-operative banks and a couple were taken over by insurance companies in the late 1930s. (More recent developments are discussed later.) In

West Germany, mortgage banks were also founded in the public banking sector during the inter-war years. German public mortgage banks have been instrumental in funding public infrastructural works and social house-building projects, particularly during the Weimar republic and the period following the Second World War.

The specialisation of mortgage banks derives from their ability to issue long-term bonds on capital markets: a privilege restricted to a small number of institutions. The Danish mortgage credit institutions and Dutch mortgage banks monopolise the long-term bond market, whereas in West Germany the specialisation of mortgage banks compares with the far greater restrictions imposed on the volume of bonds other types of banks are allowed to issue. Apart from bonds, Dutch mortgage banks can also raise funds via *onderhandse leningen* (private loans), which are loans directly provided by large investors, such as pension funds and insurance companies, without intermediation by a financial institution. This type of funding has become more important over the last two decades.

The history of mortgage banks has not been without turbulence. Failures have followed real estate booms (as in West Germany in the 1870s) or agricultural crises (like in Denmark in the 1930s). Periods of falling house prices have threatened the security of mortgage bonds for investors and led to the introduction of limits on mortgage/house price ratios. In West Germany, mortgage banks are legally confined to lending on first mortgages only, defined as the first 60 per cent of house price valuations. In Denmark, until the 1970 reform of mortgage credit institutions, lending policies of MCIs were not legally stipulated. Instead, lending limits were related to practices developed by the MCIs themselves, who offered only a particular tranche of a loan. Thus, until 1970, house-buyers had to obtain first, second and third mortgage loans from different institutions, covering respectively, up to 40/50 per cent, 40/50 - 65/70 per cent and 65/70 - 75/80 per cent of house prices. Credit institutions specialised in one of the tranches. With the 1970s' reform, MCIs were merged into four institutions, the tranche system disappeared and new, strict lending criteria were enacted. MCIs, for example, were restricted to lending up to 80 per cent of valuation prices for new houses and 40 per cent for existing ones.

Dutch mortgage banks have lacked regulation and government supervision for most of their history. While in Germany the first act to regulate mortgage banks dates from 1899, the first legislative controls were as recent as 1979 in the Netherlands. Prior to 1979, government supervision was limited and indirect via the central organisation of Dutch mortgage banks. The state savings bank also had some supervision rights, but on behalf of investors in mortgage bonds (Klein & Vleesenbeek, 1981). Regulations were only concerned with protecting bond investors: most significantly, lending was generally restricted to first mortgages, which could cover up to 75 per cent of house price valuations. The losses Dutch mortgage banks had made during the economic depression of the 1930s, unlike experiences elsewhere, had not led to more government regulation and supervision. Instead, the 'self-regulating' response was a wave of mergers within the sector and of take-overs of some mortgage banks by insurance companies at the end of the decade.

Until taken over by the Ministry of Housing in 1981, supervision over the Danish MCIs was in the main left to their central organisation. So the predominance of self-regulation for most of their existence is similar to the Dutch case, but as explained before, MCIs are not financial institutions. They only facilitate borrowing from the capital market for their individual members, without being financial intermediaries. In reality, however, the new supervision power of the Ministry of Housing is still limited, as hardly any sanctions are linked to it. Supervision by the Ministry was negotiated when mortgage lending possibilities for MCIs were liberated by parliament. Liberation particularly concerned an increase of mortgage/house price ratios for existing housing. MCIs are generally not regarded as being exposed to major lending risks, because of the regulated loan to house price ratios. Loans are tied to the house, rather than the borrower, whose financial situation is not really assessed by the MCI. In case of default, the loan is sold with the property to the next owner, or, if the selling price is insufficient to cover the debt, temporarily acquired by the MCI. House prices, so far, have not fallen enough to threaten the system. A more important aspect of adjusting lending limits of MCIs is that it is used as a policy instrument to control the volume of consumer credit that can be financed by mortgages. As MCIs not only monopolise the mortgage bond market, but also came to be the sole providers of housing loans in Denmark for both rented and owner-occupied housing, it is not surprising that they are a main target of monetary control policies.

The business of German mortgage banks was stagnant for most of the inter-war period, but it has expanded substantially since 1945. Up to the 1960s growth was linked to state-subsidised house building, for which long-term fixed interest rate loans were required. By financing West Germany's large post-war house-building programme, mortgage banks, public and private, became the largest housing finance institutions, with a 36 per cent share of outstanding mortgage loans in 1970 (Ball et al., 1986). Only in the 1970s did West German mortgage banks start to lend to individual house-buyers on a significant scale.

The Dutch situation is different again. Mortgage banks expanded substantially during the inter-war house-building boom by financing large-scale housing developments in the private rental sector. Private rental house building virtually disappeared after the war and what remained was financed and managed by pension funds and insurance companies. Most social rented house building was realised with state subsidies and state loans. Owner occupation did not develop until the late 1950s, when direct subsidies were given to house building for own use and when a government mortgage loan guarantee scheme was introduced to reduce down payments for prospective house-buyers. The guarantee scheme for owner-occupiers enabled mortgage banks, previously restricted to ratios of 65–70 per cent, to lend up to 90 per cent of house price valuations. The business of mortgage banks increased as a result, but did not really take off until the owner-occupied housing boom of the 1970s. Meanwhile, mortgage banks had incorporated other activities in their investments, such as financing commercial property developments. So it is mainly due to the peculiar post-war provision structure of rental housing that Dutch mortgage banks were confined to lending to owner-occupiers. The market share of mortgage banks was estimated at 28 per cent in 1935, with private individuals as market leaders in housing loans. Mortgage banks only regained this market share again 40 years later (Rijnvos, 1981).

Finally, the USA mortgage companies should be mentioned, as they have played a major role in post-war housing finance. American mortgage companies differ from the European mortgage banks as they do not hold mortgages in their portfolios, but only originate mortgages for sale on to other investors. Profits are made from the fees charged for mortgage origination, and through servicing mortgages for the ultimate investors. The major source of income is through servicing loans. Also, those firms which specialise in mortgage origination make a profit from selling the right to service the loans.

Mortgage companies, typically, specialise in funding single-family owner-occupied housing. They gained significance during the 1920s, when long-term loans were hard to find. The industry declined with the rise of the Thrift institutions in the 1930s and after the war, but revived again in the 1970s with the rise of the secondary mortgage market. The role of mortgage banking in mortgage originations has tended to be cyclical, rising in significance when market rates of interest increase; when Thrifts were less competitive in raising sufficient funds to meet demand, because of ceilings on their deposit rates.

Mortgage banking in the USA is not regulated and as there are no restrictions on inter-state mortgage banking, a national presence can be developed. Mortgage companies have been important in selling FHA and VA loans, and in shifting funds between states and channelling them into housing. Non-regulation includes the absence of restrictions on loan to own-capital ratios for the mortgage companies. Mortgage/house price ratios are regulated indirectly, via requirements linked to the mortgage pools held by the federally supported, secondary mortgage market institutions (see below). Most housing loans that are originated by mortgage companies are sold via such mortgage pools. These loans mainly include FHA and VA loans, but increasingly also privately insured, conventional loans.

COMPETITORS FOR MORTGAGE LENDING

Specialised housing finance institutions have never been the sole lenders of mortgages in the countries studied here, with the exception of Denmark. But until the mid-1960s, competition for mortgage lending was fairly limited as the market was divided by region or housing sector, between the active financial institutions. Table 4.1 gives an overview of the financial institutions with significant shares in housing loans in the respective countries. A brief mention will now be made of the non-specialist mortgage lending institutions, as the specialised institutions have already been discussed.

Table 4.1: Housing Finance Institutions and their Changing Significance: market shares in the volume of outstanding mortgage credit

Country	Specialised Institutions Source of Funds		Other
	Retail	Wholesale	
WEST GERMANY 1970–84	*Bausparkassen* (18% – 19%)	Mortgage Banks (36% – 25%)	Savings Banks (34% – 32%) Commercial Banks (5% – 11%) Co-operative Banks (5% – 11%)
NETHERLANDS 1975–84		Mortgage Banks, *Bouwfondsen* (31% – 8.2%)	Co-operative Banks (29% – 37%) Universal Banks (18% – 22%) Savings Banks (8% – 16%)
DENMARK		Mortgage Credit Institutions (100%)	
BRITAIN 1960–85	Building Societies (63% – 76.5%)		Clearing Banks (8% – 16.5%) Local Authorities (11% – 3%) Insurance Companies (18% – 2%)
USA 1970–84	Savings & Loan Ass. (39%–) Mutual Savings (14%–) (both 41% in '84)	Mortgage Companies (originations only) Mortgage Pools (0.7% – 21%)	Commercial Banks (13% – 15%) Life Insurance Companies (12% – about 3%) Federally Related Agencies (7% – 9%)

Note: Data for the Netherlands, the USA and Britain only concern lending
to individual home-owners, whereas in Denmark and West Germany other tenures are also included.

Sources: West Germany: Deutsche Bundesbank, *Statistische Beihefte;*
The Netherlands: Nederlands Bank nv, *Annual Report 1984* & Burgert et al., 1981;
Britain: Ball et al., 1986 & *BSA Bulletin*, no. 47, 1986;
USA: *The Report of the President's Commission on Housing* (1982) & Meyerson 1986.

Savings banks are West Germany's largest banking sector and were the second largest mortgage lenders in the early 1970s. They are owned by the local authorities or regional councils (*Kreise*) and their activities are limited to the jurisdiction of their parent authority. The ownership structure influences the role savings banks play, which is to invest in municipal projects, small companies and housing loans and to encourage moderate-income households to save. Thus savings banks mainly borrow retail funds and have most of their assets in long-term loans, about half of which are mortgages. Savings banks' substantial market share in housing finance is mainly achieved via funding variable rate, first mortgage loans to individual home-owners. Traditionally, their business was complementary to mortgage banks' lending to rented house building and to *Bausparkassen*, which only issued second mortgage loans.

In the Netherlands, competition for mortgage lending focused on the owner-occupied housing sector, as rented housing was generally financed without the intermediation of financial institutions, referred to in financial statistics as business loans. The latter are not included in Table 4.1. Rented housing loans are mainly provided by the state, insurance companies or pension funds and only occasionally by mortgage banks, when the former sources could not meet the demand.

Apart from the mortgage banks and *Bouwfondsen*,[3] Dutch housing loans are also provided by co-operative and savings banks, but in relative isolation from each other and with little competition between them (Rijnvos, 1981). The co-operative banks, with a market share of about 50 per cent in financing individual home-owners during the 1960s, are mainly agrarian based and focused on rural areas. Savings banks, on the other hand, are more orientated on the urban population. Traditionally, their main function was to secure deposits small savers made with them and savings banks were in effect rather like a social security scheme rather than a banking institution. Savings banks are legally confined to dealings in the retail sector in contrast to the co-operative banks, which are included in the commercial banking sector and allowed to issue business loans. Within the co-operative and savings banking sectors competition used to be limited, because of the regional or local specialisation of their member banks. The Dutch mortgage market was dominated by the co-operative and savings banks until the late

1960s. As mentioned earlier, Dutch mortgage banks did not substantially expand their mortgage business until the 1970s. The high costs of their funds compared to their main competitors led to their status as lenders of last resort.

The Danish mortgage credit institutions faced very little competition. Savings banks, for instance, were active in providing second mortgages in the period up to the late 1960s, following policies of MCIs of lending only 50 to 60 per cent of house prices. Housing loans offered by savings banks were more expensive than those refinanced by mortgage bonds and therefore unattractive as first mortgages; a situation which is different from many other countries. Danish banking institutions were only active in areas where MCIs' activities were restricted, such as in the second-hand housing market. Competition was also limited between MCIs, because of their specialisation by region or particular loan tranches.

Apart from the British building societies, with by far the largest market share in post-war mortgage lending, housing loans were also provided by insurance companies, local authorities and clearing banks. Again, each of them specialised in particular segments of the market. Local authority lending concentrated mainly on smaller, cheaper dwellings and was aimed at encouraging lower-income home-ownership, because, at the time, these were household and housing categories which building societies were reluctant to invest in. Insurance companies, on the other hand, primarily lent to upper-income groups. Generally, mortgages have only been a minor part of their assets (Ball et al., 1986). (The Dutch insurance companies, in contrast, are major mortgage originators, but sell them on to pension funds to maintain liquidity.) As elsewhere, insurance companies' main reason for investing in mortgages is to sell insurance policies, which accounts for their role in the growth of endowment mortgages during the 1970s.

The British clearing banks, finally, do lend mortgages, but did not have a significant presence until the 1980s. Clearing banks owe their name to their collective monopoly over the British cheque-clearing system. The sector is dominated by a handful of large private banking concerns, which had traditionally concentrated on lending to industry, trade and the public sector and only diversified into large-scale consumer lending during the 1960s. They tended to concentrate mortgage lending on the higher-priced sectors of the market.

The main competitors to the Thrift industry in the USA are the commercial banks and insurance companies. But both latter types of investor lost major market shares in mortgage lending to individual house-buyers during the 1960s (Tucillo and Goodman, 1981). Their loss of market share enhanced the role of the Thrifts in mortgage lending. But the reason for the reduced role of commercial banks and insurance companies was related to the reduction in the net return on mortgage investment relative to corporate securities (ibid.). The role of insurance companies in mortgage origination reduced to virtually nothing and the mortgage lending business of commercial banks became increasingly cyclical.

PRESSURES FOR CHANGE

Having examined the different types of financial institutions involved in housing finance in each of the countries, the remaining part of this chapter will discuss the transformations they have undergone over the past decade and the reasons for the changes. Specialisation and semi-protected financial circuits provided the key to the expansion of the mortgage finance institutions during the post-war house-building boom. But their competitive environment has changed substantially over the past two decades, and so has the political support given to them.

Pressures for change differed in their effects and in their specific outcomes. But, at a general level, the following developments contributed to the transformation of specialised mortgage lending. Each will be discussed in more detail in subsequent sections.

i) There has been a general increase in competition in financial markets, both in the business of mortgage lending and in attracting funds, particularly retail savings. Changes in the financial environment in which housing finance institutions operate include general trends towards deregulation and financial supermarkets and the impact of technological innovation on competition.

ii) Specialised mortgage lenders had to adjust to a new era of rising and volatile levels of interest rates, particularly during the 1970s and early 1980s. Particularly affected were institu-

145

tions which traditionally offered long-term fixed interest rate loans.

iii) Developments in housing markets altered the economic environment of mortgage lending institutions' investment activities.

iv) Managers of housing finance institutions, in addition, opted for continuation of the rapid expansion they had experienced throughout the post-war years.

v) Finally, commitment of central governments to maintain the semi-protected financial circuits for housing loans disappeared in many countries, or has been greatly eroded, together with the political priority given to house building.

COMPETITION IN FINANCIAL MARKETS

The 1960s brought about major changes in the competitive environment of specialised housing finance institutions. Their institutional structures did, however, not undergo major alterations until the 1980s, with the exception of West Germany's mortgage banks.

Competition grew for mortgage institutions' sources of funds in a number of countries, particularly in Europe, as a result of new attempts by commercial banks to increase their share in personal borrowing and lending. The growth in personal wealth during the post-war years made retail savings an increasingly attractive source of funding for commercial banks. Extra competition for retail funds coincided with trends to deregulate interest rate fixing. Similarly, reductions were made in tax advantages related to credit institutions traditionally operating in the retail market, and they affected the competitive position of savings banks, credit co-operatives and, in some cases, specialised mortgage lenders. As a result of these changes during the late 1960s differences between the types of banking institution reduced substantially, leading to the gradual evolution of universal banking. Again, the timing of these developments differs between countries. In Britain, for instance, specialisation within the banking sector still prevails, although it is less rigid than before, whereas the universal banking system has dominated in West Germany for over 15 years. Mortgage lending has been a major influence on the growth of universal banking.

West Germany's commercial banks saw their market share of banking business fall substantially during the 1960s (from 37.6 per cent in 1950 to 22.1 per cent in 1967) (EAG, 1981). The loss was particularly marked for the big three commercial banks following a decline in the demand for industrial credit. The 'big three' along with the credit co-operatives and their central organisation, became the most aggressive competitors for mortgage finance in the 1970s. All these institutions developed a market position in mortgage lending by acquiring majority shares in private mortgage banks during the early 1970s (see Ball et al., 1986 for a more detailed account). By integrating private mortgage banks into their banking consortia, commercial and co-operative banks were following what were already existing practices within the public banking sector. There, the savings banks offered full mortgage packages in co-operation with public mortgage banks and public *Bausparkassen*. So, within a very short period of time, the competitive environment for mortgage lending institutions changed dramatically: from a situation where mortgages were offered by institutions who specialised in particular segments of the market, to competition between the three major pillars of the universal banking sector. Commercial banks, savings banks and co-operative banks each offered similar mortgage packages (usually referred to as 'finance under one roof'), which were refinanced by a mixture of wholesale and retail funds.

The main losers from the new intense competition have been the mortgage banks, whose share of outstanding loans declined from 36 per cent in 1970 to 25 per cent in 1983 (Ball et al., 1986). Losses for the mortgage banks became gains for commercial and co-operative banks, partly because of their new ownership of mortgage banks and partly as growth in mortgage lending during the 1970s was concentrated in the area of second mortgages, which mortgage banks could not fund.

West German universal banks' policy of expanding their market share in mortgage lending was not followed by banks in other countries during the 1970s. Other diversification strategies were used instead by most commercial and savings banks. The central organisation of the Dutch co-operative banks (the Rabobank) does own the country's largest mortgage bank, but the ownership relation dates from the last century and so was not part of any new investment strategy. The Rabobank, however, has been and still is the largest single mortgage lending institution in the Netherlands, which may indicate the advantages of combining commercial and mortgage banking. The Danish MCIs, in contrast, outrank the largest banks in asset volume, which makes it more feasible for them to acquire commercial banks, rather than the other way around. But with the exception of West Germany, government policies have, so far, prevented mergers or take-overs between institutions operating in different financial sectors. Such sector policies have aimed to prevent national economies becoming dominated by just a very few financial supermarkets. But the trend towards deregulation and the development of large financial conglomerates, offering all kinds of financial services has persisted in all countries. In some cases, as will be shown below, crises within the mortgage finance sectors accelerated the deregulation process of financial markets.

For West German universal banks, mortgage lending was primarily seen as a profitable and secure form of new investment. Dutch commercial banks, conversely, developed their involvement in housing loans during the 1970s as a way of expanding their business in the personal sector and particularly in the retail savings market. Their strategy was to offer mortgages on very competitive terms if customers would accept other financial services from them. Such strategies were particularly targeted at newly built housing areas. Another new competitor in Dutch mortgage lending, the Post Office Savings Bank (RPS), now the second largest mortgage lender, entered the business for similar reasons. As with other savings banks, it has developed from an institution obliged to find secure long-term investment for small savers' deposits, to an institution providing full banking services to, in the main, personal customers.

Developments in the competitive environment of specialised mortgage lenders seem to have occurred differently in countries where savings banking forms were dominant. In both Britain and the USA, specialised housing finance institutions dominated mortgage lending well into the 1980s. The market share in housing loans of the British building societies (around 80 per cent) was, however, much larger than that of the American Thrift industry (nearer to 50 per cent). Competition was limited in Britain, at least until recently. Only during the 1970s was local authority lending to home-owners of any significance. Clearing banks started to expand in housing loans during the same period, but without acquiring a significant market share until the early 1980s. Before then, competition between banks and societies focused on retail savings and the latter were most successful, overtaking the banks as market leaders by the mid-1970s (Ball et al., 1986).

In the USA, the situation was similar in the sense that competition was fiercest in the retail savings market, i.e. for funds rather than over investments. But competition for the Thrifts was with institutions operating outside the regulated banking system, as both banks and Thrift institutions had imposed interest rate ceilings on the savings deposits they could offer. At the same time, Thrifts' market share in mortgage lending increased during the 1960s and 1970s. Rising inflation and interest rates encouraged insurance companies to leave the market, shifting to higher-yielding securities and real estate, while the banks' mortgage lending activities became more cyclical, depending on the rate of profitability of mortgage lending in comparison with other types of investment (Tucillo and Goodman, 1983).

INFLATION AND INTEREST RATE VOLATILITY

Of all the countries included in this survey, the effects of inflation and unstable levels of interest rates have been most dramatic for housing lenders in the USA. Although Thrift institutions managed to expand their market share in housing loans due to the withdrawal by insurance companies from mortgage lending, interest rate volatility periodically caused what are called 'disintermediation' problems. During periods of rising interest rates, returns on deposits with Thrift institutions increase more slowly than general interest rates, encouraging many savers to deposit their funds in higher-yielding investments elsewhere (Miles, 1983). A disintermediation crisis in the mid-1960s caused a net outflow of funds with Thrifts and commercial banks, leading to the first major pressures towards deregulation. But, rather than resulting in deregulation, Thrifts were instead put under the same regulatory powers as the banks. Before 1966, Thrifts were able to adjust deposit rates subject to supervision by the FHLBB, but deposit interest rate ceilings have been imposed on them since that year, Regulation Q, however, permitted Thrifts to offer one-quarter per cent above commercial banks' deposit rates, enabling Thrifts to continue to expand their share of the personal savings market.

Interest rate ceilings on deposits seemed only to exacerbate problems of the Thrift industry during the 1970s as outflows of funds continued to occur during high interest rate periods, and at times inflation reduced the real value of the interest rates of their savings deposits to zero or even less. Pressure for deregulation continued, particularly from the large commercial banks (Florida, 1986). Since the late 1950s there has been a succession of committees to review the legislative framework of the New Deal banking system. Large banks initially responded to the success of the Thrift industry under the regulatory system. Mortgage lending proved very profitable in the years following the war, enabling Thrifts to develop to sizeable financial institutions and Thrifts' market share in the retail savings market increased substantially. Deposit rate ceilings and Regulation Q inhibited banks from improving their competitiveness in this market. Pressure from the large banks for deregulation stepped up during the second half of the 1970s, when they faced more competition from non-banking institutions entering the business of consumer lending and from foreign banks in both international and domestic financial markets (ibid.). It was finally introduced with the Depository Institutions Deregulation and Monetary Control Act (DIDMC) of 1980.

The act responded to the policies of non-regulated institutions, like insurance companies and brokerage houses, which had introduced highly competitive money market funds for personal savers. Such money market funds again led to a net outflow of funds from the regulated institutions during the late 1970s. The DIDMC act allowed Thrifts some diversification of asset powers and — more importantly — imposed a gradual phasing out of deposit rate ceilings. But because it was introduced at a time when market interest rates were at very high levels, it resulted in a substantial increase in the costs of borrowing for Thrift institutions. The Thrifts' problems were compounded by the fact that most of their assets were in long-term, fixed interest rate loans issued during periods of lower interest rates. The consequences for the industry were dramatic. Three-quarters of Thrift institutions made losses during the early 1980s. Between 1980 and 1984, 1,200 institutions disappeared following failures and mergers. Of the 3,000 or so

Thrifts left, another 1,200 were still in 1985 technically bankrupt. Another indication of the extent of the crisis of the industry is that FSLIC, the institution which insures Thrifts' deposits, will need at least $20 billion to help the failing Thrifts, $15 billion of which is expected to be paid by the US government (*New York Times*, 30.4.87).

In effect, deregulation exacerbated the crisis within the Thrift industry. To allow Thrifts to compete more directly with their already highly diversified competitors, the 1980 act was followed by another two years later (Garn-St. Germain Act), which aimed at accelerating the deregulation process. The act accelerated the phase-out of deposit rate ceilings and allowed Thrifts and banks to offer accounts comparable to the money market funds. Deregulation was particularly stepped up on the asset side, as Thrifts were allowed to divert a much higher percentage of investments into areas like commercial and consumer lending and business loans. The massive crisis within the Thrift industry and its subsequent restructuring, however, has reduced its significance as originator and — more importantly — holder of mortgage loans. Its market share in the volume of outstanding housing loans fell from 56 per cent in 1977 to 41 per cent in 1984 (Meyerson, 1986).

The crisis of the Thrifts enhanced the role of the secondary mortgage market. Already during the late 1960s and early 1970s a new impetus was given to this market with the restructuring of the FNMA and the foundation of two new federally supported secondary mortgage market institutions, the Government National Mortgage Association (GNMA) and the Federal Home Loan Mortgage Corporation (FHLMC). Initiatives to expand the role of the secondary mortgage market aimed at the supply of additional funds to Thrift institutions when their traditional resources failed them. FNMA was privatised in 1968 and retained its secondary mortgage market function as a major buyer of mortgages from originating institutions like Thrifts, commercial banks and, most significantly, mortgage companies. GNMA is, however, fully owned by the US government and took over FNMA's function to support special federally assisted housing programmes. But more important has become GNMA's scheme to guarantee instruments which are sold to private lenders to attract additional funds into housing (HUD, 1973). The introduction of pass-through, mortgage-backed securities and mortgage-backed bonds, as these instruments are called, particularly enhanced the role of the secondary market during the 1970s. Mortgage-backed securities are made from pools of mortgage loans, which are guaranteed by GNMA in the case of FHA/VA loans. Similarly, FHLMC, a private corporation and member of the FHLB system, guarantees mainly conventional loans. The combination of risk pooling and guarantee by federally supported institutions made these securities into attractive investments.

Virtually all new loans originated by Thrifts are today passed on through the secondary market. Originating and servicing loans for the ultimate investors is now seen by many Thrifts as a securer way to earn a steady income. The secondary mortgage market has also come to the rescue of Thrifts, by allowing them to sell their non-performing, low interest mortgage portfolios. Special mortgage-backed security programmes were devised to assist Thrift institutions in selling off the old low-rate mortgage debt. In the scheme, old loans are transformed into tradeable securities and repurchased by the Thrift institutions. 'Swap deals', as these are called, are in fact no more than a creative accounting device (with a federal stamp) to improve liquidity within the Thrift sector (and apparently also a very profitable exercise for FNMA). Thus the market share of the volume of outstanding mortgage loans which the Thrifts lost was mainly a gain for the mortgage pools held by the federally sponsored secondary market institutions (see Table 4.2).

The effects of interest rate volatility and inflation in an era of increased competition in financial markets has been less devastating for the operating structure of specialised mortgage lenders in the other countries in our survey, but there have still been dramatic effects in some cases. Volatility of market interest rates has forced mortgage banking institutions to juggle between the interests of borrowers and investors. When interests rates rise, borrowers are unwilling to take on expensive, long-term fixed interest rate loans, while, at such times, investors try to sell their existing bond portfolios. Conversely, when rates are low, investors are less inclined to buy long-term bonds, expecting a future rise in interest rates, whilst borrowers try to refinance their loans.

For West German mortgage banks, the dilemma resulted in a substantial reduction in the repayment period of mortgage bonds and consequently, in the length of the fixed interest rate loan period of the loans they could offer. In the late 1960s most

Table 4.2: Home Mortgage Debt by Lenders 1975–84

Year	Savings Institu- tions[1] %	Com- mercial banks %	Federal and related agencies %	Mort- gage pools[2] %	House- holds %	Pension funds[3] %	Other[4] %
1975	55.3	15.7	8.3	5.2	8.9	0.7	5.9
1976	55.9	15.6	7.3	6.7	8.8	0.6	5.1
1977	55.8	16.2	6.7	8.2	8.3	0.5	4.2
1978	54.2	17.0	7.1	8.6	8.6	0.5	3.9
1979	51.6	17.0	7.5	10.0	9.2	0.5	4.2
1980	49.4	16.4	7.7	10.9	10.4	0.5	4.5
1981	47.2	16.1	8.0	11.8	11.6	0.5	4.9
1982	41.7	15.7	8.7	15.7	12.7	0.5	4.9
1983	40.5	15.0	8.8	19.7	10.7	0.5	4.8
1984	40.8	14.7	8.8	21.0	9.3	0.4	5.0

Notes: [1] Savings institutions include savings and loans, mutual savings banks and credit unions.

[2] Mortgages in pools backing pass-through securities issued and/ or guaranteed by the Government National Mortgage Association, Federal Home Loan Mortgage Corporation, or Federal National Mortgage Association.

[3] Includes private and public.

[4] Includes state and local governments, real estate investment trusts, finance companies and life insurance companies.

Source: Board of Governors of the Federal Reserve System, Flow of Funds Accounts, Assets and Liabilities Outstanding (from Meyerson, 1986).

housing loans issued by mortgage banks had interest rates fixed for 15 years or more, but by the mid-1980s it had fallen to eight years or less. The effect was to make the type of mortgages offered by mortgage banks much more like those refinanced via retail resources, which usually carry variable interest rates or rates fixed for a maximum of three to five years.

In Denmark, on the other hand, bonds issued by MCIs still carry long-term, fixed interest rates. This is explained by the monopoly MCIs have over the bond market, the fact that the government does not allow price competition between them, and the nature of the institutional investors in bonds. Pension funds, for example, are required to hold up to 80 per cent of their assets in bonds and have, therefore, a limited scope to divert to other, shorter-term investments, when interest rates are falling. There is, in addition, little incentive for borrowers to redeem loans early when interest rates fall, because the price of the bonds linked to the loan will have risen commensurately, and so repurchase involves higher costs.

Again, the picture is different in the Netherlands. Unlike those in Denmark and West Germany, Dutch mortgage banks have abandoned the principle of matching the volumes, interest rates and repayment structures of borrowing and lending. This happened in the post-war years, when mortgage banks gained access to short-term funds via *onderhandse leningen*. Unlike bonds, such funds include short-term borrowing, even though they are used to finance longer-term fixed rate loans. At times when the term structure of interest rates becomes inverse, so that the costs of short-term funds rise above those from capital markets, as occurred during the early 1980s, mortgage banks lose millions (Bakker, 1986). But, as will be shown below, it was not the interest rate matching problem, but developments in the housing market, that brought the final blow to the independent Dutch mortgage banks.

UNSTABLE HOUSING MARKETS

The 1970s marked the end of the post-war housing market expansion and the start of a secular decline in virtually all advanced capitalist countries. The turning point in most countries is around the mid-1970s, when an initial housing market boom turned into the most severe down-turn since the war. Subsequent housing market cycles indicate a significant qualitative change in market behaviour. Although house building rose again during the second half of the 1970s, overall production remained below the levels of earlier periods, partially because of a substantial fall in rented house building. The volume of mortgage lending, however, increased substantially due to rapidly rising house prices and a large increase in the sales of second-hand housing (see also the previous chapter). Thus, lending to individual home-owners proved very profitable during the period and, as the market was expanding, new financial institutions were induced to enter and establish niches in the owner-occupied market. Optimism over ever-rising house prices and increased competition between financial institutions encouraged more generous lending policies, such as larger mortgage to house price ratios. The new lending policies further encouraged the housing market to expand as shorter periods to save for down payments were required and younger households were drawn into home-ownership.

By the late 1970s and early 1980s, the housing market boom collapsed into another major slump, triggered off by stagnating income developments, especially in relation to housing costs. During the late 1970s boom, house price rises had been much above general rates of inflation and interest rates had risen to new post-war peaks, both in nominal and in real terms. After 1979, however, national economies were affected by world recession, leading to stagnation of real incomes and substantial rises in unemployment. With the exception of Britain, the housing market slump of the early 1980s was accompanied by sharp falls in nominal house prices, although in the USA this was confined to regions whose industrial structures were particularly affected by the economic depression. But, at national levels, housing markets recovered by the mid-1980s with the exception of the Netherlands, where the process took much longer.

The case of the Netherlands is particularly interesting, as the extreme cycle of housing market boom and slump had disastrous consequences for the mortgage banks. Dutch mortgage banks had experienced an unprecedented growth in the demand for their services during the housing market boom of the second half of the 1970s. However, during the housing boom they faced serious problems in raising sufficient funds to meet the high level of mortgage demand as competition in capital markets had become severe. In the earlier 1970s, their share of bond issues in capital markets was 60 per cent, but, by 1980, government borrowing took 80 per cent. To improve the marketability of mortgage bonds, mortgage banks had to undertake growth for growth's sake (Bakker, 1986). Competition for capital market funds further added to the costs of borrowing for mortgage banks. This raised the interest costs of their mortgages, leading to a loss of competitiveness. Solutions were tried through diversification and specialisation in up-market housing sectors. New investment outlets were found in commercial property, and — more significantly — in funding property developers in the housing sector. Thus, when house prices started to fall in 1979, mortgage banks were left with huge amounts of bad debt. Many of the property speculators they had backed went bankrupt and the outstanding debts could not be fully recovered from house sales. Although all housing lenders were affected by the down-turn in the housing market, mortgage banks were affected the worst, because of their orientation towards the two housing market sectors where house prices fell most substantially: luxury housing and previously down-market, nineteenth-century, inner-city, working-class housing. Both were high-risk sectors where property developers had been most active.

The institutions that gained by the collapse of the Dutch mortgage banks were the insurance companies, which, together with the pension funds, were encouraged by the National Bank to take over major parts of housing and other bad loans held by the mortgage banks. The National Bank sought to prevent the possibility of the collapse of mortgage banks, as this would lead to a serious loss of confidence in the Dutch financial market. Keen to gain entry into capital markets, insurance companies and also the Post Office Savings Bank negotiated major shareholdings in the, until then, independent mortgage banks. The result was a major breach of the earlier policy of the Dutch National Bank, which had aimed to keep the main financial sectors (banking, insurance and mortgage banking) separate and independent. With the housing market crisis of the 1980s, mortgage bank activities in housing loans shrank to near insignificance and all have now become integrated in either commercial banks or insurance companies.[4]

The response of the Dutch mortgage banks is not necessarily exceptional, when considering recent policies of some of the American Thrift institutions. The diversified asset powers which were given to them during the early 1980s encouraged many troubled Thrifts to engage in speculative ventures in property development in attempts to achieve quick growth. This often only added to their problems, as property development was risky and undertaken with insufficient knowledge, particularly when such investments occurred across state borders.

The down-turn in private housing markets in the early 1980s, may not have affected specialised housing lenders elsewhere as badly as the Dutch mortgage banks and some of the American Thrifts. But generally, the increasing instability of owner-occupied housing markets has meant that the profitability of mortgage lending had tended to work on an 'accordion principle'. Demand for loans grows substantially during up-turns, particularly when house prices rise and mobility increases, but during slumps, specialised mortgage lenders are adversely affected. The negative impact is heightened when specialist housing finance institutions are exposed to highly diversified competitors, which have other outlets to turn to.

A general rise in the number of mortgage defaults and forced sales has also added substantially to the costs of the housing loan business. Losses from forced sales have been particularly significant in West Germany, Denmark and, of course, the Netherlands during the first half of the 1980s, when the prices of existing housing declined substantially. In the Netherlands, however, the widespread use of public guarantees on mortgages for individual house-buyers cushioned the effect on most banks. Instead, the massive losses were covered by central and local governments and the previous home-owners, who will have to repay their debts to the public authorities.

PRESSURES FOR CHANGE AND POLITICAL RESPONSES

Pressures for the deregulation of the specialised housing finance institutions have come from both inside and outside the sector. Deregulation and the trend towards financial supermarkets is not specific to the mortgage finance industry. Competition in financial markets is still intensifying, not only at domestic, but also at international levels. It has generated a general trend towards the development of universal banking institutions, which incorporate all types of financial services that traditionally were divided between specialised institutions like commercial banks, savings banks, investment banks, brokers and insurance companies. New technological developments, and especially computerisation, are encouraging the demise of these traditional divisions (Ball et al., 1986). Pressures towards universal banking are also making state regulatory powers less effective. Crises within housing finance, as occurred in the USA and the Netherlands, put further pressure on regulatory policies. In order to save the failing Thrifts and mortgage banks without causing financial destabilisation, mergers or take-overs were generally arranged with stronger financial institutions, often outside the specialised housing finance sphere. The rescue of the Dutch mortgage banks by insurance companies, as noted earlier, caused a reassessment of financial sector policies. Similarly, large banking firms and Thrifts in the USA could develop a national presence, forbidden in principle since the

1930s, by negotiating new powers that circumvented inter-state banking laws in exchange for taking over failing Thrifts.

Attempts to transform themselves into large financial super-markets have become a goal of many large specialist housing finance institutions. The development is perhaps best illustrated by the British building societies. For them deregulation and restructuring have not explicitly been induced by crisis, as was the case with the American Thrifts, but emerged through ambitions generated in an era of prospering business.

Building societies grew to be major financial institutions after 1945. Growth occurred in a relatively sheltered environment with little competition on either retail funding or investments. Between societies competition was also limited by the interest rate fixing cartel they operated, but competition was fierce through other means, such as expansion of branch offices and advertising. Non-price competition was to the advantage of the larger societies as they could spread the costs of attracting customers over a large turnover (Ball et al., 1986). Mergers have been a major feature of growth and many societies have developed from regional to national institutions. The sector is now highly concentrated with the largest five owning more than half of the industry's total assets.

Pressures for deregulation in Britain have mainly come from the building societies. From about the mid-1970s onwards, competition in retail markets increased and societies had to adopt new strategies to secure their inflow of funds. Unlike the American Thrifts, building societies never had government-imposed interest ceilings on their savings deposits and had always offered variable interest rate loans, allowing them to adjust interest rates on mortgages to fluctuations in the cost of borrowing. But their ability to attract sufficient retail funding had become increasingly unstable and greater variations in market interest rates added to the problems. In response to competition, societies started to offer higher interest savings accounts, which were financed by charging higher interest on mortgages. Such strategies led to increased inter-society com-petition and eventually to the abolition of the interest rate cartel by the end of 1983.

The first proposal for deregulation concerned the wish of societies to secure their inflow of funds by extending their borrowing powers to wholesale money markets (Stow Report, 1980). Such funds were not only readily available, but had also become cheaper than retail funds during the high interest rate period of the early 1980s. High rates of interest also posed a new threat to the societies' dominance over the mortgage market, as it allowed other, more diversified, institutions to develop a strong mortgage presence. Clearing banks, in particular, did so successfully during the 1980–82 period, which coincided with a slump in the housing market.

There has been an up-turn in the housing market since 1983. The boom reduced the banks' market share in new mortgage lending, though their business has still expanded substantially in absolute terms. In the mid-1980s, building societies' growth was at an unprecedented rate. Their volume of outstanding mortgage loans increased by 54 per cent in real terms between 1980 and 1985. House prices rose substantially in the mid-1980s, particularly in southern England, and the scale of the government's council house sales programme further added to the housing finance boom. But despite the current rate of growth, building societies have come to realise that future expansion in mortgage lending is limited. The increase in home-ownership will slow down and has 'artificially' been raised by policies to privatise public housing. Growth through existing home-owners' capitalising on house price inflation and trading up is also less likely to be a long-term perspective with the current low general rate of inflation. In addition, house prices have started to become stagnant in some parts of those regions which are in economic decline.

Expansion in the business of mortgage lending is increasingly cyclical, which does not fit the ambitions of the managers of the larger building societies, who aim for continuous growth. Pressures for deregulation have been building up within the movement since the early 1980s, particularly for a diversification of the assets societies are empowered to hold (see BSA, 1983 and 1984). A new act became effective in January 1987, giving societies virtually all they asked for. Funds can now be tapped wholesale and investments can be extended to most retail banking and housing services. The latter include estate agency, insurance broking and lending on second mortgages. Societies can now also own and manage housing and go into land holding. Already before the 1987 act, societies had started to develop new activities, usually in co-operation with clearing banks and housing associations, depending on the type of service in question. A further indication of the 'financial supermarket' trend within the sector arises from stipulations in the act whereby diversification powers of building societies are limited to certain percentages of asset volume. As a result, mergers within the sector have continued to develop, including between the largest ten.

Bausparkassen in West Germany also had problems in maintaining their market share in mortgage lending during the 1970s in the face of increased competition from the universal banks. Commercial banks, savings banks and credit co-operatives all expanded into issuing loans above the 60 per cent house price limit, the lending area traditionally dominated by the *Bausparkassen*. The competitive position of *Bausparkassen* in attracting funds from personal savers also eroded with the general rise in market rates of interest, since the collective savings scheme they operate implies rates that are fixed at low levels. Government subsidies to *Bausparkassen's* collective savings schemes have not compensated for the rise in market rates of interest. On the contrary, from the mid-1970s onwards, income eligibility limits for savings premiums have not been adjusted to inflation and the premium subsidy itself has been reduced a number of times (Ball et al., 1986). Problems for the *Bausparkassen* culminated during the early 1980s, when market interest rates peaked and housing market activities reached a new low. Competition from other mortgage lenders intensified and the volume of new savings contracts signed with *Bauspar-kassen* declined. One implication of the closed scheme operated by *Bausparkassen* is that a reduced inflow of funds prolongs waiting periods before loans are allocated and, therefore, reduces the attractiveness of the collective savings scheme. Diversification has also been the response for the *Bausparkassen* to their problems.

Like the British building societies and American Thrifts, *Bausparkassen* are legally constrained in expanding their sources of funds and range of investments. But other solutions have been found, as is shown by the history of the largest private *Bausparkasse*, Wüstenrot. Wüstenrot decided as early as the mid-1960s to diversify, partially in response to the move towards the centralised provision of housing finance services under the dominance of the universal banks. Barred from founding financial subsidiaries (a house-building daughter was accepted by their supervisory body in early days), Wüstenrot found a solution by setting up a new holding company which would own the *Bausparkasse*. A bank and an insurance company were added to the holding company in 1968 and one year later a real estate company was founded together with the Deutsche Bank, West Germany's largest commercial bank (Schäfer et al., 1986).

Until the 1980s, the *Bausparkasse* business remained the central activity of the Wüstenrot holding company. The other subsidiaries mainly provided services in support of the collective savings scheme. The bank, for instance, specialised in building loans and intermediate loans. The latter are loans offered to the *Bausparkasse* customers to bridge the period until the contract loans are allocated. The insurance company allowed for a more efficient use of branches and sales agents linked to the *Bausparkasse* activities. But a major shift occurred during the early 1980s when market rates of interest were at unprecedentedly high levels. As a consequence, the significance of the collective saving and loan scheme reduced and the banking and insurance activities gained much importance; Wüstenrot started to present itself as a provider of comprehensive financial services, rather than as a *Bausparkasse* (ibid.).

DEREGULATION: ECONOMIC NECESSITY OR POLITICAL CHOICE?

The trends towards despecialised housing finance institutions and towards large financial conglomerates that offer all types of financial services seem to be universal, seemingly inevitable under the pressure of international competition in financial markets. Sheltered circuits of housing finance are breaking down and housing finance is developing into systems of funding from a mixture of sources. Deregulation further implies an abolition of the advantages linked to specialisation, so that housing lenders have to compete directly with other financial institutions for funds and investments. British clearing banks, for instance, recently received some of the same tax advantages linked to deposit taking as those already given to building societies. In the USA, there is still a tax incentive for Thrifts to specialise, but its effect is much reduced and only used by the smaller ones because they are not really in a position to compete with the large banks.

Despite massive competitive pressures from financial markets, there is one case in our survey which shows that deregulation of specialised housing lenders is not inevitable, but can be prevented by political power. The Danish MCIs, the country's largest type of financial institution, are prevented from extending their sphere of activities. Unrestrained, MCIs would probably diversify and acquire shares in other types of financial institutions, like banks and stock broking companies. Against the wishes of the MCIs, the Danish government argues for the economics of specialisation: the pillars of the Danish financial system are kept separate to maximise the advantages of specialisation and scale. It is argued that MCIs' specialised knowledge avoids risks and creates low overhead costs, which makes their business more efficient. Another major reason used to justify continued protection of a specialised housing finance circuit is the support that the current system gives to the construction industry. The government itself gains from the low costs of intermediation as about half of MCI bonds are issued on their behalf. It remains to be seen to what extent the Danish government can resist deregulatory pressures; these are aided by EEC directives aimed at equalising regulatory powers over financial markets between European countries.

The Danish political objectives are in complete contrast to those of successive US governments, as summarised well in a major policy document, *The Report of the President's Commission on Housing* (1982). It recommends the total elimination of the specialised system of mortgage lending. Housing, instead, should compete for funds in national and international financial markets. So, in the USA, the provision of housing finance is to become fully integrated in the capital markets from which it was so carefully separated during the 1930s.

Deregulation of financial markets in the USA can be seen as a retreat from political support for housing in general, despite the predominance of private provision in the country. But the new Building Society Act in Britain requires a different interpretation. The act complies with the current housing policy objectives of the Thatcher government, which aim at encouraging heavily subsidised, private provision with extended involvement of the building societies. Of central concern here is the extended housing service powers given to the societies. After individual council house sales peaked in 1982, a new stage in privatisation policies has been designed and introduced in a new Housing and Planning Act, allowing for the sale of whole council housing estates to private developers. Building societies can now directly participate in such schemes, not only as providers of finance, but also as buyers and housing managers. In conjunction with developers, they can further undertake the rehabilitation of these estates for sale to individual home-owners. Housing investments urgently need to be done in Britain, but contrary to earlier post-war policies, the government hopes to leave this largely to the private market.

Why Should Deregulation Interest Consumers and Housing Policy-makers?

A well-known argument for deregulating specialised housing finance institutions is that it will benefit consumers. There will be more choice between financial institutions in the types of mortgage and housing related service they offer. Competition will make the market more efficient, it is argued, and will therefore reduce lending costs. The British National Consumers' Council, for instance, welcomed the proposed new Building Society Act for these reasons. In practice, however, real interest rates on mortgage loans are higher now than ever. Increased competition for funds, particularly in retail savings markets, has pushed up the costs of borrowing for all financial institutions. Anyone offering more attractive deposit instruments is soon followed by others, not wishing to lose their market share. In the early 1980s, the costs of short-term funds exceeded those from capital markets for the first time since the war. Competition also had other cost effects which were passed on to consumers, in the expenses of branching networks and advertising campaigns to attract extra customers, and in the massive investments in new technology, which did not always raise efficiency as hoped for.

Another aspect of diversified lending powers is that housing finance institutions have become less dependent on the fortunes of housing markets. Investments are only likely to be made there when the rate of return is highest (Meyerson, 1986). Thus during periods when the housing market expands and mortgage lending proves very profitable, funds are readily available. In a competitive environment, extra lending to lower-income house-holds is taken on and mortgage debt ratios pushed up. But, during market down-turns, other, more profitable investment outlets will be looked for and the introduction of restrictive and discriminatory policies on housing loans becomes more likely. High house prices and down-payment requirements then inhibit access to home-ownership for lower-income households generally. But, in addition, there may be a recurrence of red-lining or of restrictive lending policies applied to areas where there are high concentrations of low-income households and ethnic minorities. Such policies usually affect inner-city working-class areas, but may well include badly serviced parts of suburbia. In the Netherlands, this is already the case. Restrictive lending policies were introduced, particularly in older inner-city areas, where house price falls were most substantial. It also followed government policies to limit the issuing of public mortgage guarantees to individual buyers of second-hand dwellings in 'high risk' areas.

Discriminatory lending policies may also be imposed via instruments which link mortgage loans to capital markets. At least for the USA, it has been suggested that the increased reliance on secondary mortgage markets as a source for housing credit may well lead to greater inflexibility in mortgage lending. Properties that do not conform to a standard secure type may well become discriminated against (Meyerson, 1986). Such policies may also enhance inequalities in housing markets between regions. Housing lenders have generally developed a national presence and become less dependent on the fortunes of local housing markets. Their ability to draw funds from different sources and shift these around may well enhance gentrification processes in one area by making credit readily available, whilst developments in areas of stagnating house prices may be inhibited.

Generally, it seems that increased competition in housing finance further increases affordability problems. Upper-income households may benefit from the greater availability of finance and the wider range of services provided, but the advantages for other housing consumers are less clear cut. Housing loans may be easily available for lower-income households during housing market booms, but rising house prices and an upward trend in real costs of borrowing reduce access in the longer run. High-income debt ratios, in addition, make home-owners far more vulnerable to default and may increase the risk of them eventually losing their home altogether. Default on mortgage payments and repossessions by financial institutions, in fact, have already increased substantially in all the countries included in our survey in the 1980s, irrespective of the state of their national housing markets.

The long-term effects of the mortgage finance 'revolution' are, of course, difficult to predict and it is also not our aim to make such forecasts. Instead, this chapter has described the traditional specialised mortgage finance systems of five countries and analysed some reasons for their recent transformation. The existence of specialised mortgage lenders has been a major condition for the growth of private housing markets (and in some countries also for social housing provision). But without wishing to give unqualified support for the traditional institutional system of mortgage lending, we have tried to outline some of the, in our view, likely consequences of deregulated housing finance systems for housing consumers and for future developments of housing markets. Features that may emerge in the future include sharper fluctuations in housing market cycles; an upward pressure on the costs of housing loans; an increased likelihood of the introduction of discriminatory lending policies during market down-turns; and higher risks of home-owners defaulting on mortgage payments. Also, the transformation of institutions active in mortgage lending is not likely to be over yet, due to the changed nature of the environment in which they operate.

NOTES

1. The findings of this chapter are based on two research projects, which were conducted by the author in conjunction with Michael Ball and Michael Harloe. One project, funded by the Anglo-German Foundation studied recent changes in housing finance systems in West Germany and Britain. The Economic and Social Research Council funded a study of mortgage finance institutions in the USA, the Netherlands, Denmark and Britain. Much of the information discussed here is based on interviews we had with representatives of financial institutions in the various countries. British and German developments in housing finance systems are described in more detail in Ball, Martens & Harloe (1986).

2. Mortgage banks were, however, never set up in Britain, even though they were made possible by the 1865 Mortgage Debenture Act. But, as the act was never put into practice, it was eventually abolished in 1958. The only bond-issuing institution Britain has known was the Agricultural Mortgage Corporation, founded in 1928 (see Pleyer & Bellinger, 1981). Very recently the founding of the National Home

Loans Corporation has for the first time introduced mortgage lending refinanced by securities issued to investors in capital markets.

3. *Bouwfondsen* are specialised housing lenders. Their market share of housing loans is around four per cent. There has been little change in either this share or their operations. *Bouwfondsen* were founded after the war by the Dutch Council of Local Authorities. Their main shareholders are the local authorities and regional specialisation has limited competition between them. Funds are derived by borrowing directly from pension funds and insurance companies (*onderhandse leningen*). There is no legal context in which supervision over *Bouwfondsen* takes place. They are not regarded as financial institutions, as a result of which *Bouwfondsen* are not allowed to attract funds from personal savers. Mortgage loans issued by *Bouwfondsen* traditionally carry long-term fixed interest rates and they specialise in lending to individual buyers of newly built, premium subsidised housing.

4. 'The Postbank gambled and lost' was a succinct newspaper headline about the affair (*Volkskrant*, 21.1.87). The former Post Office Savings Bank, it was announced, had to write off all of its shares in the FGH, the second largest independent mortgage bank, to a major insurance company, Aegon. Problems for the FGH were much worse than initially expected and a new financial rescue operation had to be arranged by November 1986, which this time included Aegon. In the process Aegon managed to buy out all minor and major shareholders (at extremely low current nominal market values), and after the Postbank had allocated to the mortgage bank a substantial, low interest rate loan. Apart from money, the Postbank also lost its entry to capital market borrowing, which it had hoped to realise via its stake in the mortgage bank.

REFERENCES

Bakker, M. (1986) 'Ondergang Hypotheekbanken: Voorgeprogrammeerd Drama', *FEM 1*, 64–7

Ball, M., Martens, M., Harloe, M. (1986) 'Mortgage Finance and Owner Occupation in Britain and West Germany', *Progress in Planning, 26*(3), 187–260

BSA (1983) *The Future Constitution and Powers of the Building Societies*, Building Societies Association, London

—— (1984) *New Legislation for Building Societies*, Building Societies Association, London

Checkoway, B. (1980) 'Large Builders, Federal Housing Programmes and Postwar Suburbanisation', *International Journal of Urban and Regional Research, 4*(1), 21–45

Cleary, E. (1965) *The Building Society Movement*, Elek, London

Craig, P. (1986) 'The House that Jerry Built? Building Societies, the State and the Policies of Owner Occupation', *Housing Studies, 1*(2), 87–108

EAG (Economists Advisory Group) (1981) *The British and German*

Banking System: A Comparative Study, Anglo-German Foundation for the Study of Industrial Society, London

Florida, R.L. (1986) 'The Political Economy of Financial Deregulation and the Reorganisation of Housing Finance in the United States', *International Journal of Urban and Regional Research*, 10(2), 207–31

HM Treasury (1984) *Building Societies: A New Framework*, HMSO, London

HUD (Department of Housing and Urban Development) (1973) 'Housing Finance' in *Housing in the Seventies* (Draft Report), HUD, Washington DC

Klein, P.W. and Vleesenbeek, H.H. (1981) 'De Geschiedenis van het Hypotheekbankwezen', in R. Burgert, J.L. Bouma, H. Visser (eds), *75 Jaar Nederlandse Vereniging van Hypotheekbanken*, Nederlandse Vereniging van Hypotheekbanken, Den Haag, 9–30

Meyerson, M. (1986) 'The Changing Structure of Housing Finance in the United States', *International Journal of Urban and Regional Research*, 10(4), 465–96

Miles, B. (1983) 'Housing Finance: Development and Evolution in Mortgage Markets' in Committee on Banking, Finance and Urban Affairs, *Housing — A Reader*, US Government Printing Office, Washington DC

NCSI (National Council of Savings Institutions) (1985) *National Fact Book of Savings Institutions*, NCSI, Washington DC

Ornstein, F.H. (1985) *Savings Banking, an Industry in Change*, Resting Publishing Inc., Virginia USA

Pleyer, K. and Bellinger, D. (1981) *Das recht der Hypotheekbanken in Europa*, CH Bech'sche Verlagsbuchschandlung, Munich

Price, S.J. (1958) *Building Societies, their Origin and History*, Franey, London

Rijnvos, C. (1981) 'Maatschappelijke Plaatsbepaling van Hypotheekbanken in Nederland', in R. Burgert, J.L. Bouma, H. Visser (eds), *75 Jaar Nederlandse Vereniging van Hypotheekbanken*, Nederlandse Vereniging van Hypotheekbanken, Den Haag, 129–54

Schäfer, O. Seuferle, W. and Wocher, C. (1986) 'Tradition und Perspektive — Wüstenrot im Wandel' in G. Hahn and K.-F. Otto, *Ein Zuhause für Menschen*, Helmut Richardi Verlag, Frankfurt/Main

Tucillo, J.A. with J.L. Goodmann Jr (1983) *Housing Finance, a Changing System in the Reagan Era*, The Urban Institute Press, Washington DC

US President's Commission on Housing (1982) *Report of the President's Commission on Housing*, US Government Printing Office, Washington DC

Wijk, H. van (1984) 'Een Nieuwe Kans voor Hypotheekbanken', *Intermediair*, 20(34), 39–43

Wilde, J. de (1977) 'Een Eeuw Financiering van Onroerend Goed', G. Bolle and G.A. Snepvangers (eds), *Spiegel van Onroerend Goed*, Kluwer, Deventer

Wytzes, H.C. (1981) 'De hypotheekbanken als Financiele Intermediairs', in R. Burgert, J.L. Bouma, H. Visser (eds), *75 Jaar Nederlandse Vereniging van Hypotheekbanken*, Nederlandse Vereniging van Hypotheekbanken, Den Haag, 155–74

5

The International Restructuring
of Housing Production

Michael Ball

INTRODUCTION

At varying times, from the mid-1970s through to the early
1980s, virtually every advanced capitalist country experienced a
collapse in its housing output. Unlike previous post-war house-
building cycles, it was obvious that this particularly dramatic
slump was not a temporary setback. The world of housing
production was about to change. Output would recover, at least
partially, from the depths of recession, but it would be
produced under different forms of provision.

New forms of housing provision may imply changes in the
ways in which housing is produced. Some of the biggest
transformations of housing production, for instance, have
occurred in countries with previously large social house-
building programmes. But it would be wrong to see the current
transformations of production simply as part of a general back-
to-the-market trend for housing. Housing production, whatever
the tenure, has always been overwhelmingly market based.
More subtle, but no less dramatic, transformations within
capitalist house building, therefore, are of concern here.

Changes in housing production depend on a wide constellation of pressures and on the nature of pre-existing building
industries. There is little international competition in house
building; although one of the characteristics of the current
restructuring is that such competition is growing. In housing
production, international competition plays little part in forcing
the building industry to adopt new techniques and organisational forms. Most pressures for change derive from the country
in question itself.

When comparing changes in housing production, each country will have its own peculiarities. Yet it is still possible to highlight some general trends. Two interlinked trends form the core themes of this chapter, though their consequences for housing production in individual countries are highly variable.

First, it will be argued that there has been a downgrading within house-building firms' accumulation strategies of continual transformations of the labour process. In part, the reduced emphasis arises from previous successes in moving house building ever further away from the skilled handicraft ideal of popular imagery. More importantly, the downgrading has occurred not because there is less concern to reduce production costs, but rather because of the new environments in which such changes are occurring. Those environments demand increased flexibility in production, which has forced building firms to move away from attempts to increase labour productivity in ways that limit flexibility, most notably the large-scale concrete systems devised for the mega-housing projects of the 1960s.

The nature of that changed environment for housing production is the second general conclusion. In a variety of mixes between and within countries, there has been greater market volatility; an increased fragmentation of demand, locationally and by dwelling type; and rising real interest rates. Housebuilders in different ways have reacted by increasing their activity in product marketing; by altering the ways in which production is financed; and, in a number of instances, by emphasising the speculative elements of their operations. Similarly, there has been a shift towards renovation and repair away from new building, with substantial implications for labour processes. On the labour side, firms have resorted to indirect forms of employment as a way of cheapening and disciplining their workforces and of forcing through changes in methods of production.

Explanations given by house-builders for changes in housing production are usually couched in terms of the changing structure of demand (e.g. by house-builders' trade associations, like the US National Association of Home Builders or the British Housebuilders' Federation). Though important, demand cannot be said to be the only factor leading to change; instead a complex interweaving of factors has occurred. One of the reasons, for instance, for the shift towards a more demand-orientated type of production regime is that the position of building workers has deteriorated in virtually all advanced capitalist countries. The building booms of earlier years are over, leaving workers in a much weaker position. Building firms have had less need to confront labour unions directly through such means as transformations of the labour process, but are more concerned to make labour power as flexible a productive force as possible. Flexibility fits in with the new demand orientation, but is not simply an automatic product of it. The new conditions of production have had to be created, and in a variety of ways in different countries.

The outcome of the constellation of changes is that new forms of productive enterprise are coming to dominate housing production. In some countries, they are big, all-purpose house-builders, active in all spheres of housing production. The Netherlands, Denmark and Sweden exemplify such enterprises. Elsewhere, large speculative house-builders have emerged. Britain, in relation to the size of its housing market, has the most centralised producers — the result of over a decade of takeovers and internal expansion. Big speculative builders have also emerged in the USA, but their market share is still relatively small. In other countries, fragmentation seems to dominate, as, for instance, in France and West Germany, where large producers have found it difficult to operate in the new housing markets.

One area which has encouraged a greater use of small-time builders has been the enormous growth in housing renovation, conversion, repair and maintenance, noticeable in most advanced capitalist countries since the mid-1970s. The trend towards renovation in part is a consequence of the failures of earlier production-orientated strategies. Firms in the building industry have found it impossible to transform housing provision and the urban environment in ways in which they, architects, planners and state officials, once thought possible. Mass-produced suburban housing has not proved cheap to build. The 'technological breakthrough' once dreamt of for housing production failed to materialise. Production techniques have changed considerably, but they have slowed down rather than reversed the long-term tendency for the cost of house building to rise relative to other manufactured products. New patterns of urban living associated with gentrification and a movement of certain sections of the new 'middle class' back to the central city, in other words, are not quite as consumption-related as some people would have us believe, because at least in part they reflect the cost of suburban living.

A major problem when analysing the house-building industry, particularly at an international comparative level, is that the available information is often poor. The precise forms of the restructuring of housing production are consequently difficult to decipher, and this chapter must remain speculative over many important issues, though the information available indicates that some changes have been quite dramatic.

What follows is divided into three main sections. The first looks at the general trend of housing output over the past 20 years for a variety of European countries and the USA. The second explores the new types of market and their impact on producers. The third, and most substantive section, then evaluates the restructuring of building capital and how it has adopted accumulation strategies that are more product-market orientated and productively flexible. Not all countries are covered, and of those considered only illustrative changes are given, partially because of the data problems mentioned earlier, but also because the object of this chapter is to give an illustration of the types of change taking place rather than to present an exhaustive and exhausting list.

A final introductory comment should be made. It concerns the almost bewildering variety of ways in which housing production is organised, both between countries and within one country. Following one of the themes of this book, no attempt will be made to distil a small number of generalisations from such variety. There is no reason to expect that housing production is moving towards some common, universal organisational form. Changes may have taken place in all the countries considered, and they may all in some direct or indirect sense have something to do with the difficulties of the world economy after the earlier 1970s, and with underlying forces in the sphere of production itself. But beyond that a variety of responses can be seen, rather than a single common one. Such a conclusion is not surprising, given that in each country there were distinct social relations in house building prior to the crisis, and it is those social relations which have had to change. Such changes are obviously intimately tied up with the political processes of each country, and politics above all can never be effectively reduced to a simple common denominator.

HOUSING OUTPUT: THE QUANTITATIVE DIMENSION

When looking at overall trends in housing output, the early 1980s in most advanced capitalist countries can be seen as representing the trough of a decline that had been going on for a decade or more. As in so many other areas of economic life, Britain led the decline. There, the long post-war house-building boom started to tail off in the late 1960s, whereas in countries like the USA, France and West Germany output was to peak in speculative booms of the early 1970s. Since the early 1980s, there has been a revival of output in a number of countries, including the USA, West Germany, Denmark and the Netherlands, but in no country is output expected to return to the levels achieved in the 1960s and early 1970s.

HOUSE BUILDING IN THE BOOM

A crude general description of the nature of the post-war housing boom and its aftermath will help explain why certain features of production are going to be emphasised in what follows. No attempt to explain the boom will be made, the point is to demonstrate the changing relations of the building industry to housing.

After the war, most advanced capitalist countries experienced unprecedented rates of economic growth up to the early 1970s. Since then growth has been far more variable, and house building has followed a similar trend. The long boom was associated with the introduction of new products and labour processes, changed household structures, and with new spatial organisations of society. The economic and social changes associated with the long post-war boom put unprecedented demands on many countries' house-building industries. Record levels of housing production, in turn, helped to fuel further economic growth.

In virtually all countries, new housing production was heavily subsidised by the state. The form of the subsidy generally depended on the tenure for which the housing was being produced. But, in all cases, high, state-subsidised, demand made house building a profitable activity and facilitated experiments with new ways of producing housing. Of course, the high house-building rates were not simply natural outcomes

173

of economic forces, nor should the forms of provision that were adopted be endowed with a fatalistic inevitability. Post-war house-building booms had key social and political aspects. Pre-existing housing crises, combined with rising living standards and the restructuring of urban labour forces, induced substantial state intervention in attempts to increase new housing output in areas where it was most needed. Extra output also had to be achieved without compromising either national or local dominant interests, or generating social instability. Housing tenures and the spatial location of those tenures became key strategic political issues. The outcomes of these political conflicts had feedback effects on housing production. They forced central government to take an interest in the building industry, as bottlenecks could hold up politically essential housing drives. Debates over housing tenures and their location also affected many aspects of production. Influences were felt in housing density and design form, the types of feasible labour process, the means through which firms could make profits and even the types of enterprise active in housing production. Each aspect will be considered in detail later.

State intervention into housing production took many forms. Direct production subsidies were the most obvious, but others were important. Out of fears that it would hamper house-building programmes, attempts were made to solve the 'labour problem', through legislation, government attacks on building trades unions, and extensive training programmes. (Governments felt it ideologically impossible to subject capital to the same treatment.) Enormous sums were spent on infrastructure, to which housing frequently related in direct or indirect ways. Urban renewal projects and new towns blossomed. Land-use planning was souped up, among other reasons in order to provide more readily available, high-quality housing land, and, in many cases, generous land profit inducements. Housing subsidies, low-interest rates and tax reliefs were used in a variety of mixes to encourage individuals to consume more housing, or to induce private landlords and non- or low-profit institutions to provide more rental housing. With rising living standards, and such government inducements, it is not surprising that builders found mass house building so profitable. In addition, although there were cyclical variations, demand was remarkably stable when looked at in a broad historical context (Gottlieb, 1976).

House-builders did not have to worry much about their product markets, though they still frequently complained about them in ways reminiscent of farmers and the weather. The demand conditions for accumulation were good, and all the infrastructural investment and planning made them even better. Building firms' accumulation strategies concentrated on producing as many houses as possible. 'It was like shelling peas out of a pod', as one UK suburban developer once remarked to me. The scale of suburban developments in the USA in the postwar years became world famous, as developers erected whole towns at one go (Checkoway, 1980 and Eichler, 1982). In Europe, large-scale social housing projects changed the face of many urban areas, or led to new satellite suburbs and towns (Hall, 1974).

In such an environment, materials and particularly labour shortages became pressing. Virtually all European countries sent delegations to the USA in the 1940s and early 1950s, to discover why the 'productivity gap' between Europe and the US existed (e.g. Bemis, 1936, Anglo-American Council on Productivity, 1950 and White, 1965). The gap was almost certainly misunderstood and exaggerated, but the success of the US house-building industry was interpreted in terms of far greater on-site mechanisation, the prefabrication of building components and the deskilling of labour. One outcome was the industrialised, heavy, concrete building systems pioneered in Sweden, Denmark and France in the 1950s.

During the house-building boom years, the breaking of the power of skilled workers was regarded by building firms and governments as one of the keys to solving labour shortages; though generally the solution was not couched in such direct language. Encouragement was frequently given to the use of non-union labour, especially in Britain and the USA (Austrin, 1980 and Ball, 1988). Elsewhere corporatist consensus was tried as well, often in conjunction with the introduction of revolutionary new industrialised building techniques. Sweden exemplified the approach (Dickens et al., 1985), though other Scandinavian countries, West Germany, France and the Netherlands used it to varying degrees. Immigrant labour was also used as a way of keeping down wages. Most West European countries relied heavily on cheap immigrant workers during their building booms. Campinos-Dubernet (1985) highlights a famous strike in France in 1962, after which large numbers of North African workers were introduced into the French building industry.

House-builders in the years of the long boom were keen to use their workforces intensively. The interlinked issues of pace of work, discipline and productivity structured site relations. In the main, construction companies followed the fashionable management strategies of the day: the growth of detailed work study in the 1950s and 1960s, superseded by more flexible incentive schemes and a growing reliance on subcontracting and 'just in time' dovetailing of materials, equipment and specialist gangs of workers in the 1970s and 1980s. In this respect, the greater merging of house building with the rest of the construction industry in a number of European countries was significant. Management techniques devised for large, non-housing sites could be applied to social housing and urban renewal projects. The infrastructural requirements of house building also encouraged general builders to enter the housing sphere.

In Britain, for example, virtually all the major general contractors were involved in council house building in the 1960s, using traditional and non-traditional techniques. Even in private house building, site works can encourage builders to take over the whole development process. Wimpey, which has built more homes in Britain than any other building company, entered housing production after the First World War when its owner recognised there was more money to be made out of building houses rather than just site access roads.

The collapse of new housing output in the mid-1970s changed the general picture described above, but it is important to be aware that house building even during the long boom period was in a continual state of flux. As methods of house building and particular tenure forms went in and out of fashion in each country, there were enormous implications for house-building capital and the workforces they employed. Similarly, firms external to the industry have from time to time decided it was a good place to invest. Most of the industrial giants of US manufacturing industry, for instance, have since the war had house-building subsidiaries at one time or another (Grebler, 1973). Sometimes they attempted to use revolutionary production or management techniques, and generally they did not stay in the business for long. House building has remained a fairly independent industry in all countries.

TYPES OF MARKET STRUCTURE FACED BY HOUSE-BUILDERS

In order to explain how countries' house-building industries have changed it is useful to be aware of the types of market in which they sell their product.

The extent to which housing provision involves capitalist producers

Countries with as diverse systems of housing provision as Sweden and the USA share one common feature, that housing production is overwhelmingly capitalist in nature. Even advanced capitalist countries with significant provision of social housing conform to the norm. Social housing institutions are only the promoters and owners of completed dwellings not their producers. With the exception of a small proportion of the British council housing stock (DLC, 1978), all social housing production has been undertaken by capitalist or quasi-capitalist organisations (like the Nordic building co-operatives).

Self-building, where households provide all or part of the building labour themselves, would seem to contradict the pervasiveness of capitalist housing production. Self-building is common in the Third World (Ward, 1982), though often the expression is a misnomer for the household as promoter/ developer rather than as direct builder. A number of advanced capitalist countries also have significant self-build sectors. The majority of West Germany's owner-occupied housing is created in this way. Though there is a tradition of doing some of the work, like painting and decorating, it would appear that self-building is primarily concerned with instigating production through buying a building plot and organising the production of a dwelling rather than the actual building (see Chapter 3). Generally, self-building in the advanced capitalist countries of Europe is more akin to the custom building prevalent in the USA than to real non-capitalist forms of production. Often the dwelling will be a catalogue one, tailor-made in its details, but prefabricated in its prime structural elements and delivered to the future owner's site for erection and completion by a mass housing producer.

'Self-building' and custom building, nonetheless, are significant for the housing producer as they imply a break between

177

the purchase and development of a land plot and the production of the dwelling itself. Of relevance here is the fact that households themselves may directly provide the land, or be able to acquire it through non-market processes. In countries with a significant fragmentation of landownership, the phenomena can have important implications for the nature of housing production. Cheap and easy access to individual building plots can render uncompetitive speculative building of the British form, where a builder undertakes the whole development operation from greenfield site to sold dwelling. Even if large-scale developers tried to compete in such localities, they might find that the multiplicity of landowners made it virtually impossible to assemble sufficiently large greenfield sites. A number of major European countries have many rural localities dominated by small-scale peasant holdings. Fragmented landownership patterns are important in regions of France, West Germany, Italy, Spain and Greece.

Classifying institutions as capitalist is important when trying to understand the response of housing producers to crisis. Petty commodity producers will react very differently from large-scale capitalist enterprises, while different forms of housing provision favour certain types of capitalist enterprise over others. Such basic distinctions help considerably in explaining the variety of responses to the mid-1970s housing down-turn in different countries. If house-builders are capitalist enterprises, economic crises force them to restructure or go out of business; whereas non-capitalist producers might respond to crises in other ways, depending on the precise circumstances. Petty producers can hold off production temporarily more easily than a capitalist builder; alternatively they may try to maintain their incomes by building more at lower returns; and some may temporarily switch to wage labour in construction or other industries, or go back to agriculture.

Impact of personal sector wealth

Of growing importance for housing demand in a number of countries is personal wealth, particularly that associated with home-ownership. Almost half of personal sector net wealth in Britain, for example, is the net wealth of owner-occupied dwellings. In the USA and Britain, where owner occupation has been substantial for 40 years or more, there are large 'trade-up' markets of home-owners using their money gains from house price inflation to fund better quality accommodation. Alternatively, such wealth enables moves to smaller accommodation on the part of the elderly, resulting in much reduced housing expenditure and the growth of 'retirement' housing markets. Increasingly, in addition, there is inter-generational transfer of housing-related personal wealth. Each of these elements helps to structure the market faced by house-builders. Builders may attempt to cater, for instance, to the trade-up market, altering their product profiles accordingly. Yet, they also discover that markets dominated by second-time buyers can be highly volatile (Ball, 1983 and 1986), making house building a more risky venture than it might otherwise have been.

Correlation of housing market to the general level of economic activity

Mass home-ownership of the type known in Britain and the USA is now closely tied to the general macroeconomy in terms of the levels of output, because of the dependence of such market forms of provision on the contemporary ability of households to afford the move to a new home. Other forms of housing provision tend to be more independent of the general cycle of economic activity. The building of rental housing in the nineteenth century, for example, depended on factors influencing housing landlord's investments. Household incomes had only an indirect effect via their influence on rent levels, which anyway were seldom reduced whatever happened to incomes. Such economic factors gave rise to the famous counter-cyclical patterns of nineteenth-century housing investment over which there has been so much debate (Dyos, 1961; Parry Lewis, 1965 and Gottlieb, 1976). The current West German 'self-build' sector is also relatively immune to economic recession. In response to economic difficulty, self-build households scale down their plans or delay final completion rather than abandon their projects altogether. State subsidies to housing production can be used in a counter-cyclical way. Subsidies to social house building have been used as such a Keynesian-style economic regulator by many West European governments since the war.

For some countries, the health of economies other than their own has the greatest influence on housing output. Greece is a good example. The 1970s saw two major periods of boom, peaking in 1973 and 1978 respectively; while the overall level of output per 1,000 inhabitants is remarkably high, averaging 17 new dwellings per 1,000 inhabitants in the 1980s compared with between 3 and 8 for most European countries. Such high house-building rates in Greece are explained by the subordinate role of the Greek economy in Europe, and the characteristics of its house-building industry and landownership. Both the latter are highly fragmented. There is widespread ownership of individual apartment buildings in the major Greek cities, and most of them have been built by petty capitalist speculative builders, who undertake one apartment building development at a time. A significant part of the repatriated incomes of the large number of Greeks working in northern Europe has been invested in housing and has helped to swell the funds available for apartment building (Emmanuel, 1981). Repatriated incomes vary with the demand for wage labour in northern Europe, reinforcing the Greek economy's and its housing sector's dependence on the general pattern of European economic activity. The peculiar social relations of housing provision in Greece consequently explain the distinctiveness of its aggregate output.

The extent of social housing production

Social housing production has been one of the main items subject to public expenditure cuts since the mid-1970s. Much of the decline of output in Europe since the 1970s, therefore, can be attributed to the collapse of social housing output and the inability of other forms of provision to take up the missing production, as earlier chapters have shown.

Social housing may have a different organisation of production from other sectors. Distinct types of building enterprise may be involved, as in Britain, and the sector is often deliberately used as a test-bed for new building technologies. Its decline, therefore, has had major implications for the restructuring of housing production.

The role of owner occupation

As Chapter 3 showed, owner occupation is the major housing

tenure in Britain and the USA and is growing elsewhere. Though heavily subsidised in virtually all countries, housing provision in owner-occupied sectors depends essentially on the contemporary state of the relevant macroeconomy rather than on specific government strategies. When households' real incomes are rising the tenure expands, unless that growth is choked off by rising house prices or high interest rates. Generally, when incomes stagnate, as for example in a recession, owner occupation and the institutions associated with it come into crisis (see Chapter 3 above, Ball, 1983; BSA, 1981; Florida, 1986; and Meyerson, 1986).

The consequences of the expansion of home-ownership for housing production depend on the extent of stock transfers from other tenures, particularly the private rental sector. Stock transfers are often associated with the rehabilitation, or the conversion, of single-family or non-housing structures into owner-occupied flats; a process frequently described as gentri-fication. So, in part, the growth of owner occupation has been associated with a shift within the building industry towards repair and renovation away from new building. Sometimes stock transfers are wholesale and dramatic. One of the clearest instances is the council house sales programme in Britain of the Thatcher government in the 1980s. After 1979, over three-quarters of a million council dwellings were sold to sitting tenants in the space of a few years. Not only did this change the public rental sector, but also owner occupation. Paradoxically, one of the consequences of that change was that house-builders lost part of their market, because some of the purchasing tenants would have moved into owner occupation anyway, encouraging new house building rather than stock transfer.

Overall owner-occupied new output is given for a selection of countries in Figure 3.2. Despite the shift towards home-ownership, in many countries it can be seen that the shift has only been a relative one, in that new building for owner occupation has either failed to replace output losses in other tenures (e.g. Denmark and France) or it has simply managed to decline at a slower rate than other tenures (e.g. Britain).

The frenzied real estate boom of the early 1970s was strong in private housing as well as in commercial property markets and this led to a revival of housing output (Britain) or all-time peaks in it (the USA, West Germany, France and Denmark). New owner-occupied house building tumbled everywhere in the slump years of the early 1980s, but output revived in the subsequent up-turn. In some cases, as in Denmark, the Netherlands and West Germany, government reflationary policies helped to stimulate the upswings.

For house-builders, a secular decline in house building for owner occupation does not necessarily lead to falls in profitability. Real house prices are generally higher in the 1980s than they were in the 1960s. Firms' real turnovers consequently have declined less than their physical output, and during housing market up-turns both turnover and profits can rise rapidly. It is clear, however, that building for owner occupation has become more speculative, in that builders now have to undertake investment decisions in the face of sharp fluctuations in total demand and significant variations in geographic and sectoral market activity. When owner-occupied markets collapse, builders are forced into bankruptcy, as occurred in Denmark, the Netherlands and France in the late 1970s, in Britain in 1974, and in certain US regions in the early 1980s.

Some building and building materials firms were able to ride the crisis in their own countries' housing markets in the late 1970s and early 1980s by switching to export markets either within Europe or in the Third World; a move that was most notable for Scandinavian producers. Others were able to shift towards supplying catalogue housing for the more resilient self-build markets. Such shifts, in combination, with the growth of repair and renovation weakened the impact of the new house-building slump on building materials producers, although simultaneous crises in other construction sectors did adversely affect them.

IMPACT OF THE NEW MARKET STRUCTURES

Given the severity of the output declines and tenure shifts, new demand patterns have played leading roles in forcing a restructuring of housing production.

A major reason for the importance of changing patterns of demand is that different tenures (and sometimes sectors within tenure markets) are generally associated with different structures of provision. Within each tenure, there are particular ways in which housing is financed, built and allocated, each of which involves different forms of building enterprise. Sometimes building enterprises may straddle different tenures using essentially the same production methods, but often shifts in demand from one tenure to another force substantial changes on the nature of the house-building industry. In some tenures, furthermore, distinct types of builder may compete for the same market. Owner occupation, for instance, may involve self-building in a variety of forms, or speculative developers who convert greenfield sites into housing developments (which may involve one co-ordinating enterprise or several at various stages of the development process), or builders who specialise in stock conversion and improvement. Given these factors, it is not surprising that demand shifts between tenures, and changes within any one of them, can have considerable effect on the types of builder in existence.

Tenure forms may affect the production methods used. Design styles, types of dwelling structure, and acceptable materials are cases in point. Owner-occupied dwellings are predominantly single-family dwellings which require minimal load-bearing structural walls and use up expensive land (with implications for building company finance when land is acquired by them). Rental housing, on the other hand, is more likely to be land efficient, multi-dwelling structures necessitating substantial load-bearing elements, for which concrete is usually the ideal material. Tastes, of course, vary between countries. Brick is a popular cladding in some places, while elsewhere timber is more acceptable or concrete more easily tolerated. The greater acceptability of timber systems in some countries has knock-on effects on new production methods. Modern timber-framed, single-family housing systems are common in North America and Scandinavia, but shunned or disguised in brick-and-block loving ones, like Britain.

Production methods are also market influenced in terms of their scale and the speed at which a development can be sold. With rental housing, particularly in the social sectors, developments generally are large scale (though usually smaller in the 1980s than the monster schemes of the 1960s and early 1970s). Scale enables substantial on- and off-site economies to be achieved, so a reduction in the size of projects tends to raise unit costs. Rental projects are built on a contractual basis, which means that for the builder the houses are sold before production starts; whereas in the home-ownership market, houses are often sold only when completed on a piecemeal basis. Custom building is even more fragmented. Owner occupation consequently weakens or removes the advantages of continuity in production. The flow of materials and workers must be accommodated to the speed at which houses are sold, unlike the social sector. Moreover, certain production methods require a large number of dwellings to be built at the same time, which means that they cannot be used in owner occupation, whereas they can be used in the rental sectors.

Production methods are not universal but depend on specific social relations and market structures. Such differences within housing production are recognised in the building literature, though rarely taken account of in the housing literature itself. A good example is the difference between the horizontal and vertical methods of building (Hillebrandt, 1984 and Ball, 1983). The horizontal approach to building treats a site as essentially one continuous production process, where the object is to complete the dwellings in the most expeditious way possible. The structures consequently are built as a unity, with the building being produced in a sequently layered way, so that the project as a whole is gradually assembled from the groundwork upwards. With vertical building, each separate dwelling is treated essentially as a different development, to be constructed when required for sale. If sales are brisk, a degree of continuous building is possible, but production must be organised in a way that makes sudden cessations of work feasible without leaving half-completed structures tying up working capital. Each approach to building imposes considerable limits on what is possible within the production process, albeit with some potential variations in techniques and the organisation of the work. The difference between the vertical and horizontal methods of construction in Britain parallels closely the division between building council housing and owner-occupied housing. It should be stressed, however, that the difference arises from market structures and types of enterprise, not from innate characteristics of the tenures themselves. Not surprisingly, therefore, there are considerable differences between countries in the actual ways in which housing production for a tenure is organised.

THE RESTRUCTURING OF HOUSE-BUILDING CAPITAL AND THE REDRAWING OF CLASS RELATIONS

Changes in housing markets and production techniques have helped to alter the nature of enterprises operating in house building. The changes are not entirely market led, internal accumulation pressures and shifts in the types of capital investing in house building have played their parts as well. What is clear is that there are contradictory pressures at work, and the current nature of firms reflects them. In each country, the pressures have produced different outcomes. It is easiest to list the contesting features that will be considered here, before considering them in more detail and assessing their impact on the structure of countries' house-building industries:

- a tendency towards greater fragmentation and flexibility of the construction process;
- an increased role for construction and consumer credit;
- increased emphasis on product marketing;
- technological change geared to flexibility in production;
- growing roles for subcontracting and on-site planning;
- competitive pressures leading to further market stratification;
- a decline of the independent medium-sized producer.

More emphasis on owner occupation and the demise of the large house-building projects of earlier years have helped to encourage a fragmentation of the construction process. Many site-related economies of scale must have been lost in the drift to smaller schemes. Such economies can be quite significant, especially when it is remembered that building's site-based nature means that transportation costs can be higher and the dovetailing of the flow of inputs more problematic on today's smaller, spread-out sites. The loss of scale economies has weakened some of the earlier productive advantages of large house-builders over their smaller competitors. Now the pendulum in this respect has swung in favour of the smaller concerns with lower overheads and greater management flexibility.

Such trends have helped to encourage greater flexibility on the part of larger firms in their control over production and in the way in which they orchestrate the assembly and use of construction inputs. Extra productive flexibility in house building

185

reflects trends elsewhere in construction, where there is a movement towards flexible management systems and detailed management accounting control. Large-scale projects have changed over the past decade at least as much in their management and site planning systems as in the technologies used (see for example Ball, 1988). The use of such strategies in housing production, even on small-scale sites, has helped producers to adapt to their new market environment.

Perhaps the most well-known aspect of greater productive flexibility is the growing use of subcontracted labour and equipment. Both specialist and general building tasks have been subject to this tendency, and it has been a common trend in countries where the workforce was not previously organised in this way. In some, like Denmark, labour gangs have always prevailed. In house building, the trend should not be exaggerated, as this sector of construction has always had a high proportion of subcontract labour in most countries, especially in speculative house building and repair and maintenance. New management techniques, however, have brought a greater sophistication to the control of the flow of subcontractors through a site. In addition, the combination of more subcontracting and tighter site procedures have enabled producers to minimise the working capital required for production, and, in the case of speculative house sales, enabled producers to gear production rates more closely to sales achieved.

House-building firms have always been sensitive to the extent of their borrowings. Recessions, which force up interest rates and lower turnover, often bring overgeared builders into liquidation. Speculative house building and housing promotion have always been the worst in this respect, as firms have to borrow to finance land purchase and to fund completed or semi-finished houses. Even so, rising world interest rates and their increased volatility since the late 1970s have exacerbated the problem.

A variety of effects can be noted. One of the most spectacular consequences of rising interest rates has been the rise and fall of the independent promoter of owner-occupied housing in France during the 1960s and 1970s, as documented by Topalov (1983 and 1985). Initially encouraged by the advent of generalised systems of mortgage credit for house purchase in the early 1960s, French housing promoters built speculatively for sale to owner occupiers on a large scale. During the peak periods of the mid-1960s and mid-1970s, such promoters were altogether building a quarter of a million dwellings a year. Topalov argues that they were highly dependent on borrowing from the banking system, so that rising interest rates in the late 1970s resulted in widespread failures and much reduced building rates. Custom-built houses are not subject to the same financial constraints. Their output grew steadily from 80,000 units a year in the early 1960s to over 200,000 by the early 1980s. Now, therefore, erection of dwellings for personal use dominates owner-occupied production in France.

In other countries, the reaction has been different. The growing importance of access to plentiful supplies of credit, for example, has been one of the principal causes of a rapid centralisation of capital in the British speculative house-building industry over the past 15 years. From being an industry dominated by small- and medium-sized producers in the 1960s, the British house-building industry is now one of the most centralised in the world with about ten large producers building over half of the annual owner-occupied output. Moreover, mergers are still taking place, so the current process of centralisation does not seem to have run its course yet. One explanation for the speed and extent of the growth of giant housing producers in Britain could be the role played by land banking. In no other country have the large house-builders been able to control the supply of building land to the extent they have in Britain (Hall et al., 1983 and Ball, 1983). Their success has been achieved through the high land prices which they are prepared to pay and the time for which they are prepared to hold land, if necessary, before building on it. Obviously, access to large and plentiful supplies of capital are necessary for such operations, and the British banking system is notorious for its failure to provide long-term capital to high risk-ventures (Ingham, 1984), so centralisation at the level of the enterprise has been necessary to generate sufficient internal funds and external sources of capital.

In the USA, a different picture emerges, as Table 5.1 shows. In comparison to the overall size of the market, American speculative builders are extremely small. The largest are only as big as the British ones for a market that is over four times as great. The top 20 US builders altogether produce less than 8 per cent of total output (NAHB, 1985), and many of them are located in the south and have been hit by the collapse of the US oil industry in the wake of the oil price falls of the mid-1980s. Widespread custom building (according to Grebler and Mittle-bach, 1978, 46 per cent of new single-family starts were for own use in 1976) and extensive land development by independent estate developers has limited the size of US house-builders.

Table 5.1: Market Shares of US House-builders

In total, 1,713,000 dwellings were started in 1983

— 8% were started by the top 20,
— 7% by the 21st to 100th largest,
— 26% by the 101st to 2,614th largest and
— 59% by the rest.

Source: NAHB (1985).

In contrast to Britain, where centralisation has been induced by the need to engender capital to finance land banking and development, in the US many large builders have been running down their land operations to minimise working capital. Instead, they increasingly purchase finished lots from local developers and builders (NAHB, 1985). Yet, easier access to capital is still cited as the biggest advantage that the larger US producers possess. It enables them to set up their own mortgage companies, and so provide an improved market package to the purchaser. In addition, it gives them access to the rapidly growing secondary mortgage market, and a greater ability to raise capital for their own internal operations. Through a quirk in the US tax laws, builders in the 1980s have gained consider-able tax advantages by issuing their own mortgages to house purchasers, financed through the secondary mortgage market (Ball and Martens, 1988).

Small- and medium-sized builders in the USA have coun-tered the financial innovations of the large house-builders by forming direct partnerships with financial institutions. The National Association of Home Builders has estimated that, in 1984, financial institutions participated in 20 per cent of the homes started: a figure that could rise to 40 per cent over the next decade.

Other countries are also showing indications of greater involvement of financial institutions in various aspects of the land development process. Commercial and co-operative banks and *Bausparkassen* in West Germany have taken a growing role in land holding and development over the past decade (Ball, Martens and Harloe, 1986). British building societies are moving into house building. The largest, the Halifax, aims to become one of the country's largest house-builders over the next ten years, according to recent press reports.

Moves by financial institutions into house building reflect a dual process. On one side, there is a need for financial institutions to find new investment outlets, because of limited profit opportunities in their traditional areas of business. On the other hand, there are shortages of long-term credit for key agencies currently involved in housing provision, because of the risks of such lending for creditors. Financial institutions presumably hope to reduce the risk by undertaking the investment themselves. Whether the growing involvement of a broad range of financial institutions in housing provision is just a fashion of the 1980s or a sustained realignment of the relationship of housing production to financial capital is currently unclear. After Third World debt problems, 'as safe as houses' seems to be a contemporary catch-phrase of the financial community. But housing investments are in reality often risky investments. Losses on speculative housing ventures, as experienced by the Dutch mortgage banks in the late 1970s and some US savings and loans institutions in the 1980s, may become more generalised and, once again, encourage financial capital to have a more distanced and secured relation to housing development.

House-builders of all types have had to put greater emphasis on marketing their products. The product may be a management skill, a distinctive technology, or a completed dwelling; in all cases builders have learnt the importance of going out and selling them.

The new emphasis on marketing is obvious given what has happened to the volume and nature of housing demand. Gone are the days of chronic housing shortages and plentiful funds to tackle them. Builders can no longer expect to see continually expanding markets. They have to be capable of spotting ever-shifting market gaps, and of finding new ways of encouraging clients to undertake housing developments or of inducing purchasers to buy their homes. The shift towards owner occupation has compounded the trend, and home-owners tend to be more diverse than the archetypal 'young (or not so young) marrieds' of yesteryear. In addition, given the growing importance of existing home-owners as house-builders' customers, builders find that the composition of demand varies with the state of the housing market, so they have to adjust to cyclical shifts in the pattern of demand.

Extra emphasis on marketing is not simply a response to changes in demand. The reconstitution of house-builders and the new environment in which they operate has helped considerably. Greater flexibility in production makes it economically possible to put more effort into marketing. The proliferation of marketing agencies has opened up expertise at minimal fixed cost to the producer. The growth of the big builder has also aided the marketing emphasis. Marketing capabilities are one of the major advantages of large firm size. Builders with a major national or regional presence are likely to gain far more from it than a small, ephemeral concern.

Technological developments in the 1950s and 1960s emphasised the importance of scale in housing production. The organisation and planning of the labour process was one aspect of technical change (for building in general, see McGhie, 1982 and Campinos-Dubernet, 1986). Another aspect was the more well-known one of prefabricated, concrete technology. The possibilities opened up by social housing projects, particularly in a number of European countries, for such technological developments were discussed in an earlier section. The question of concern here is what has happened to technical change in the face of the more recent restructuring of production? New techniques have had to come to terms with modern builders' concerns to minimise capital tied up in production, to keep their productive operations as flexible as possible, and to search the market for new opportunities.

Contradictory tendencies can be seen in the adjustments required of technology by the new economics of house building. Flexible production is achieved most easily by reducing the labour process as much as possible to a simple on-site assembly of pre-manufactured components. In this way, a relatively unskilled labour force can be used, minimising the need to train and retain skilled workers as permanent staff. Manufactured components also avoid the stockholding of materials and semi-fashioned components, with the traditional builders' yard losing much of its earlier role and costs. The principles of reducing building work as much as possible to simple assembly with limited holding of materials and equipment have been the essence of capitalist house building since its inception, but modern materials and the industries producing them have freed the builder from virtually all the on-site fashioning of super-structural elements. Developments in timber machining and manufacturing are the most obvious, but concrete, clay, plastic, block and even brick components can, and have been, transformed in similar ways, especially in the 1970s and 1980s, although to varying extents in different countries.

There are crucial differences between trends in technological change in house building in the 1950s and 1960s and modern-day approaches. In that earlier period, building technology was seen overwhelmingly from a productionist perspective. On both sides of the Atlantic, the idea existed that housing production could eventually be reduced to 'Fordist' style mass-production, virtually identical to that of motor cars. Industrialised systems would eventually create standardised, low-cost housing that would satisfy officially laid down, basic housing standards. In trying to achieve lower building costs, the general goal was seen as one of creating conditions where site work was deskilled and total on- and off-site labour time minimised. That goal and its means of achievement were formulated on the basis of principles derived from simplistic views of what constituted factory-style production.

Modern house building with its emphasis on marketing, financial control and productive flexibility is totally at variance with productionist principles. Production now has to conform to the requirements of other aspects of the economics of house building, while the productionist approach assumed that the direction of determination would be the other way round. So the industrialised technologies that had evolved by the end of the 1960s have either had to be abandoned or drastically modified. The demise of the big concrete industrialised systems of the 1960s most dramatically illustrates the consequences of the shift. But it is wrong to think, as is frequently assumed, that techniques have gone back to 'traditional' methods, even if house-builders' advertising blurbs often try to generate such reassuring similies (Cullen, 1984; Ball, 1983; Schlesinger and Erlich, 1986; and NAHB, 1985).

Danish industrialised building illustrates the process of adapt-ation and refinement that has taken place in some of the earlier high-rise concrete systems of the 1960s.[1] Danish industrialised building started in the early 1950s. The reasons for the drive to industrialise building were similar to elsewhere. There was a chronic housing shortage, whilst the building industry had low productivity and skills shortages; added to which a small group of Danish architects and engineers were influential in the Modern Movement's ideologies towards rationalisation of the building process and workers' housing. The state was also keen to facilitate means through which high levels of housing output could be quickly achieved and a key component of Danish industry pushed to the forefront of technological advance. Subsidy schemes as a result began to favour industrialised building over traditional methods.

Initial experiments in the early 1950s were facilitated by the large-scale construction of military barracks. Techniques could be tried in an environment where dwelling comfort could be sacrificed and costs were virtually unrestrained. Experiments were made in the use of heavy pre-cast concrete slabs and the best means to achieve the rationalised planning of site operations. Planning of the on-site production process was regarded by many Danish experts as the most difficult part of the innovatory process — a lesson not learnt in Britain, which helps to account for the appallingly low standard of industrialised building there.

Throughout the late 1950s and the 1960s, large numbers of industrialised social housing flats were built in Denmark, generally of a high structural quality, although frequently situated in the bleak physical and social environments of new towns and suburbs. Building companies undertook all of the fabrication and site assembly processes, while architects and engineers prospered out of the refinement of technologies and designs. The systems were also exported to other countries.

The post-1973 economic crisis brought a halt to Denmark's industrialised building boom, and with it the end of an era of major technological advance. Many producers folded with the collapse of social house building, but those that remained have been remarkably successful in adapting their products to suit the needs of mass owner occupation. Today, most owner-occupied housing in Denmark is prefabricated, except for the most expensive houses, and Danish prefabricated producers have aggressively expanded into foreign markets, not only in the Third World but also in Europe. It has been suggested to me by one Danish interviewee that Danish producers now have 20 per cent of the West German single-family home market, for example.

Modern Danish concrete systems have notable differences from those of the 1960s. The concrete panels are now lightweight, an innovation made possible by the fact that they have to carry far less structural weight in a single-family dwelling than in blocks of flats. The panels are made of composite materials, including insulation and facing materials (the latter frequently consisting of a 'brick' skin a few centimetres deep to give a traditional look). The panels can be assembled in a wide variety of combinations to enable variety in design, and their light weight enables them to be transported considerable distances. Internal fittings take a flexible, pre-manufactured, modular form. Builders can order a dwelling complete to be assembled by their own staff, or by the manufacturer (usually a big building company) or by subcontractors. Modern Danish concrete systems, in other words, have been adapted to conform to the requirements of the current housing market and the contemporary economics of house building with its overriding need for flexibility.

'Industrialised' house building is not simply about changing materials and the ways they are put together to form a dwelling. Such technical changes in many respects are means by which to transform the more fundamental aspect of building — the relationship between the building employers and workers. Much modern house building, whether it uses industrialised technologies or not, has been influenced by the rationalisation of site processes, albeit with inter-country differences. One of the major emphases of modern housing production is site planning — the streamlining of the actual process of building.

Traditional building work contains large amounts of handicraft activities, whose execution ultimately is under the direct control of the workers involved. Given the nature of building sites and tasks, it is extremely difficult to have detailed management supervision of the labour process, while the ability of building workers to resist management directives is enhanced by their autonomy. Traditional management objectives on building sites prior to the 1950s were to devise means which struck a balance between minimising the degree of autonomy open to individual workers in the way in which they undertook their tasks and utilising the autonomy still left to workers as a way of inducing key strata of the workforce to assent to management targets. Craft pride could be encouraged, for instance, in order to lower the amount of detailed supervision required, and pay differentials could be used to play off sectors of the workforce against each other (for Britain, see Postgate, 1924; Price, 1980 and Ball, 1988).

Management strategies, since the war, have involved different tactics. They have relied less on craft hierarchies and more on adjusting forms of employment and on adapting contemporary factory-based management techniques to a construction site. The shift arose partially because of the opportunities opened up by technological developments, like new building components, and the advent, especially from the 1960s onwards, of extremely flexible, hydraulic equipment. The hierarchy of building skills, in particular, was restructured by such developments, so that many of the old crafts lost their pre-eminence. The other principal reason, at least up until the early 1970s, was the acute shortages of building labour experienced in most countries. Labour shortages weakened management's hand, and state-induced controls on welfare payments and working conditions to varying degrees increased the costs of pre-existing employment practices. One common technique of labour management was implicitly to guarantee permanent employment and good wages to a core of skilled workers, and to offer worse conditions to less vital strata. The distinction could be achieved through co-operation with building unions in the key crafts (as in the USA and Sweden), the use of foreign workers in many West European countries, or by distinguishing between directly employed and subcontract workers, as in Britain.

Two features of site practices evolved with these new types of management strategy. The first was an attempt to break down the centrality of traditional skills and replace them with the site assembly of factory-manufactured components and a greater use of plant and machinery on site. It was noted earlier that this was a central concern of industrialised building technologies, but it applied also to traditional building techniques. The second centred on 'Taylorist' style work evaluation and incentive schemes as a way of increasing the pace of work and of tying remuneration to productivity (for France, see Campinos-Dubernet, 1986); though crude work-study related pay schemes tended to fail because of the hostility of building workers towards them.

The lowering or absence of labour shortages since the mid-1970s has had profound effects on the nature of employment relations in house building. Although it is difficult to assess because of limited information and the qualitative nature of the changes, it would seem that building unions have been considerably weakened in all countries, though to varying degrees. In house building, the shift towards owner occupation and building firms' increased emphasis on flexibility have played important contributory parts. Rarely now do building unions in the USA form the conduit through which construction labour is hired. In virtually all countries, there has been a shift away from the direct employment of workers to the hiring of them on a subcontract basis. Building employers thereby increase the flexibility of their own operations and avoid the additional labour costs associated with sick, pension and holiday schemes, which grew as part of post-war state-orchestrated social welfare schemes. In subcontract piece rates they have one of the most direct forms of payment by results to ensure speedy execution of tasks, and the use of subcontract labour has helped to break down, in a number of countries, the power of the trades unions.[2]

CONCLUSIONS

This chapter has tried to draw out some general features of change in housing production in advanced capitalist countries. Although many pieces of information necessary to make a systematic investigation of the topic are tantalisingly absent from the literature, what is available does indicate that significant changes are going on. Shifts in tenure patterns, sharp falls in output in the late 1970s and early 1980s, and the redrawing of building firms' accumulation strategies have led away from the mega-building of the 1950s and 1960s and from the ideologies that went along with it. A new flexibility in building enterprises has ensured renewed conditions for accumulation in house building in many countries, but with highly variable consequences. In some countries, large-scale capitalist house-builders seem a thing of the past; being replaced by an amalgam of petty producers and housing component producers. Elsewhere, big house-builders have gone from strength to strength.

One factor that does seem certain is that the process of change is far from over, although it is difficult to predict the directions it might take. The processes of restructuring in house-building industries have generally gone through two classic phases. First, there were periods when workloads collapsed, leading to dramatic bankruptcies of firms and a redrawing of the social relations of production. Then came periods of retrenchment and the formulation of new conditions for accumulation. In most countries, the latter have occurred during periods of rising demand for owner occupation such as in the 1980s. Yet, the owner-occupied market is highly cyclical, and in the next down-turn many carefully assembled business plans might face ruin. Greater flexibility on the part of producers should ensure that a future crisis is not so bad as the last one. But the old adage that nothing ever changes in the house-building industry is clearly far from the truth.

NOTES

1. Discussion with Knud-Eric Skouby helped considerably with my understanding of the development of the Danish house-building industry, though he is not responsible for any factual or interpretative errors I may have made. Bonke and Jensen (1982) is a useful, published reference source.

2. Subcontracting is only one element of the weakening of the power of building unions. In Britain, it was crucial, while in some other countries unionisation amongst subcontracted labour has always been, and remains, high (Austrin, 1980). Danish workers, for example, operate on a gang basis, yet the gangs are highly unionised.

REFERENCES

Anglo-American Council on Productivity (1950) *Building*, Anglo-American Council on Productivity, London

Austrin, T. (1980) 'The "Lump" in the UK construction industry' in T. Nichols (ed.), *Capital and Labour*, Fontana, London

Ball,M. (1983) *Housing Policy and Economic Power*, Methuen, London

—— (1986) *Homeownership: a Suitable Case for Reform*, Shelter, London

—— (1988) *Construction Rebuilt? Economic Change in the British Construction Industry*, Routledge and Kegan Paul, London

Ball, M., Martens, M. and Harloe, M. (1986) 'Mortgage finance and owner occupation in Britain and West Germany', *Progress in Planning, 26*(3), 189–260

Ball, M. and Martens, M. (1988) *As Safe as Houses? The International Mortgage Finance Revolution*, Wheatsheaf Books, Brighton

Bemis, A. (1936) *The Evolving House*, MIT Press, Cambridge, Mass

Bonke, S. and Jensen, P. (1982) 'Technical development and employment in the Danish building industry', *Production of the Built
Environment*, 3, 4–4 — 4–9, University College, London

BSA (1981) *The Determination of House Prices*, Building Societies
Association, London

Campinos-Dubernet, M. and Grando, J. (1985) 'The French construction industry from 1945 to 1980: progressive changes in conditions
of employment and work', mimeo

Campinos-Dubernet, M. (1986) 'The rationalisation of labour in the
construction industry: the limits of orthodox taylorism', *Production
of the Built Environment*, 7, 117–29, University College, London

Checkoway, B. (1980) 'Large builders, federal housing programmes
and postwar suburbanization', *International Journal of Urban and
Regional Research*, 4(1), 21–45

Cullen, A. (1984) 'Speculative housebuilding in Britain. Some
comments on the switch to the timber-frame production method',
Production of the Built Environment, 3, 4–12 — 4–18, University
College, London

Dickens, P., Duncan. S., Goodwin, M. and Gray, F. (1985) *Housing,
State and Localities*, Methuen, London

Direct Labour Collective (1978) *Building with Direct Labour*, Conference of Socialist Economists, London

Dyos, H. (1961) *The Victorian Suburb*, Leicester University Press,
Leicester

Eichler, N. (1982) *The Merchant Builders*, MIT Press, Cambridge,
Mass

Emmanuel, D. (1981) *The Growth of Speculative Building in Greece*,
PhD Thesis, London School of Economics

Florida, R. (1986) 'The political economy of financial deregulation and
the reorganization of housing finance in the United States', *International Journal of Urban and Regional Research*, 10(2), 207–31

Gottlieb, M. (1976) *Long Swings in Urban Development*, NBER, New
York

Grebler, L. (1973) *The Large Builder. Growth of a New Phenomenon*,
Praeger, New York

Grebler, L. and Mittlebach, H. (1978) *The Inflation of House Prices*,
Praeger, New York

Hall, P. (1974) *Urban and Regional Planning*, Penguin, Harmondsworth

Hall, P., Gracey, H., Drewett, R. and Thomas. R. (1973) *The
Containment of Urban England*, George Allen and Unwin, London

Hillebrandt, P. (1984) *Analysis of the British Construction Industry*,
Macmillan, Basingstoke

Ingham, G. (1984) *Capitalism Divided?*, Macmillan, Basingstoke

McGhie, W. (1982) 'The implications of project management',
Production of the Built Environment, 3, 3–1 — 3–9, University
College, London

Meyerson, A. (1986) 'The changing structure of housing finance in the
United States', *International Journal of Urban and Regional
Research*, 10(3), 465–97

197

NAHB (1985) *Housing America — The Challenges Ahead*, National Association of Home Builders, Washington

Parry Lewis, J. (1965) *Building Cycles and Britain's Economic Growth*, Macmillan, London

Postgate, R. (1924) *The Builders' History*, The Labour Publishing Co., London

Price, R. (1980) *Masters, Unions and Men*, Cambridge University Press, Cambridge

Schlesinger, T. and Erlich, M. (1986) 'Housing: the industry capitalism didn't forget', in R. Bratt, C. Hartman and A. Meyerson (eds), *Critical Perspectives on Housing*, Temple University Press, Philadelphia

Topalov, C. (1983) *Tous Proprietares!*, CSU, Paris

—— (1985) 'Prices, profits and rents in residential development: the case of France' in M. Ball et al. (eds), *Land Rent, Housing and Urban Planning: a European Perspective*, Croom Helm, London

Ward, P. (1982) *Self Help Housing: a Critique*, Mansell, London

White, R. (1965) *Prefabrication: a History of its Development in Great Britain*, HMSO, London

6

Towards a New Politics of Housing Provision

Michael Harloe

In this book we have been concerned with the exploration of a limited set of issues arising from a period of restructuring of the housing markets and policies of advanced capitalist countries. Our analyses are limited in two respects. First, because in a book of this length many issues have simply had to be ignored — for example private rental housing (but see Harloe, 1985), landownership and various aspects of changing demographic structures. Second, because many of the changes that we have described (and others that we have ignored) are still in progress. New structures and social relations of housing provision are still emerging, we can only now make a preliminary assessment of their patterns and consequences.

However, this much is clear:

1. With the collapse of the long post-war boom and the accompanying political consensus on matters such as the extent and nature of state intervention in economic and social processes, a major restructuring of housing provision is occurring. In any one country at any one time the changes may *appear* to be no more than a series of disconnected, piecemeal or marginal shifts in markets and policies. But when viewed in *cross-national* and *historical* perspective much more may be seen to be at stake.

2. However, while the cross-national focus of our work has enabled us to comprehend the *generalised* nature of the restructuring which is now occurring, it has also highlighted the considerable degree of *variation* in the manner in which each nation is experiencing these changes. As we have insisted throughout this book, structures and relations of housing provision are nationally specific (and there are also, of course,

considerable local variations as, for example, Barlow (1987) has recently argued). One consequence is that the nature of, and possibilities for, a new politics of housing — whether it be of the Left or of the Right — also varies from country to country.

In drawing the first of these conclusions we are implicitly taking issue with much of the limited, consumption-oriented tradition of housing research and policy discussion which we criticise in the first chapter of this book. But our second conclusion equally implies a criticism of some of the more recent, Marxist-inspired research which, oblivious to much historical and contemporary evidence, attempts to simplify and reduce the variation and complexity in structures of provision via the use of ideal constructs and universally applicable hypotheses (see, again, the discussion in Chapter 1). Such approaches are neither intellectually valid nor very useful as a basis for the constructive critique and reformulation of proposals for housing reform.

In this final chapter we will briefly set out some of the broad conclusions which we have been able to reach about the nature and consequences of those aspects of the restructuring of housing provision examined in this book. Also, drawing on more recent research in some of the countries with which we have been concerned, we shall outline some of the most important innovations in housing markets and policies now occurring. Innovations are indicators of responses by households, housing market institutions and governments to housing market restructuring. We shall consider some of the implications, both positive and negative, of these innovations for housing consumers and touch on the shift which has occurred over the past decade or so in the broader agenda of housing politics under the impact of pro-market ideologies and 'New Right' governments. Finally we shall outline some possible directions for more radical reform.

HOUSING RESTRUCTURING — KEY ASPECTS OF CHANGE

There are five main aspects of change which we wish to highlight:

1. There has been a sharp alteration in the circumstances of the owner-occupied housing market over the past decade. Despite short-term fluctuations, house building has been in

secular decline. Housing markets have become much more unstable and sensitive to general economic changes. The real cost of house purchase has increased since the 1970s and is unlikely to return to the very low levels of that decade.

2. A centrally important reason why owner occupation has become so costly (which may seem surprising in an era of deflation and mass unemployment) relates to the dramatic changes which have occurred in mortgage finance. Semi-protected, relatively low-cost circuits of housing finance have been breaking down and there has been an increasing integration of the housing finance market into general financial markets. The consequences are that funds tend to be more expensive (although possibly more available for those who can pay the price) and more volatile, flowing into and out of the housing market according to its profitability with respect to other national and international investment opportunities. Volatility and costliness are key factors helping to perpetuate the instability of owner-occupied housing markets which we have already noted.

3. Unstable housing markets have had profound consequences for the production of housing. As we have shown in Chapter 5 these consequences vary, depending on the pre-existing structure of the house-building industry and its relation to housing markets. In some cases large-scale enterprises have virtually disappeared from the sector, in others they are becoming more dominant. But a common trend seems to be that large-scale structures of building *organisation* and *management* are giving way to smaller-scale, more flexible and fragmented arrangements. Housing producers now have to give far more attention to marketing their products, to seeking out profitable sub-markets and sectors of demand. The relatively easy years when private demand continued to expand and, at times of temporary crisis, social house building provided relief, now seem to be over.

4. In the post-war period increased social rented housing production was often used to counteract a down-turn in private building or in the economy generally. With few and limited exceptions such counter-cyclical policies are not happening any more. Instead social housing production has been cut back by governments of a variety of political persuasions, sometimes simply to reduce public expenditure, sometimes because they find it ideologically objectionable as well. A *trend* towards

limiting social housing to a residual provision for those excluded from the private housing market is apparent. Most governments wish to limit or reconstitute the tenure in this way, but, as is discussed in Chapter 2, not all of them are able to achieve their objectives. However, it is generally the case that social housing rents have risen, often sharply, and income-related housing allowances have not fully protected many who are on the lowest incomes from this trend. Furthermore, there seems to be an increasing degree of segregation occurring in social housing, between areas of better quality housing inhabited by somewhat better-off tenants and areas of deteriorating housing to which the very poor and other socially marginalised groups are confined. (Although it is important to note, as Forrest and Murie (1986) have recently stressed, that this marginalisation is not necessarily confined to social or even all rented housing — certainly it is not in countries such as Britain and the USA where low-income owner occupation is substantial.)

5. While there is a great deal of cross-national variation in housing politics and policies, there are also some common trends. All governments aim to reduce public expenditure on housing, although this does not mean that they always succeed. They also wish to disengage in other ways, for example by reducing the regulation of circuits of housing finance and cutting back on indirect subsidies through the tax system. In some cases housing policies are changing because the governments concerned see this as a sheer necessity, others also believe that state involvement in housing is economically and socially damaging. But there are many obstacles hindering state disengagement. For example, there is powerful political opposition to reductions in tax subsidies for owner-occupiers, indeed in some countries governments have been forced to increase assistance to owner occupation. In some cases there is sharp opposition to cuts in social housing subsidies. Moreover, beyond these housing-related pressures, there are other problems — for example, the deregulation of financial markets has, as was shown in Chapter 4, led to a continuing crisis in the US Thrift industry which could have serious knock-on effects on that country's financial sector as a whole. And collapsing employment in the building industry has contributed a great deal to the overall levels of unemployment in many countries. But, in the context of political strategies for housing provision, the objective of relying increasingly on the private market is in

contradiction with the decline in the ability of this market to provide decent and affordable housing for considerable sections of the population, at least without continuing major state support. This is the central dilemma which current policy formation ought to address. However, most governments, and even many of their critics, fail to see the difficulty or are open to rethinking the strategy. We shall return to this issue below.

INNOVATIONS IN HOUSING MARKETS AND POLICIES

The many changes which have occurred in housing markets and policies in the past decade have, of course, not affected all households or all housing-related institutions equally. Large sections of the population, especially those lucky enough to remain employed, continue to be reasonably well housed. They may pay rather more for their housing, or accept a rather lower quality of accommodation. As we note later, they may become involved in innovatory forms of housing provision, perhaps because otherwise they can no longer afford the standard of housing that they formerly expected or because these means are ill suited to particular needs. But the process of adaption to change in housing provision and its consequences have not been severe compared to that experienced by lower-income households. The experience of housing market institutions has also varied. Some have suffered; builders, mortgage institutions, social and other landlords and so on have collapsed or had to undergo radical changes. But some have benefitted from these changes and expanded their roles and operations.

Lower-income housing consumers have been most seriously affected by the increased cost and reduced affordability of housing. Promises made during the post-war housing boom to end the sharing of accommodation, substandard and deteriorating property, insecurity of tenure and homelessness and excessive housing costs are no longer being met. In every country which we have studied there is a growing mass of housing disadvantage and stress, accompanied by the continuation of much better housing conditions for those whose economic security continues to be relatively assured, both by their position in the labour market and because of their continued receipt of housing subsidies (one indicator of this is the increasing recognition of homelessness as a problem which is affecting 'normal' households, not just those who have particular social or psychological problems which affect their ability to gain access to housing).

Adaptions to worsening housing opportunities by, for example, increased sharing of accommodation, the acceptance of cripplingly high housing payments and so on can hardly be called innovations. At best they might be called 'negative innovations'. They are, in fact, a reversion to forms of low-income housing 'solution' which were common in the nineteenth-century cities of capitalist Europe and the USA. However, there are more genuine innovations, many of them still on a small scale, which, it is argued by their promoters, do constitute a more positive response to the manifest inability of the established structures of housing provision to deliver adequate housing to significant sections of the population.

In a recently completed study in the USA, the Netherlands and West Germany we have examined some of these new developments and their impact on housing consumers.[1] They can be grouped under three broad headings: reductions in the cost of new housing, changes in social housing provision and changes in the relations between housing agencies.

Reducing the cost of new housing

This includes schemes to reduce land costs by promoting higher building densities, by land leasing and by the provision of subsidies. In the USA there are some schemes in which new free market housing cross-subsidises a smaller proportion of low- to moderate-income housing. However, such schemes are currently fairly rare as they only work where there is some positive means of inducing private developers to participate.

A major aspect of policies which aim to reduce construction costs (apart from various ways of depressing construction industry wages) is the lowering of the quality, equipment and size of new building. There is a considerable degree of loosening of housing and building standards and some government-financed research into how to reduce costs. These changes raise questions about the physical and psychological limits of the extent to which housing quality and standards can be reduced, and the future costs in terms of repair and maintenance which are being incurred.

Another development is the increasing use of self-help in

house building. One Dutch scheme which has yet to be fully utilised in connection with self-build, but which offers opportunities for it, is so-called 'open building'. In such schemes the shell of the building and the service connections are delivered to the householders who then determine the nature and hence the cost of the 'infill' and may install some elements of this themselves using modular packages.

Self-help can reduce housing costs and enable households to fulfil desired types of living arrangements (for example, communal forms of living — which are being demanded by groups of young people and some elderly people in particular) but its scope is limited. It is often oriented to the middle ranges of the owner-occupied housing market, it does not cater for the needs of many poorer households unless substantial subsidies are available. Experiences with urban homesteading (self-help rehabilitation of older housing) in the USA, which was aimed at low-income households, have not proved very successful since many of the poor lack the skills and resources necessary to organise the rehabilitation process. It is not necessarily efficient either, completion times are often very lengthy and economies of scale are often lost. Despite self-building, the costs remain relatively high. Also it is a stressful and time-consuming activity which can reinforce family tensions and divisions. In the USA at least, where there has so far been the greatest experience of low-income self help, this has mainly been entered into as a last resort — for example by tenants of buildings which have been abandoned by their landlords and who have no other option but to run the property themselves if they wish to remain there. Relatively few households feel able or are willing to get involved in major self-building projects. However, some of the problems can be eased when such projects are based on collective organisation and are aided by technical and other support. On the whole such collective projects tend to attract younger, more educated and politically active individuals who have the time, the motivation and the resources to participate.

Finally there are innovations in mortgage instruments, some reduce initial housing costs, although others reflect the lenders' wish to shift the risk of fluctuations in the cost of funds from themselves to the borrowers. Examples of the former include 'low start' and equity sharing mortgages and of the latter various forms of variable interest rate mortgage (in countries where long-term fixed interest loans have been the norm in the past). The general fall in interest rates from their peak levels in the early 1980s is likely to have had more effect on lowering housing costs than any of these innovations in mortgage instruments.

Changes in social housing provision

Sales and other means of converting social housing to the private sector are increasing. In some countries this is explicit government policy but in other cases it is more the product of the financial pressures that social landlords now face, especially for sources of capital to meet the costs of rehabilitating their older stock.

Another major innovation is the introduction of decentralised housing services and tenant management schemes, although neither of these is necessarily a cost-saving exercise. Decentralised management is also introduced with the objective of democratising formerly bureaucratic and centralised organisations. The claim is that such management can respond more effectively to tenants' needs. But there are many problems to solve such as the degree of financial autonomy and liability of tenant managers and who has tenancy allocation responsibilities. Self-help management requires considerable resources for training and technical advice. It is also time consuming and many tenants are unwilling or unable to get involved. The scope for self-management may be rather limited, although much still remains to be learnt about how and when it can be successful. The question of who really benefits from such schemes and where their costs lie cannot be determined except by a careful examination of each new development. In some cases tenants may obtain cheaper and/or better management. In other cases it may be the social housing landlords and/or governments that benefit by a reduction in their financial and other responsibilities for such housing. Rather than self-management, our research suggests that what tenants really desire is a greater degree of *control* over, and *accountability* by, existing housing management. Self-management is only one option for achieving this.

Changes in the relations between housing agencies

With central governments reducing their direct responsibility for low-income housing provision, the role of local authorities, which are directly confronted with growing housing needs, is becoming more pronounced. But fewer funds are available for meeting these needs. Where there are explicit policies of decentralisation it is often claimed that they are a means of returning greater power of decision-making to the local level, reducing the bureaucratic rigidities of centralised control and so on. But a desire to reduce central government expenditure and responsibilities often seems to be the more fundamental motive.

With limited finances local authorities have to look for new policies. These can involve increased housing market controls or co-operation with the private sector. Private market controls are usually a matter of great political controversy. On the one hand, they are strongly opposed by private housing interests and in several countries national or state governments have prevented or inhibited such controls. On the other hand, many grass-roots groups campaign, for example, for controls over the gentrification of formerly private rented housing. Innovations by such groups address themselves to the negative conse- quences of the adaption to changing housing market conditions by one group of consumers — those who are relatively well off — for those who are at the bottom of the housing market. Insofar as governments have assisted such efforts, their assist- ance has often been severely limited and outweighed by other policies (for example, relating to improvement subsidies) which have encouraged tenure conversion and gentrification.

Lack of resources encourages local authorities and non-profit social housing agencies into closer collaboration with the private sector. There are experiments which bring together voluntary and community groups, landlords, builders and financial institutions for new house building and rehabilitation. State and local authorities may offer technical expertise, cheap land, housing loan guarantees, limited subsidies or tax reliefs. Especially in the USA, there is a wide and often very sophisticated variety of combinations of public and private agencies and sources of finance and subsidy. But few schemes have benefitted low-income households, more are targeted at moderate- to middle-income groups. In some cases these new schemes result in the direct displacement of low-income tenants. In others they have the same effect via a reduction of the available lower rented stock.

Private sector housing institutions are looking for new market opportunities and the privatisation of social rented housing and joint public/private schemes can have a considerable attraction for them. But there are obvious limits in the extent to which they will accept publicly imposed restrictions on, for example, the resale prices of this housing or the groups to whom it is allocated.

Although there is not space here to discuss these innovations in any detail, a number of preliminary conclusions may be drawn:

1. Few of the schemes which add to the supply of housing seem to benefit low-income households, except when they receive substantial subsidies. They are more likely to benefit moderate- to middle-income households. The limitations of low-income self-help have already been noted.

2. Apart from housing consumers, both governments and private sector institutions have their own interests in promoting innovative developments. These interests may well determine the parameters within which innovations develop; without a close examination of these developments, it is impossible to determine where their costs and benefits fall.

3. Some innovations, while they do not increase housing supply or accessibility, may improve the quality of housing services already being received. Some developments in co-operative housing/tenant management have been successful in these terms. But there are also some instances where such innovations have been imposed on tenants who were neither able nor very willing to take on new roles in housing management. Successful experimental schemes, based on grass-roots campaigning and organisation by housing consumers, may then be taken up by governments and imposed on other groups 'top down'.

4. Some innovations benefit certain groups of housing consumers but at the expense of other, often more disadvantaged groups. Conflict over access to scarce housing occurs not only between consumers and governments or private sector agencies, it also divides consumers along lines which may be demarcated by income, class, gender or ethnicity.

THE POLITICS OF HOUSING IN THE 1980S

When viewed as a whole, these piecemeal and often small-scale innovations are indicators of a more general change in the politics and ideology of housing provision. Ideological concepts began to shift in the 1970s, particularly in response to a growing critique from both the Left and the Right, of the bureaucratic, paternalistic and rigid structures of social housing provision. In addition, the Right was increasingly critical of almost any form of state involvement in welfare, believing that market-based provision was inherently superior. In recent years this critique of state provision has been given extra impetus by the pressure to cut government expenditure. So concepts of self-help and self-reliance are now enthusiastically promoted by political parties which range from the Right through the Centre to the reformist Left.

The growing emphasis on self-reliance also reflects changing attitudes on the part of some sections of the middle class (including those, such as groups of young people, who may be poor but who, in terms of their origins and education, have a similar class background). These groups have, although much less severely than the poor, been faced with growing housing costs and difficulties of access to desired forms of housing. This is one reason why they have become involved in collective schemes, such as co-operatives. In addition, some private housing developers and financial institutions are interested in introducing more consumer participation into their developments (by, for example, 'open building' or various forms of housing with collective services provision) as a means by which to open up new markets.

So, together with the current privatisation trends in housing provision, issues like consumer participation, decentralisation and self-help are being taken up by the middle class, politicians and the private housing sector. The value of these concepts is more ambiguous for lower-income households who often desire better housing services (or indeed access to *any* housing services) but who, for the reasons which we have discussed above, can only take limited advantage of the new trends in housing provision.

Although many of these innovations are, as yet, of marginal quantitative significance, many of them have been enthusiastically promoted by political parties and governments — in words if often not with much money. There is often a degree of tokenism involved in this promotion. The existence of some small-scale innovatory projects, most of which are relatively cheap to finance, suggests that government is concerned with meeting housing needs and is actively seeking new and more effective ways of carrying out this objective. At the same time major housing programmes, which in quantitative terms have been, and may still be, much more significant, especially for low-income households, continue to be cut back.

Therefore, in commenting on the nature of the politics of housing in the 1980s, we cannot just look at the innovatory trends, some of which we have reviewed above. We also have to consider the broad or strategic thinking which lies behind governmental and party programmes and policies. There is no doubt that in the USA and in many West European countries the agenda has been dominated by the Right. The main elements of this agenda are:

1. that the operation of the private market is the most efficient and effective means of producing and distributing housing;
2. that government intervention in housing distorts this mechanism and has a variety of adverse consequences. Intervention: a. leads to a misallocation of investment in the economy, with too many resources going into housing, encouraging 'overconsumption'; b. stifles beneficial private enterprise by, for example, excessive land-use planning, housing and other regulations, rent controls, etc.; c. especially where government itself is directly involved as a landlord (or in setting the terms of operation of other landlords), it reduces consumer choice and autonomy, subjecting the population to centralised, bureaucratic and inflexible controls over what housing they get and how they live in it;
3. that most groups of the population are now well housed, largely due to the past successes of market-oriented provision, and that there is no need for major further expansion of the housing supply. Housing is, therefore, no longer a particularly important political priority;
4. that many consumers have paid too low a proportion of their incomes for housing in the past, and that this should rise. Insofar as there is still a need for some households to be assisted with their housing costs, limited income-related allowances should be the means of supplying this assistance.

From this perspective the state's role should in future be no more than the provider of a minimal 'safety net' for those quite unable to provide for themselves. Beyond this there should be the minimum of regulation necessary to prevent some of the worst excesses of unrestrained private market activity. As Marian Bowley once described a similar period of attempted state withdrawal from housing in Britain, in a phrase which harks back to the nineteenth-century conception of housing policy, this is a form of 'new sanitary policy' (Bowley, 1945).

In practice there has in fact been a considerable gap between ideology and practice. Some of the objectives which have been listed above have been less easy to achieve than others. Governments have found some of the more radical changes set by the agenda too politically and economically costly to pursue. The central problem is that, as we have tried to show in this book, the private market has, in the years of recession, become a *less* not a *more* effective means of supplying decent and affordable housing, especially to low- and moderate-income households. Unless governments are willing to provide more financial support — not less — this position is unlikely to change more than marginally. There are other difficulties as well. In some countries, the Netherlands and Denmark for example, there is a wide gap between the objectives of right-wing politicians and what is politically acceptable (for example, regarding the mass sale of social rented housing). There are also various economic and social constraints. In some countries right-wing governments have, at least for brief periods, actually expanded subsidised house building, to prevent a total collapse of the building industry and/or to stem the increase in unemployment. Moreover, even in Britain the government has shown some concern about the potentially disastrous impact of the risks which might be run by major housing finance institutions as a consequence of radical deregulation and unrestrained competition.

At the heart of the right-wing approach to housing is the belief that 'free' markets function most effectively with a minimum of state involvement. In fact, especially in an era of economic recession, they can only function even semi-effectively with a continuing and substantial level of state support (if effectiveness is to be measured in terms of delivering decent and affordable housing for the mass of the population). However, the *form* which this support takes has been changing. Economic and social interests which are marginal to this

211

maintenance of the private housing market — principally lower-income households and those organisations which have supplied housing to them, have been, in practice, the main victims of the new approaches to housing policy. Their ability to resist this exclusion from the centre of housing politics varies a good deal from country to country and even from locality to locality. But, even under social democratic or 'liberal' governments, their loss of effective power in policy-making is clear.

With the collapse of the post-war consensus on the role of the state in the 'mixed' economy and in social welfare provision, the social democratic parties of Western Europe (and the Democratic Party in the USA) have been plunged into considerable confusion. To varying degrees, they have accepted many of the essential propositions of the right-wing theorists and political parties, or, when in office, have been unable to resist the pressures from powerful economic and social interests for austerity policies (the history of the French Socialist government and earlier the British Labour government illustrate this). At the same time social democrats have come to recognise that there are valid criticisms of the model of bureaucratic and centralised housing and other welfare provision which they had previously championed. But, instead of attempting to develop new and distinctive policies which retain former objectives of, for example, achieving greater social and economic equality, policies have often been adopted which are little more than watered down versions of the policies being advocated and implemented by their right-wing opponents. In some cases social democrats still promise a reversion to the policies of yesteryear (such as major increases in social house building together with the maintenance of existing subsidies and support for private housing) despite the fact that, when and if they come to office, such policies are most unlikely to be implemented.

Above all, there is, as yet, little recognition of the need to move policy considerations beyond a concern with making marginal changes to the existing system of housing provision. Most research and policy formation still concentrates on a limited range of consumption-oriented issues, as we discussed in Chapter 1. As we have tried to show in this book, a wider concern with the social relations of housing provision as a whole, with the agencies and structures of this provision, is necessary to an understanding of the current nature of housing provision and how it is changing. It follows that those who wish to change the outcomes of this system — for example, to improve housing conditions for those who have suffered most in the past decade — also need to consider and make proposals for changes in these structures and social relations of housing provision. Not only is there a need to continue to question and develop new policies relating to the state's role in housing but also to question and seek to alter the role of the private market and its institutions.

This requires a far deeper analysis of the nature of housing provision, of its social relations and structures, than is presently incorporated in policy discussions, whether by the Left or the Right. In a recent critique of theories of social policy Hindess has repeated a point made earlier by others when he notes that most such theories 'essentialise' publicly and market-controlled provision (Hindess, 1986). By this he means that they assume that the 'market' and 'state provision' necessarily produce certain effects. As Hindess points out, this is not so, for both markets and state provision operate under 'specific institutional conditions' which determine their outcomes.

TOWARDS A NEW POLITICS OF HOUSING PROVISION

As we have stressed throughout this book, the social relations of housing provision are nationally and in some cases locally specific. This means that both the circumstances which determine the form that proposals for radical, new policies should take and the likelihood of their having an impact on mainstream political thinking vary a great deal. It would therefore be pointless to present a neat blueprint for change in this section and hopelessly impractical as well. But it is possible to point to some of the main issues which any radical programme for housing will have to confront.

The central issues concern who is to *control* structures of housing provision and *in whose interests*. In the past the dominant role has been played by the private market, assisted by extensive state support. For many years this has seemed a relatively successful way of providing the necessary housing for large sections of the population. But in this book we have argued that this 'solution' is beginning to fail. If present policies continue, even with all the innovations which have already been mentioned, current problems of housing quality, affordability

213

and accessibility will remain and even intensify. Changing this pattern requires a strategy which has as its objective a fundamental restructuring of housing provision to meet housing needs, rather than to ensure the profits of those who provide it. While this may seem a utopian goal, and will certainly be very hard to achieve, except perhaps on a fragmentary and localised basis, two factors need to be borne in mind. The first is that radical shifts in social provision, with a sharp reduction of the role of the private market, have occurred in the past in areas other than housing, in health and education for example. Indeed, in some countries, in the first few years after the last war, there was a similar, though temporary shift in at least the ownership and management of housing provision. So there is no reason to believe that a radical shift in the basis of housing provision is necessarily incompatible with the continuation of the existing political and economic systems of capitalist societies (as some on both the Left and Right have tended to assert).

The second point is that, if we are correct in our contention that the ability of the private market to provide for mass housing needs is and will remain seriously constrained (indeed may become more so), then it is conceivable that new and more radical proposals for reform could attract considerable political support from groups which, unlike many of the poor, do have some effective political voice in society. Finally, there is an acute need for the development and discussion of radical options for housing reform. Even though the difficulties of moving towards the implementation of new policies may be very great, there is a dearth of ideas about housing reform which might be drawn upon if or when the opportunities for major change do occur. Although the coming to power of right-wing governments in the late 1970s and early 1980s may have been largely the consequence of the failures of their social democrat predecessors, rather than because of the successful propagation of a new agenda for economic and social reform beforehand, this agenda has provided an important influence on policy-making since. It has to be recognised that ideas concerning, for example, the role of the private market in welfare provision, which were treated with ridicule a decade or so ago, have now had a very real impact on policy.

The central objectives of a radical new approach to housing provision might, on the surface, be rather similar to those which most governments profess to be attempting to achieve, namely to ensure an adequate stock of affordable housing with the widest variety of choice for the consumer. But it would break with existing policies by recognising that the current means of achieving these ends, consumption subsidies, support for existing market institutions, plus various forms of regulation and so on, are often ineffective and sometimes positively harmful in this effort. At the same time there can be no reversion to the bureaucratic, paternalistic and rigid structures of the traditional welfare state. Many of the interests which this system has fostered are not those of housing consumers but of those who are involved in one form or another in administering, controlling or otherwise providing housing through its mechanisms. In addition, as has been widely pointed out, some aspects of this mode of welfare provision have often been a means of social control and have, either by design or intention, had stigmatising effects.

There is therefore considerable potential in some of the experiments in new, decentralised structures of housing provision, although solutions need to be found to the various problems mentioned earlier. Likewise, the general principle of shifting the locus of control away from the providers of housing towards the consumers is also important, but on the basis of educated consent and the provision of the necessary financial, technical and other resources — not as an alternative to such provision and by being imposed 'top down'.

But control over the supply of housing also has to be shifted in ways which are not encompassed by present policy trends. The link between housing tenure and the existing forms in which these tenures are created and sustained needs alteration. There is no necessity, for example, for social housing only to be provided in a limited range of rental forms. These forms could even be expanded to include socially controlled individual ownership in which the freedom and autonomy (as well as the responsibilities) which this form of housing occupation provides can be retained, while its role as a medium of capital accumulation and profit making is much reduced. There are, in fact, a few small-scale experiments in such housing, in the USA and the Netherlands for example.

Finally, there would have to be extensive changes in the control and planning of house building, landownership, housing finance, taxation and subsidies (see Ball, 1986; Achtenberg and Marcuse, 1983 for specific examples of such changes, relating to

215

Britain and the USA respectively).

New agendas for housing politics are beginning to emerge in several of the countries in which we carried out our research. In some cases there are groups which are developing radical and comprehensive programmes, thus seeking to inform and influence public and political opinion. In addition there is the growth of the small-scale practical experiments in alternative forms of housing provision, some of which have been briefly referred to in this chapter.

Of course such proposals and projects are no more than a first stage in the development of a progressive housing politics. The means by which such a politics could be implemented, the extent to which it could be achieved and the pace of progress would depend both on the nature of the existing structures and relations of housing provision and, crucially, on the degree of political mobilisation in favour of change. We recognise that these issues are not addressed in this book which is intended to help stimulate a radical rethinking of the housing agenda, not be a substitute for such work. Nor are we so naive as to believe that ideas often have more than a somewhat tenuous connection with political action, even when such action is justified in terms of such ideas. But, as we have suggested in this chapter, housing policies *are* being influenced by certain ideas at the current time, as well as by the sorts of change in housing provision which we have described in the rest of the book. If we are unhappy with the nature of these changes we need to develop an alternative analysis and critique of present social relations and structures of provision and stimulate fresh thinking about how these might be refashioned. These have been the principal purposes of this book.

NOTE

1. This is a project, funded by the Joseph Rowntree Memorial Trust, to examine a range of innovations in housing markets and policies in the USA, the Netherlands and West Germany. A full account of the results will be published in 1988. A preliminary paper is Harloe and Martens (forthcoming).

REFERENCES

Achtenberg, E. and Marcuse, P. (1983) 'Towards the decommodification of housing: a political analysis and a progressive program' in C. Hartman (ed.), *America's Housing Crisis*, Routledge and Kegan Paul, Boston and London

Ball, M. (1986) *Home Ownership. A Suitable Case for Reform*, Shelter, London

Barlow, J. (1987) 'The housing crisis and its local dimensions', *Housing Studies, 2*(1), 28–41

Bowley, M. (1945) *Housing and the State, 1919–1944*, Allen and Unwin, London

Forrest, R. and Murie, A. (1986) 'Marginalisation and subsidised individualism: the sale of council houses in the restructuring of the British welfare state', *International Journal of Urban and Regional Research, 10*(1), 46–66

Harloe, M. (1985) *Private Rented Housing in America and Europe*, Croom Helm, London

Harloe, M. and Martens, M. (1987) 'Innovation in ·contemporary housing markets' in B. Turner et al. (eds), *Between State and Market: Housing in the Post-Industrial Era*, Almquist and Wicksell, Stockholm

Hindess, B. (1986) *Freedom, Equality and the Market*, Tavistock Publications, London and New York

Index